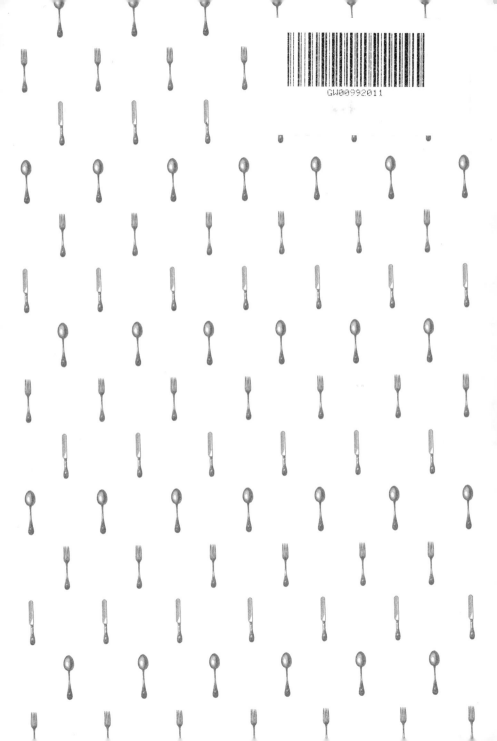

GW00992011

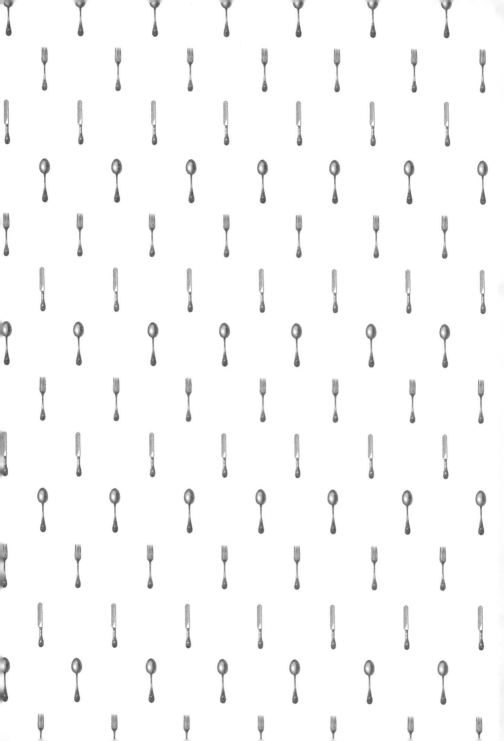

EATER'S DIGEST

LORRAINE BODGER

EATER'S DIGEST

400 DELECTABLE READINGS ABOUT FOOD AND DRINK

STEWART, TABORI & CHANG

NEW YORK

Editor: Jennifer Levesque
Designer: Pamela Geismar
Production Manager: Kim Tyner

Library of Congress Cataloging-in-Publication Data
Bodger, Lorraine.
Eater's digest : 400 delectable readings about food and drink / by Lorraine Bodger.
p. cm.
Includes index.
ISBN 1-58479-449-6
1. Food—Miscellanea. I. Title.
TX355.B597 2006   641.3—dc22
                          2005029810

Excerpt on page 85 ("My 'Hood Is Bad for My Health," by Pauline Gordon) reprinted from *Represent: The Voice of Youth in Care*, January 2005 © 2005 Youth Communication. All rights reserved. Reprinted with permission.

Excerpt on page 149 ("Mastering Mac 'n' Cheese," by D'nashia Jenkins) reprinted from *New Youth Communications*, December 2004 © 2004 Youth Communication. All rights reserved. Reprinted with permission.

Excerpt on page 277 ("It Ain't Easy Eating Greens!" by Omar Morales) reprinted from *New Youth Communications*, January 1998 © 1998 Youth Communication. All rights reserved. Reprinted with permission.

Published in 2006 by Stewart, Tabori & Chang
An imprint of Harry N. Abrams, Inc.

The text of this book was composed in Joanna, Trade Gothic Condensed, and Gill Sans Shadowed
Printed and bound in the United States of America

10 9 8 7 6 5 4 3 2 1

HNA
harry n. abrams, inc.
a subsidiary of La Martinière Groupe

115 West 18th Street
New York, NY 10011
www.hnabooks.com

ACKNOWLEDGMENTS

Authors frequently divide their acknowledgments into *thanks* and *special thanks*. All the thank-yous here are emphatically (and alphabetically) very special thanks:

Karen Baar; Carole Bodger, especially for the title of the book; Delia Ephron; Pamela Geismar; Keith Hefner and Youth Communication; Barry Hoffman; Gordon Javna; Jerome Kass; Ted Kerasote; Jennifer Levesque; Angela Miller; Marnie Mueller; Grace Shibata; Peter Small; Jenny Snider; Hallie Ephron Touger; Molly Touger; Naomi Touger, for clever and persistent research (as well as memoir); Jane Weiss.

EATER'S DIGEST

INTRODUCTION

Americans love food. Eating is the great American pastime, and we think and talk about it day in, day out. We chat about where we ate, when we ate, what we ate, and who we ate with. We argue over where to get the best pizza, pasta, burger, barbecue, dim sum, fried clam, taco, Caesar salad, apple pie, and chocolate chip cookie. We discuss how our food was prepared, what the ingredients were, and where to buy everything from hot sauce to bagels. We reminisce about family meals, holiday feasts, restaurant dinners, party food, road food, foreign food, regional food—we're insatiable. Time in the kitchen may be at a premium, but we spend hours talking and thinking about every facet of food.

We love to read about food too. There's hardly a newspaper or magazine in America that doesn't have its food section and its food columnists, read avidly by cooks and noncooks alike. Even the most dedicated gourmets buy cookbooks as much to read them as to cook from them, and the rest of us gobble foodie memoirs, foodie mysteries, and other foodie lit as if they were popcorn.

Eater's Digest is really great popcorn, a collection of short, delicious, original pieces about our favorite topic. It goes in every fascinating food direction you can think of—serious food, pop food, funny food, quirky food, food history, food lore, food celebrities, food science, food advice, food everything. Open the book and start reading on any page. Choose a story at random or pick one that suits your mood: a piece on candy bars or the food service at the White House, a brief essay about astronaut food or weight-loss diets, an article about Iron Chef or how to behave when you're taken out for dinner, a checklist for bakers or one for bartenders. Take a pop quiz (or take several), ponder the great food films, learn how to buy a knife.

Each short piece is complete unto itself, readable on its own. Read one, read four, read ten—snack as much or as little as you like, then keep *Eater's Digest* handy for the next time you feel like grazing. Dip into it for the delicious pleasure of being totally entertained by food.

HOW DO SUMO WRESTLERS GET SO FAT?

How do they get so fat? They work at it. Japanese sumo wrestlers pack on the pounds just as assiduously as fashion models unpack them, and they do it the same way: by working out like mad and eating a special diet. That's where the similarity ends, however.

Success at sumo wrestling is contingent on skill, strength, and bulk. The skill and strength come from constant, rigorous training, and the bulk is acquired by equally rigorous eating. The members of the *heya*—the stable of wrestlers—start work early in the morning on an empty stomach (sumo training is not something you want to do on a full one), so by lunchtime they're hungry. After a huge lunch they take naps to slow their digestion, and then they eat a huge amount again at dinner.

The food they eat in such gigantic quantities is a one-pot dish we'd call *nabemono*: *nabe* for "pot," *nabemono* for "things in a pot." When sumo wrestlers prepare this dish (and it is indeed prepared by the junior members of each *heya*) it's called *chanko-nabe*, or just *chanko* for short.

There are no recipes or rules for making *chanko*. The basic idea is to take a very large cooking pot full of rich miso-based broth seasoned with sake, mirin, and other things, and gradually add to it a variety of

AMAZING FOOD EVENT: 1930

Invention of the Twinkie

If you're looking for someone to blame (or thank), try James A. Dewar, manager of a bakery near Chicago, who invented the little cream-filled sponge cakes in 1930 and named them after Twinkle Toe Shoes. He filled his cakes with banana cream right up until World War II made bananas scarce, then switched to the vanilla cream most of us remember so fondly (how *did* they get the cream inside the cake, anyway?). A Twinkie, you'll be happy to learn, is included in America's millennium time capsule, and it will probably still be edible whenever it's removed.

meats, seafood, tofu, and vegetables that have been prepared ahead. The ingredients that take longest to cook go into the boiling broth first, and the rest are added one by one. Once the cooking begins, it's a quick and easy process. As the pot of chanko is depleted by the senior members of the heya, noodles, rice, and eggs may be added to extend the chanko for the juniors. Everyone gets their fill—no one goes hungry—but the juniors may not get quite all the goodies that the seniors get, since seniors always eat first.

Eating chanko to bulk up seems almost counterintuitive; after all, the main thrust of the dish is toward protein and vegetables, not carbs. But as Mom always said, if you eat enough of anything, you'll get fat.

SUMO NOTE: Sumo is surrounded by secrecy and ritual, and visitors are rarely permitted in the heyas; a fan sitting down to a bowl of authentic chanko in a heya just doesn't happen. But the immense fascination with and devotion to sumo in Japan has produced the next-best thing: the chanko-nabe restaurant, serving highly refined versions of the chanko eaten by real sumo wrestlers.

THE GRAPEFRUIT DIET AND OTHER WEIRD WEIGHT-LOSS SCHEMES

Fad diets have been with us for as long as chubby thighs and hips have been an issue. Some of the diets are pretty strange, and most of them are short-term, unreliable, and not too much fun. And the minute you go off them, the weight may sneak back. The infamous Grapefruit Diet was based on the supposed "fat-burning" property of grapefruit. For breakfast you had half a grapefruit and a cup of black coffee. For lunch, half a grapefruit, an egg, some salad, a piece of dry toast, and tea or coffee. For dinner, half a grapefruit, two more eggs, lettuce, tomato, and more tea or coffee. Ugh.

The main thrust of fad diets seems to be either a severe reduction in the amount of food you eat, an elaborate system of what you may and may not eat, or an equally elaborate system of what you may eat with what. The Cabbage Soup Diet, for instance, has you slurping lots of the soup, along with very specific foods on each of seven days: on day four you have cabbage soup, eight bananas, and fat-free milk. The Seven-Day All-You-Can-Eat Diet sounds exciting until you see what you may eat all of: on Tuesday you get all the vegetables you want and that's it; on Thursday, five bananas and five glasses of milk; on Saturday, four steaks and fresh vegetables.

The Raw Food Diet: nothing cooked. The Peanut Butter Diet: four to six tablespoons of PB per day, but not at dinner. The Popcorn Diet: a healthy food plan, plus unsalted, unbuttered popcorn for snacks. The Chicken Soup Diet: a healthy breakfast and nothing but chicken soup for the rest of the day. The Apple Cider Vinegar Diet: up to three teaspoons of apple cider vinegar before each meal. (If you've ever downed a spoonful of apple cider vinegar, you know this could be heavy going.)

There are loads of diets to consider rejecting: the Three-Day Diet, the Russian Air Force Diet, the Detox Diet, the Chocolate Diet, the Hay Diet (Dr. Hay, that is), the Subway Diet, the Negative Calorie Diet, and oh so many more. Why not try moderate amounts of plain old healthy food with a good dollop of exercise on the side?

POP QUIZ!

1. Which ingredient is not in homemade mayonnaise?
   A. egg yolk
   B. oil
   C. sour cream
   D. vinegar
   E. salt

2. What is *cuitlacoche*?
   A. a variety of chile
   B. corn smut
   C. a tool for grinding masa flour
   D. goat meat
   E. liqueur in Mexican cocktails

3. *True or false*: Kumquats are grown mostly in South America.

4. Sapsago is
   A. the syrup from a specially cultivated maple tree
   B. an American Indian dish
   C. a kind of beer
   D. starch derived from sago palms
   E. a Swiss cheese

5. If you were a sous-chef in a restaurant kitchen, would you be
   A. in charge of everyone
   B. in charge of no one
   C. next in line after the head chef
   D. the person who preps the salads
   E. the person who garnishes the plates

6. How many Americans drink coffee?
   A. 4 out of 10
   B. 5 out of 10
   C. 6 out of 10
   D. 8 out of 10
   E. 9 out of 10

7. *Name that cuisine*: What's the national origin of egg foo yong?

8. Jansson's Temptation is a dish made of
   A. chocolate ice cream, cookie crumbs, and whipped cream
   B. buttered toast and creamed chipped beef
   C. flaked poached salmon mixed with rice, cream, and fresh dill
   D. potatoes, onions, and anchovies
   E. yellow cake layered with strawberries and vanilla buttercream frosting

Answers: 1. c; 2. b; 3. false; 4. e; 5. c; 6. d; 7. the United States (it's a pseudo-Chinese egg pancake); 8. d

13

LOLLIPOPS AND CHOCOLATE BARS: CANDY IN AMERICA

In 2002 the Department of Commerce reported that retail sales of candy (or confectionary products, to use their all-purpose terminology) were a whopping $24.3 billion. That's a whole lot of sweet stuff.

But wait a minute. Didn't Mom tell us that candy was a *special treat?* A reward? Maybe even a bribe (if you stop that shrieking, I'll buy you a Mars bar)? If we're spending billions of bucks on candy, how can it be a special-occasion treat? The numbers suggest that for millions of Americans candy is less a treat than an everyday pleasure.

Well, it is an everyday pleasure, but it's also a special-occasion treat. Most holidays (not to mention birthdays and anniversaries) demand candy; some holidays are totally identified with certain candies. Name the holiday: (a) chocolate bunnies, marshmallow chicks, and jelly beans; (b) candy corn and mini candy bars; (c) candy canes and chocolate Santas; (d) big red satin boxes of filled chocolates and little conversation hearts. No way do you do these holidays without candy.

Candy brings back memories—of scarfing down sweets at the movies when you were a kid, of the Whitman's Sampler your first boyfriend gave you or you gave your first girlfriend, of the bowls of cellophane-wrapped peppermints your great-aunt Sally put out in the living room when you visited. Candy is *fun.* It's *comforting.* You and your friends stopped for candy after school. Your mom sent you a candy-

---

15 OF THE MOST POPULAR CHOCOLATE CANDIES IN THE UNITED STATES

Snickers	Mounds	M&Ms
3 Musketeers	Almond Joy	Baby Ruth
Milky Way	Twix	Butterfinger
Oh Henry!	Hershey Bar	Pay Day
Kit Kat	Hershey's Kisses	Reese's Peanut Butter Cups

stuffed care package when you were homesick at sleep-away camp. You bought yourself some candy comfort when you were on the way home from a bad date, a dentist appointment, a job interview, the bar exam.

Candy is all wrapped up in nostalgia, too. Remember malt balls and Junior Mints? Bazooka bubblegum and Chuckles? Bubblicious and Skittles? Abba Zabbas, Kit Kats, Razzles, and Zotz? Your favorite candies define your time, or so you think. Actually, dozens of candies have bridged the decades and the generations. They're as familiar to your granny as they are to you. Life Savers, Juicy Fruit gum, Hershey's chocolate bars, Baby Ruth, Necco Wafers, Mary Janes, red licorice strings, M&Ms . . .

And candy is so-o-o-o easy to get to. Every other store on the block or in the mall sells candy: drugstores, bookstores, coffee shops, Internet cafés, gourmet shops, supermarkets, delis, bodegas, newspaper-and-magazine stands, even the local Blockbuster. Candy is everywhere (including online), in almost unbelievable variety.

What other edible comes in so many flavors, sizes, shapes, combinations, colors, and price points? An egg is pretty much an egg, but candy is out there in hundreds of forms, from the lowliest sour ball to the most exalted chocolate truffle. And new products just keep coming. Candy is affordable, accessible, and abundant—it belongs to everyone. What's on your Ten Best list?

THE PERFECT MARTINI

Ask for a vodka martini in front of a gin martini man and he'll recoil in horror; ask for a gin martini in front of a vodka martini woman and she'll roll her eyes at your dearth of cool. Gin or vodka, twist or olive, straight up or on the rocks—what is the perfect martini, anyway?

The facts about martinis are few, but we do know that the most popular early versions, before World War I, were made with equal amounts of gin and either sweet or dry vermouth, with a twist of lemon. As the years marched by, less and less vermouth made its way into the standard martini and the ratio of vermouth to gin dropped precipitously—one to five, one to six, one to seven. Dry, drier, driest. Drinkers have been known to ask the bartender simply to swirl a little vermouth around the martini glass, ditch the vermouth, and pour in the gin. Or simply to glance at the vermouth bottle and then pour the gin.

Nowadays we've expanded the definition of a martini, that's for sure. Never mind lemon twists versus green olives, how about a dirty martini? An apple martini? A watermelon martini? Martinis are what you make them, and the answer to the "perfect martini" question is this: a perfect martini is the one you like best.

7 Great Martinis

Blue Moon (gin, blue Curaçao)

Dirty Martini (gin, dry vermouth, olive juice, olives)

Pear Martini (vodka, pear liqueur)

Emerald Martini (gin, dry vermouth, Chartreuse, lemon peel)

Cosmo Martini (vodka, Cointreau, cranberry juice, lime)

Apple Martini (vodka, apple schnapps, apple juice)

Paisley Martini (gin, dry vermouth, scotch, lemon peel)

PROHIBITION AND SPEAKEASIES

A strange thing happened in America in January 1919: the Constitution was amended to prohibit the sale of alcoholic beverages anywhere in the United States. As of January 1920, with the passage of the Eighteenth Amendment, making, selling, and transporting liquor was going to be illegal. Cosmopolitans? Martinis? Margaritas? Mojitos? No way. Not even a nice glass of wine or a cold brew. Proponents called Prohibition "the Noble Experiment," and hoped that control of alcohol would result in less poverty and crime.

In anticipation of the big day, Congress passed what came to be called the Volstead Act—the Prohibition Enforcement Act. Lawmakers (among whom there were more than a few drinkers) knew that serious enforcement was going to be necessary if Prohibition was going to work.

Prohibition did not work. Oh, did it not work. The law was broken regularly, drinking *increased*, and the number of alcohol-related deaths shot up—in part because so much contaminated or poisonous liquor was produced (with no controls on the industry any longer) and consumed (by people too desperate to care what they were drinking). And gangsters quickly began bootlegging (dealing in liquor illegally) because there were gigantic profits to be made: Congress or no Congress, a lot of Americans wanted their alcoholic beverages.

Where there had been legal bars, saloons, and clubs before, now there were illegal speakeasies, reputedly over 100,000 of them in New York City alone. Whisper softly—"speak easy"—at the door of one, give the secret password or knock, and you entered a world of hard

---

10 THINGS TO DRINK AND EAT
THAT MAY ACTUALLY HELP WHEN YOU'VE GOT A HANGOVER

water	sports drinks	honey
fruit juice	toast or bread	cereal, oatmeal
tomato juice	crackers	broth
	muffin	

drinking. The entrance to a speak might look like the plain door to an ordinary shop or apartment; it might look like the fancy door to an exclusive club. The clientele varied according to the city, neighborhood, and style of the speakeasy, although rich folks could be found slumming at lowdown haunts on the wrong side of town.

Some speakeasies were just smoky rooms accommodating quiet, determined drinkers, but some were nonstop parties. And since there was fierce competition among them to attract customers, the owners often provided tempting entertainment. Jazz thrived in speakeasies (they didn't call it the Jazz Age for nothing), and so did sultry torch singers, cabaret, vaudeville acts, piano players. Patrons danced and drank and carried on even more wildly than they had when alcohol was legal; the thrill of the illicit was a powerful stimulant.

Prohibition lasted for thirteen long years, but speakeasies finally lost their reason for being in 1933, when the Eighteenth Amendment was repealed by the passage of the Twenty-first Amendment. Thirty-six states ratified it, and alcohol became legal in America once again.

HISTORICAL NOTE: In spite of the Twenty-first Amendment, twenty-two states and a slew of counties stayed on the wagon by passing statutes that kept them dry without the help of the federal government.

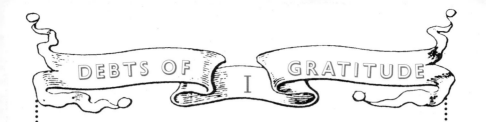

In 1895 **PEARL B. WAIT** (a guy who made cough syrup) bought the patent for a gelatin dessert and turned it into a *commercially packaged* gelatin dessert. What to call it? Pearl's wife, May, suggested Jell-O. Great idea, but it still didn't fly—until a clever marketer named Frank Woodward bought the business, almost gave up on it, and eventually turned it around big-time.

ROBERT COBB (who died in 1970) owned the original and famous Brown Derby restaurant in Hollywood. One hungry midnight in 1926 he went to the fridge and started pulling out ingredients for a big salad. Chop, chop, chop—lettuce, watercress, tomatoes, Roquefort cheese, cold chicken, hard-cooked egg, crisp bacon all went into a bowl with French dressing, and the delicious, classic Cobb salad came into being and became a staple on the Brown Derby menu.

In 1843 (or possibly 1846) Philadelphian **NANCY JOHNSON** patented a hand-cranked "artificial freezer" for making ice cream much more easily. Turning the crank agitated a narrow cylinder of ice cream mix that was set into a taller cylinder of ice and salt. The mixture froze quickly and voilà! Homemade ice cream.

Whenever you say, "Wow, that's the greatest thing since sliced bread," think of **OTTO FREDERICK ROHWEDDER** (1880–1960). He's the guy who invented the bread-slicing machine, in 1928 in Chillicothe, Missouri. Actually he had invented one earlier than that, but until he came up with a machine that would slice *and* wrap (to keep the bread from going stale), no one was interested.

CLASSIC SANGRÍA

Sangría gets its name from the Spanish word for blood—*sangre*—but there's nothing gory about sangría except the color. Basically it's a chilled mixture of red wine and fruit, with options. It's usually served from a glass pitcher, because this is a very pretty concoction and it would be a pity to miss the visuals.

When you make sangría, the wine you use should be a not-too-fancy medium- to full-bodied red (rioja is a good choice, in keeping with the Spanish theme). Don't use a cheap and disgusting wine because that will produce a cheap and disgusting sangría; there's no point in using expensive wine, either, because you're going to be adding flavor enhancers. (You may, if you like, use white wine, in which case you'll be making *sangría blanca*, white sangría.)

Now comes the according-to-taste part: To your glass pitcher of decent red wine add fresh fruit juice and fresh fruit. You may add the juice of an orange, a lemon, or a lime—or all three. Citrus is important in sangría, so even if you add the juice of some other fruit (peach or apricot nectar, apple juice, or even something exotic like pomegranate juice) be sure to toss in at least six slices of something citrus. And while you're tossing, toss in more fruit: chunks of peach, pear, plum, apple; whole blackberries or raspberries; sliced or whole strawberries.

Some sangría aficionados stop right there, with wine, fruit juice, and fruit, but others add a splash of Cointreau, Triple Sec, brandy, or rum to give it a bit more wow. And at the opposite end of the spectrum are the folks who add some bubbly water to lighten the sangría and give it a little less wow. You may let the mixture rest and marry in the fridge overnight (assuming you haven't added the club soda yet) or you may get started on it right away, poured over ice in tall glasses. Be sure everyone gets some fruit in his or her glass.

FRESH FRUIT JUICE NOTE: Some people prefer to add no fruit juice at all to sangría, and this is perfectly acceptable too. The beauty of sangría is its versatility.

```
┌──────────────────────────────────────────────────┐
│                12 TRADITIONAL TAPAS                │
│                                                    │
│   mixed olives        marinated squid      skewered chicken
│   Spanish cheese      stewed octopus       sweet and sour mari-
│   Serrano ham         Spanish omelet         nated onions
│   shrimp in garlic sauce  (also called Spanish  stuffed peppers
│   mussels in white        tortilla)        mushrooms in garlic
│     wine sauce                               and olive oil
└──────────────────────────────────────────────────┘
```

A MOMENT OR TWO WITH...

WRAPS

Wraps are a phenomenon in the food industry, and that doesn't happen very often. Existing products are often improved, tweaked, expanded, low-fatted, repackaged, refocused—but new products are news. Wraps began to catch on in the mid-1990s for a number of reasons. They were, well, new. Also inexpensive, fast, and fun. Also portable: You could eat a wrap on the go, striding down the street, standing on a line—or with the wrap in one hand and a mouse, a baby, or a cell phone in the other. They had flexibility, too; wraps were excellent for breakfast, lunch, or even dinner. They could be stuffed with just about anything, from scrambled eggs to barbecued chicken, smoked salmon, tuna, sliced steak, or roasted veggies. And they were cool. Kids of all ages loved them and still do.

WRAP FACT: As part of Awareness Week in 2003, the kids at Dixie State College of Utah made the (then) largest wrap in history (311 feet, 7 inches long) to "alert students to hunger both globally and locally," according to the *Dixie Sun*, and the giant wrap became a "major lunch giveaway" for students and faculty. Aha! *That* must have been the local hunger they were so concerned about.

RATTLESNAKE, ANYONE?

Now we're really going to mess up our heads, but first a disclaimer: this is a piece about unusual, strange, and weird foods from all over the world, so if you can't take it, don't read it.

Weird food is like pornography: we may not agree on the definition, but we each know what we think it is. Kangaroo sashimi, tapioca bubble tea, deep-fried grasshoppers—who's really to say? It's all in the eyes, nose, and taste buds of the eater, and your assessment of what's weird is almost entirely a function of what you're used to. But don't worry: even if you're an intrepid diner there'll probably be something here that will creep you out.

Let's start our Weird Food World Tour gently. First course: Chicken feet. Deep-fried rattlesnake. Gorgonzola cheese. Geoduck. Haggis. Scrapple. Snails (or escargots, if you insist). Frogs' legs. Chicken fat. Blubber. Jellyfish. Pigs' ears. Menudo (yes, boiled tripe soup). Yak milk. Kimchee (fermented cabbage with strong chiles). Goat's head. Monkey brains. Silkworm grubs.

Are you warmed up yet? Then here we go, second course: Fugu (highly poisonous Japanese blowfish). Fermented tofu. Durian (a very, very stinky fruit). Rat. Dog. Maggot cheese. Tequila worms. Sago (palm tree) worms. Thai water bugs. Lutefisk. Sheep's eyeballs. Jellied (animal) blood. Camel tendons. Mountain oysters (you know, bull testicles). Fufu (slimy balls of pounded yam). Baalut (egg containing a partially developed chick).

Still with me? Okay, third course, winding down: Poi. Bull penis. Pig snout. Fish bladder. Fermented herring. Fried spiders. Baby mouse wine. Fried dill pickles. Sea slug (or sea cucumber). Jellied eel. Iguana. P'tcha (jellied calves' feet, with garlic). Blood pudding. Smoked bats.

And for dessert: fruitcake.

18 Foods You'll Find at the Minnesota State Fair

Right out there with the ordinary wild-rice pancakes, chicken drummies, funnel cakes, and elk burgers, you'll find a huge food field to graze in. Think sticks, lots of things on sticks. Think batter-dipped, chocolate-dipped, deep-fried, and excessive. And you've got to love the names of some of these snacks, regardless of their culinary merit.

★ Cob Dogs

★ Bull Bites

★ habanero pistachios

★ yak meat sticks

★ wild-boar-and-bacon sticks

★ alligator sausage-on-a-stick

★ teriyaki ostrich-on-a-stick

★ Gizmos

★ Dogzilla

★ Pig Wings

★ cheesecake-on-a-stick

★ Dippin Dots

★ Fudge Puppies

★ deep-fried Milky Ways

★ deep-fried Oreos

★ sweet potato sundae

★ Supercalifragilistic Sundae

★ Custard Cyclone

FOOD ALLERGIES
AND FOOD INTOLERANCES

Let's not confuse the two. You probably know plenty of people who eat certain foods and then develop itchy little hives, have indigestion, throw up, or get diarrhea. Why, they wail, did I eat those strawberries (or chocolate or tomatoes or cheese)? Yes, those folks are extremely uncomfortable after munching strawberries, but they're not necessarily allergic. More likely they're intolerant.

There's a real difference, though the difference may seem moot when a person is suffering the consequences of eating the wrong food. A food allergy (or hypersensitivity) is, by definition, an abnormal response to a food, triggered by the immune system; a plain old food intolerance has nothing to do with the immune system. Food allergies affect only 1 to 2 percent of the population; food intolerances affect far more people (and sometimes when you're planning the menu for a dinner party it seems as if you've invited most of them). Food intolerances aren't fun, but food allergies can cause *severe* hives, eczema, or asthma, or even be fatal—a reaction called anaphylaxis, in which the airways in the lungs constrict, blood pressure drops, and suffocation can occur from swelling of the tongue and throat.

The most common adult food allergies are to peanuts, tree nuts (like walnuts and pecans), fish, shellfish, soy, wheat, milk, and eggs, but almost any food can be a potential stimulus. In children the foods most likely to cause allergic reactions are milk, soy, wheat, eggs, and peanuts. (Heredity can play a part: if both your parents have food allergies, there's a 75 percent chance that you will too.) Adult-onset food allergies are likely to stay with you for the rest of your life; kids often outgrow their allergies to milk, eggs, soy, and wheat—but they don't usually outgrow their allergic reactions to peanuts, tree nuts, shellfish, or fish.

So what's a food intolerance? Usually it results from a deficiency of a certain enzyme needed for digestion of a particular food. For instance, you've probably heard about lactose intolerance, which affects about one in ten people: the body needs the enzyme *lactase* to break down the sugar *lactose* in cows' milk; people with insufficient lactase have intolerance to lactose, so they react badly to milk and many products that contain milk. There are other kinds of food intolerances, as well: you might have an adverse reaction to food additives such as flavor enhancers (remember Chinese Restaurant Syndrome, a reaction to MSG?), food dyes, sulfites, and other preservatives.

And then there's psychological intolerance to certain foods. If your parents forced you to eat every morsel of liver on your plate before you were permitted to leave the dinner table, the stomachache you got when you ate that nice dish of liver last week could have started in your head.

✦✦

And Speaking of Food . . .

Delia Ephron, *How to Eat Like a Child*, 1977

HOW TO TORTURE YOUR SISTER

She ate her jelly doughnut at lunch. You saved yours. It is now two hours later:

Sit down next to your sister on the couch. Put the jelly doughnut on a napkin in your lap. Leave it, untouched, until she asks you if you still want it. Then begin eating: "Mmmmmmmmmmmmmmmmmmm. This is soooooooo good." Take a large bite and chew with mouth open so she gets a good view. Swallow and run tongue over lips. "Mmmmmmmmmmmmmmmmmmm." Stick tongue in jelly center and wave it around in the air before pulling it back in mouth. "Don't you wish you had some?" Take tiny bites. Lick fingers in between. "Boy—there's nothing like having a jelly doughnut in the middle of the afternoon!" Pop last bite in mouth and pat stomach.

BEING BEN AND JERRY

The official Ben & Jerry's Homemade, Inc., history states that Jerry Greenfield and Ben Cohen—high school buddies—were "two of the widest students in their school." Widest? Don't they mean "wildest"?

No, they don't. They mean widest. As in broad, the way a pair of dedicated ice cream guys should be. And their story is as much about a great guy friendship as it is about making great ice cream and running a unique and socially conscious business.

Thirteen years after the boys met in gym class in Merrick, Long Island, after Jerry had graduated from Oberlin and Ben had left Colgate, Skidmore, the New School, and NYU behind, they moved to Vermont and took a correspondence course in ice cream making. They opened their first ice cream shop in Burlington in 1978. From the beginning, their attitude about business was different from many: it was vital to Cohen and Greenfield to give their workers living wages and benefits; to use high-quality ingredients, such as milk from cows that had not been fed growth hormones; to participate in their community through, for example, Community Action Teams; to support environmental causes, like the preservation of the rain forest; to help nonprofit organizations via the Ben & Jerry's Foundation; and to get involved in political groups they believed in, like Businesses for Social Responsibility.

---

10 Weird Ice Cream Flavors (Past and Present)
AND A FOOTNOTE

French Lavender	Computer Chip	Sweet Potato Pie
Curry	Muddy Sneakers	Dastardly Mash
Black Licorice	Frozen Tundra	Grape Nut
	Miller Family Malt	

FOOTNOTE: And then there are the Japanese ice creams: fish, octopus, squid, ox tongue, crab, fried eggplant, eel, corn, shrimp, wasabi, cactus, and chicken wing. Really.

No outsider can know exactly what was going on inside the company, but it appears to have been a place where employees were respected, innovation was encouraged, and the owners lived their social values. Customers, in their turn, loved the product and the quirky, uncorporate nature of the company, and for quite a long time the enterprise was able to retain both its independence and its profits. In 2000, when Ben & Jerry's finally succumbed to corporate takeover, the new owner, multinational conglomerate Unilever, promised that the old company would maintain its independence and be free to continue its social activism. Whether that happens in the long term remains to be seen.

Bottom line, the story is great, but what's especially endearing is the sheer exuberance of Ben and Jerry. This is a pair of guys who, in 1986, crossed the country together in the "Cowmobile," handing out free samples of their ice cream. Who invented the Ben & Jerry's Joy Gang, "dedicated to bringing more joy into the workplace through fun activities." Who treated their community to free film festivals and Free Cone days. Who invented flavors as great as Cherry Garcia and Chunky Monkey, and as weird as Kiwi Midori and Ice Tea with Ginseng. Who sent their ice cream truck all the way down to Wall Street, in New York City, to hand out free scoops after the stock market crash in October 1987. Who sponsored the Newport Folk Festival, sent a Circus Bus on a national tour, held One World, One Heart festivals, joined the Children's Defense Fund, supported family farmers—the list is exhaustive and exhausting.

And it all started with a frivolous product that no one needed but everyone wanted—really great ice cream.

FOOD TRIP ACROSS AMERICA

Marnie Mueller, novelist

Every summer the three of us, my mother, my father, and I, would drive from Burlington, Vermont, to the West Coast to visit family. We would aim first for the Bay Area, where my aunt and cousins lived, and from there drive the coastal route to Seattle to see both my grandmothers as well as my maternal great-grandmother. We had the usual two-week vacation to cram all of this into, and a very limited budget. Our car was the property of the Vermont Farm Bureau, my father's employer, provided to him for his travel around the state. The bureau allowed us to use it for our yearly journeys across America in the latter part of the 1940s, with the caveat that we would be responsible for repairs and gasoline.

We couldn't afford to pay for a motel, and in order to save time my parents drove day and night, each taking a turn at the wheel while the other curled up in the sedan's back seat. I, being the smallest party, perched in the front passenger seat watching out for cowboys and Indians in the daylight hours and waking during the night to search for rabbits caught in our headlights as they hopped across the empty road.

One summer our car broke down in Ohio in a small town on Lake Erie. My despairing parents practically emptied their wallets to pay for the major repair, leaving us with just enough money to keep the gas tank full and another twelve dollars for food. They phoned my aunt, asking her to wire some money, but the first place it could reach us was at the Western Union office in Las Vegas, a minimum of three days' drive away. Twelve dollars had to cover our food for those three days. Doing the simple math, my mother calculated that this meant four dollars for three meals a day for the three of us, or twenty-seven meals for twelve dollars. Her solution to the dilemma: "We'll drink milkshakes with raw eggs stirred in!"

And so it was. Every meal, breakfast, lunch, and dinner, we sat at the picnic tables of roadside stands slurping our shakes. We alternated between vanilla and chocolate, "for variety's sake," my mother enthused, as the wafting aroma of hot dogs and fried chicken tormented us, and families chowed down, biting into juicy burgers, emptying ketchup onto golden French fries, gnawing round and round buttery corn cobs, and—the final affront—leaving uneaten pickle slices on their otherwise empty plates.

"This isn't so bad," my mother chirped. "And remember, it's nutritious. We're getting our protein in the eggs."

Try as I might to remain stoic, on the second day tears flooded my seven-year-old cheeks.

"Only one and a half more days, only four more milkshakes," my mother comforted, dabbing at my tears with the free paper napkin. "And we'll eat chicken-in-the-basket, I promise."

"Thank god," my father muttered. "Much more of this and I'll be laying the eggs."

Finally, on the morning of the fourth day, my parents came out of the Western Union office, all smiles as they walked to our car, where I waited with growling stomach.

"Let's go, kid," my father said, gunning the car. "Let's eat up a storm."

Never has any meal approached such a level of deliciousness and aesthetic delight as that fried chicken and French fries nestled in a red plastic basket lined with crisp white paper. Everything about it, the greasy smell, the tender chicken squirting juice when I bit through the thick crusty coating of batter, the finger-licking-good French fries slathered with ketchup, and the tingly taste of the sweet-sour pickles on the side. And it was all washed down with a genuine sassafras root beer float in a tall icy mug, frothing at the top with vanilla ice cream, the remains of which I spooned slowly from the bottom after the root beer was gone, savoring each sweet, eggless drop.

✳✳✳

15 Fun and Fascinating Food Web Sites

HometownFavorites.com
Hard-to-find groceries, nostalgia candy, and gift baskets

Kitchen101.com
*Links to all sorts of cookware, kitchen gadgets,
small appliances, foods*

http://www.virtualquincy.com/quincy/recreation/recipes.html
Hundreds of cooking and recipe links

chowhound.com
*For those who love and live to eat: quirky articles,
reviews, reports, opinions, books, and products,
from Alpha Hound Jim Leff*

reluctantgourmet.com
*The Reluctant Gourmet's cooking techniques,
cheese guide, pantry suggestions, chef interviews, tools,
terms, and recipes galore*

http://www.welton.net/nana/index.html
*Grandmother Norma Welton's recipes, with a
special emphasis on chocolate*

messygourmet.com
*Down-home recipes, tips, and chat from a pair
of delightfully wacky ladies*

✳✳✳

localharvest.org

Resource for the Buy Local movement, including info on local food, small farms, farmers' markets, and restaurants

lileks.com/institute/gallery

From James Lileks, author of the hilarious
Gallery of Regrettable Food

homecooking.about.com/od/newspaperfood1

Links to food articles appearing in newspapers all over the country

melissas.com

Specialty and staple produce from around the world

http://www.Sheboygan.lib.wi.us/pages/
linksfood.html#Anchor-Food-47383

Terrific (and varied) food and cooking links

moms-kitchen.com/kids_cook.htm

Recipes for kids

outlawcook.com

Commentary, recipes, and book reviews from the author of the "Simple Cooking" newsletter

Lagomarcinos.com

Chocolate Easter eggs, chocolate assortments, toffee, and more

SPORTS FOOD

You've heard about the carbo-loading food that's recommended to participants in heavy-duty athletic events such as marathons—plates of pasta, bananas, rice, bagels, waffles, pancakes, potatoes. A dieter's nightmare, a glutton's dream. But serious endurance athletes such as cyclists, swimmers, and runners need energy from huge amounts of calories, and carbs are the first line of supply. In fact, carbs generally make up 60 to 70 percent of total calorie intake for an A-list athlete.

Here's why: during strenuous exercise, the body draws on the glycogen that's stored in the muscles. If glycogen is depleted and not replaced, fatigue is the result and performance suffers. Carbohydrates supply quickly available energy by raising glycogen levels (and also have the added benefit of warding off dehydration; for every gram of carbohydrate stored, the body stores three grams of water). Athletes need protein (for repairing broken-down muscle tissue), fats, vitamins, and minerals, too, but calories are still, ultimately, the issue. So some athletes drink liquid supplements or eat power bars to keep their calorie intake high.

And then there's the big day, the big competition. Let's take a look at the Tour de France diet for the American cyclists, during which they each take in about six to seven thousand calories per day and some-

WHAT IS THIS THING, ANYWAY?

It's a giant serrator: an unusually large and sturdy tool for making rippled slices of carrot, potato, or other dense vegetables.

times even more. They eat all the time: breakfast, pre-race meal, and dinner, and plenty of snacks between meals and while they're cycling. Their carbs come from pasta, potatoes, rice, whole-grain breads, cereal, fruits, and vegetables; proteins come from eggs, meat, chicken, and yogurt; fats are from butter, cheese, and olive oil. (Lance Armstrong's pre-race breakfast is, reportedly, a bowl of tagliatelle topped with an egg, a sprinkling of Parmesan cheese, and chopped basil.) Water is crucial, and so are sports drinks, which provide some carbs and, more importantly, help replace electrolytes. Consuming all this stuff is practically a career in itself, and these champions have to manage it without getting a stomachache. Six hours on a racing bike with an upset tummy? Not a fun prospect.

OLYMPIC NOTE: According to the Olympic Training Center in Colorado Springs, here's what gets scarfed down in the dining hall in a single year: 584,000 pounds of pasta, 56,400 pounds of beef, 16,800 loaves of bread, 39,500 pounds of fruit, 29,000 pounds of potatoes, 10,800 gallons of juice, and 14,250 dozen eggs.

10 Great Novels about Food

Dinner at the Homesick Restaurant, Anne Tyler

Heartburn, Nora Ephron

Like Water for Chocolate, Laura Esquivel

The Debt to Pleasure, John Lanchester

La Cucina: A Novel of Rapture, Lily Prior

Friendship Cake, Lynne Hinton

Fried Green Tomatoes at the Whistlestop Café, Fannie Flagg

Hunger, Jane Ward

The Persia Café, Melany Neilson

Five Quarters of the Orange, Joanne Harris

WHAT DO ASTRONAUTS DINE ON?

Space food has come a long way, in more ways than one. Back in the days of the Mercury spacecraft, it was strictly freeze-dried tidbits and aluminum toothpaste-style tubes of semiliquid. In the Gemini missions the guys added water to plastic containers of pulverized dried food and squeezed the resulting purees directly into their mouths. With Apollo, the method was the same but the variety of food was greater and the newly available hot water made the food taste better when it was rehydrated. Still, mealtimes couldn't have been all that much fun or even much of a break from routine.

NASA aims to make eating an easier, more pleasurable, and less alienating experience for the astronauts, along with making sure they get the calories and nutrition they need on lengthy flights. A lot of time and energy go into providing food the crews actually want to eat. And then it has to be safe, light, compact, and packaged in a way that makes it simple to handle and quick to prepare—in zero gravity. Skylab, for instance, was like a luxury restaurant compared to those earlier missions. It had a dining table, food-warming trays, flatware (and scissors for snipping open the packaging), a freezer, and a (very small) refrigerator. Collapsible plastic bottles replaced plastic drinking bags, and the "spoon-bowl" package, from which rehydrated food could be eaten with a spoon, made the process of space eating more like normal earth eating. Best of all, the menu had grown to seventy-two items.

Whatever the mission, astronauts plan their own personal menus, within the bounds of nutritional requirements and the choice of foods. (Meals repeat, but not that often—every eight days on the Space Station, for example.) Here's a sample breakfast menu, per the NASA Web site: raspberry yogurt, sausage patty, picante sauce, tortilla (bread is a no-no, because aspirated crumbs could cause health problems and free-floating crumbs could get into the computers), oatmeal and raisins, granola bar, orange-pineapple drink, coffee. Lunch might be beef jerky, grilled pork chop, mac and cheese, tortilla, almonds, trail mix, cherry-blueberry cobbler, candy-coated chocolates, and orange-mango drink. Salt (suspended in water) and pepper (suspended in oil) are bottled, and there are little packets of mustard, ketchup, and sauces, too. Salsa is a big favorite.

10 MAIN COURSES FROM MILITARY MREs

The military now feeds mobile troops with MREs: meals, ready-to-eat. Most MREs contain an entrée, side dish, spread, crackers or bread, dessert, beverage, and some other odds and ends such as cookies, nuts, sauces, candy, seasonings, and so on. Here are some main dishes:

chicken with salsa	beef ravioli	jambalaya
chili and macaroni	beef enchiladas	chicken Tetrazzini
beefsteak with mushrooms	Cajun rice, beans, and sausage	chicken with cavatelli
		pork ribs

Here's one more tricky thing: food can taste different to the astronauts when they eat it in space, even after they've tested it on earth—which they do, extensively. An astronaut can arrive in space expecting to enjoy his favorite chicken à la king eight times in a row and suddenly discover that out in space it tastes bland or weird or he just doesn't like it. There's no way to exchange it for something else; the food he's chosen is the food he gets, and since he has to eat (for the calories as well as the nutrition), he's stuck unless a space pal will switch with him. That's what happened to astronaut Peggy Whitson: the Russian cosmonauts on the International Space Station loved the shrimp cocktail she had come to hate, and they traded their meals for hers. (Peggy had another interesting food jolt: peanut butter, which she never ate on earth, was delicious to her in space.)

Notice a lack of fresh fruit and vegetables in these menus and anecdotes? Refrigeration, storage, sanitization, and packaging are serious problems with fresh produce, and odor is, too: the scent of bananas, for example, can permeate the cabin and nauseate the crew. But NASA is working on this because crewmembers want fresh produce, and it improves crew morale. So would pizza, but they haven't yet figured out that one, either.

POPULARITY CONTEST: NASA says these are the top ten foods astronauts want to take on the Space Shuttle: butter cookies, dried beef, orange-mango drink, granola bar, lemonade, cashews and macadamia nuts, trail mix, shrimp cocktail, potatoes au gratin, and chocolate pudding.

The Story of
THE FOOD NETWORK

I have a friend who, instead of taking a nap in the afternoon, wraps herself in an afghan and watches the Food Network. It doesn't matter what's on; she's there for the delightful distraction, not the quality. Watching the shows doesn't make her cook more, cook differently, eat more, or eat differently (though she does occasionally crave something she sees on air). It simply entertains her with its unabashed and joyful dedication to her favorite topic—food.

The man who got the Food Network onto its feet was not a cook. Reese Schonfeld didn't know a damned thing about cooking, but he understood television. He'd been co-founder of CNN and, after Ted Turner booted him out, he went right on to develop other enormously successful TV programming. Nonetheless, the Food Network wasn't his brainchild. According to Schonfeld, in 1991 Johnson & Wales University (a huge culinary arts school) had an idea for a food network, took the idea to the *Providence Journal*, and the Providence Journal Company took it to Schonfeld at Time Warner.

Schonfeld said, in the September 2003 issue of *Gourmet*, "There were two reasons I thought [the Food Network] would work. The programming is quite inexpensive, and the advertisers were lined up." What about the fact that its focus was food? What about the fact that it was entertaining? "I'm not even gonna pretend I would have been smart enough to know how to meld food with entertainment," Schonfeld continued. "When we started, it was very much a food service magazine."

Maybe so, but not anymore. Now its scope is broad, if not deep. The Food Network is "committed to exploring new, different, and interesting ways to approach food," their press release informs us. In addition to diet, nutrition, and technique, the FN is into cuisines from all over the United States and the world, food history, pop culture, travel, loads of entertaining, and plenty of lifestyle.

When the first fledgling cooking shows went on public television (remember Julia Child, the French Chef?) they were a small part of a large and varied lineup that included news, drama, and kids' programs—and no advertising. But nonpublic television is a business that makes money by selling audiences to advertisers, and the Food Network is no different. In order for it to survive and prosper, the programming has to grab audiences. Which it does, around the clock. The Food Network now makes its way into over 80 million homes, and the Web site (foodnetwork.com) is used by several million fans.

PROGRAMMING NOTE: Did you know that the star chefs you see on the FN are far too busy to sit around deciding what dish to make for each half-hour TV slot, to buy and prep ingredients, set up the kitchen, and attend to all the other details of television cooking? That (and about a million other critical details like sticking to schedule and budget, getting the visuals right, and keeping the talent happy) is the job of the producer and staff. The chef's job is to be a star, so viewers will view and advertisers will advertise.

---

15 Songs about Food

"Food Glorious Food"

"Goober Peas"

"Alice's Restaurant"

"One Meatball"

"Chicken Soup with Rice"

"On Top of Spaghetti"

"My Boy Lollipop"

"Eat It"

"Country Pie"

"Cheeseburger in Paradise"

"Thanksgiving Song"

"Hot Dog and a Shake"

"Ice Cream"

"Cornflake Girl"

"Buttermilk Biscuits"

ALICE WATERS

Alice Waters, the mind, heart, and hands behind Chez Panisse restaurant and café in Berkeley, California, is arguably one of the two Mothers of Modern American Cooking. Julia Child made the home kitchen a friendlier, more interesting place to be; Alice Waters raised our standards of what to expect from the ingredients we find in restaurants and the ones we use to make our own meals, too.

According to her Web site (chezpanisse.com), Ms. Waters was born in 1944 in New Jersey, the Garden State. Perhaps that had lasting effects, because one of her most important claims to fame is her insistence on and her crusade for the very best of the garden, from baby lettuce to strawberries. What she's after is the best of every ingredient, which is— by her definition—local, organic, free-range, fresh, seasonal, and/or grown in accordance with the principles of sustainable agriculture.

Back in 1971, when she opened Chez Panisse, that was a pretty big chunk to bite off as a concept for a restaurant, but Alice Waters has always been a passionate advocate of the healing power of food and was

7 Good Reasons Not to Open a Restaurant

1. You'll work twenty hours out of every twenty-four.

2. You'll work seven days a week, including holidays.

3. If you're single, you'll have no time to date,
   much less have a relationship.

4. If you're married, you'll narrowly avoid divorce—maybe.

5. If your restaurant fails, your investors will hate you.

6. If it succeeds, your friends would hate you if you had any
   friends left after months (or years) of burying yourself
   in your work and having no social life whatsoever.

7. Nine out of ten restaurants fail in their first year.

clearly not going to be discouraged by a big concept. Her search for the best-tasting high-quality food extended to fishmongers, mushroom foragers, chicken raisers, and every other purveyor of ingredients for her now world-famous establishment.

The concept may not sound so unusual to you today, but you're spoiled—by Alice, among other pioneers. When she first set her sights on her goal of tracking down, cooking, and serving the very best from local suppliers, the pursuit of this concept in America was anything but common. Most high-class American restaurants took the best of what they were offered by their purveyors and rarely went on the offensive. Alice Waters did. She demanded the most delicious *everything*, and only if it met her standards of "environmental harmony and optimal flavor," as her Web site puts it. Somewhere along the way word got around, first about the brilliance of the restaurant's food, then about Waters's rigorous standards, and finally about the concept itself.

Celebrated extravagantly by her colleagues, adored by her public, she has used her unique position to advance her cause. She does not market or franchise herself, nor does she have a TV show, but a generation of chefs have learned from her and a generation (or two) of eaters have come to share her enthusiasm. And she gives back to her community: just ask anyone involved in the Edible Schoolyard Project she sponsored at the Martin Luther King Middle School in Berkeley, where children learn about, harvest, and eat the foods they grow in their own school backyard, with Alice Waters's support and blessing.

It's a coil whip, simply another version of the wire whisk. Use it for beating egg whites, mixing liquids, and smoothing sauces and gravies.

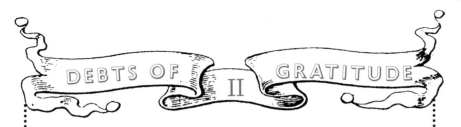

DEBTS OF GRATITUDE
II

JULIUS MAGGI (1846–1912) eventually got around to inventing the bouillon cube, but he started in 1884 with a powdered pea-and-bean soup mix that provided good (and easy) nutrition to factory women who had neither time nor money for cooking hearty meals. A few years later he came up with bouillon concentrate in capsules, which were soon redesigned into the cubes we know today.

GENNARO LOMBARDI opened America's first pizzeria—Lombardi's—in 1905, on Spring Street in New York City (where it still lives today, though not in the original spot). He made his delicious pizza in a coal-burning oven, from a recipe he'd brought from Naples in 1897.

ELIZA ACTON (1799–1859) revolutionized the concept of *cookbook*. Her *Modern Cookery for Private Families*, published in London in 1845, was addressed to real women—housewives—not to chefs with full staffs. It was written clearly and simply, with ingredients listed separately so that the much-tested (by Acton) recipes were easier to use.

E. W. "BILLY" INGRAM and **WALTER A. ANDERSON** founded the White Castle hamburger chain, the oldest in America, in 1921 in Wichita, Kansas. The burgers were pretty thin (unlike other burgers of the time), but they only cost a nickel. The business expanded rapidly, and by 1933 Ingram had bought out his partner. Part of the company's success was due to the standardized, highly recognizable White Castle building, fifty-five of which were built between 1928 and 1956.

40

11 Foods Named for (Mostly) Real People

MELBA TOAST
for Nellie Melba, opera star

PEACH MELBA
ditto

MELBA SAUCE
and again

OYSTERS ROCKEFELLER
for John D. Rockefeller

CHICKEN TETRAZZINI
for Luisa Tetrazzini, another opera star with a big appetite

VEAL OSCAR
for King Oscar II of Sweden

DAGWOOD SANDWICH
for Dagwood Bumstead, perpetually starving husband
in the old *Blondie* comic strip

EGGS BENEDICT
for a pair of bored patrons of Delmonico's Restaurant,
Mr. and Mrs. Legrand Benedict

EGGS SARDOU
for French playwright Victorien Sardou

BEEF STROGANOFF
for the Russian diplomat Count Paul Stroganov

BANANAS FOSTER
for Richard Foster, faithful patron
of Brennan's Restaurant in New Orleans

The Oscars of the Food World:
THE JAMES BEARD FOUNDATION AWARDS

James Beard was in all ways a giant of a man. Tall, broad, and immensely talented, with boundless energy and creativity, he made an impact on American food and cooking that persists to this day, not least in the form of the James Beard Foundation Awards that are the highlight of every year in the American culinary world.

Beard was born in 1903 in Portland, Oregon. After a thwarted stab at an acting career, he backed off and started a catering business. From catering it was a short hop to opening a small food store, writing a pair of cookbooks, and arriving at the realization that his real life would be in the world of food. Between 1945 and 1955, he produced many more cookbooks (*The Fireside Cookbook* is a particularly charming one), spoke and appeared on radio and TV (where his earlier theatrical training undoubtedly paid off), wrote prolifically for magazines, consulted for restaurants, ran his own restaurant in Nantucket, and generally towered head and shoulders above most other food personalities.

In 1955 Beard started his own cooking school in New York City,

---

25 FAVORITE COMFORT FOODS

hot oatmeal	creamed spinach	hot cocoa
cinnamon toast	stuffing	rice pudding
chicken soup	hot biscuits	macaroni and cheese
mashed potatoes	grits	tuna casserole
chocolate ice cream	bread pudding	tomato soup
warm apple pie	brownies	chocolate fudge sauce
vanilla pudding	sugar cookies	soft-boiled eggs
grilled cheese sandwich	peanut butter	spaghetti and meatballs
	sticky buns	

but he also taught all over the country, sharing his enthusiasm (and vigorously proselytizing) for regional American cooking. Even more new cookbooks came out, and continued to come out almost to the end of his life, in 1985. He was a tireless proponent of fine but sensible cooking.

His home in Greenwich Village was the center of a vibrant round of food, friends, and learning, and so it remains today—a monument to a monument, and the heart and headquarters of the James Beard Foundation, which is now a world-famous resource for food and wine professionals, a gathering place for food lovers, and the primary sponsor of the James Beard Foundation Awards. The awards have become, since their first presentation in May 1991, the industry standard. No cash prizes are involved; the currency is only (only!) recognition for what the judges deem to be excellence and great achievement.

The awards for 2004, for example, were divided into six overall categories: book, journalism, chef and restaurant, broadcast media, lifetime achievement, and restaurant design. Within each category there were at least two and as many as sixteen separate awards. In the book category there were awards for the outstanding baking cookbook, international cookbook, and single-subject cookbook, among others; in the chef and restaurant category there were various best restaurant awards, awards for rising star chef, best pastry chef, best chef in America, regional best chefs, and so on.

Though there's no prize money involved, this kind of prestige can be worth quite a lot: a cookbook bearing a sticker that proclaims it a Beard Award winner looks a lot better than one without. Among chefs, publishing houses, restaurants, and journalists there's fierce competition for the honors, and there's often a certain familiarity about the names of the winners—hot chefs are more likely to win than unknowns, major cookbook publishers generally sweep the book field, well-known restaurants are frequently at the fore, and big-city newspaper reporters are singled out more times than small-town reporters. It's not surprising at all; it's logical. But most years—same as at the Academy Awards—there's some delicious surprise, some dark horse nominee who emerges an unexpected winner and keeps hope alive for all aspirants.

SOUND BITE FROM HOLLYWOOD:
EATING, THEN AND NOW

E-mail from a longtime Angelino

Sweetheart, you ask me what I remember about eating in Hollywood? Back in the old days (and we're talking thirties, forties, and fifties here) the hot spots for dining were Chasen's, the Brown Derby, Ciro's, the Trocadero. Drop-dead glamorous, where the stars came out to see and be seen. They're gone now, along with most of the stars. All gone, except for Musso and Frank's. Oh, yes, Musso and Frank's is a good one. The only other old glory days restaurant I remember is Romanoff's. Equal to Chasen's when I was a kid. Chasen's and Romanoff's were the big ones.

Canter's is an old deli on Fairfax. Current big deli is Nate 'n' Al's. When I was a kid, it was little, more of a counter, now it's a big deli on Beverly Drive. I wouldn't say that famous people eat in it, as famous people don't eat deli anymore. But it's an old-timer's place, and Larry King is always there. And they have the world's greatest franks. And if a person did want to eat deli, that's where they'd eat.

Spago is the main place now. For glamour. But Giorgio's has a lot of heat. But not the glamour of Spago. Giorgio's is near the beach on West Channel Road. Italian. The Ivy is also a biggie. There are two. The Ivy and the Ivy at the Shore.

I'm not really into the show business thing out here. All I remember about Chasen's is a dessert, Dobosch Torte, and the chili and I think marrow bones. But I'm not sure.

CHILI ACROSS AMERICA

Chile is a Spanish word; a chile—poblano, chipotle, habanero, serrano, jalapeño—is a pepper. Chili is an invented (okay, transmuted) word for that North American (not Mexican!) bowl of, well, of what? You'll find chiles (or chili powder) in chili, that much is pretty consistent, but travel from state to state in the United States and you'll find not much else that is, including which chiles (or chili powder) are used and how hot the chili should be.

In Texas a bowl of red will contain beef, onions, garlic, tomatoes, chile, and herbs, but *no beans*. In Cincinnati it's beef, onions, tomatoes, garlic, chile, herbs—and cinnamon, allspice, and cocoa powder; beans can happen, or not. Oklahomans like their chili made with beef, tomatoes, onions, garlic, chile, herbs, and finely ground cornmeal for

U.S. Cities with the Best and Worst Tap Water

According to recent research on levels of contaminants such as arsenic, bacteria, and lead, conducted by scientists at the University of North Carolina, Rutgers, and the Natural Resources Defense Council, the three cities with the best water were these:

St. Louis, Missouri
Toledo, Ohio
Honolulu, Hawaii

The worst water is in these cities:

Las Vegas, Nevada
Los Angeles, California
San Francisco, California
Houston, Texas
Glendale, California
Washington, D.C.
Wichita, Kansas

thickening. In New Mexico there's green chile (spelled with an *e* at the end), with no meat at all, or green chile with pork. In the South and Midwest, beans are definitely the thing. And so it goes across the country.

Competition has grown up around chili, and there are fierce verbal and culinary battles between cooks, counties, cities, states. The "true" definition of chili has, for some reason, become a matter of contention and the subject of a lot of newspaper articles. Truth, honor, and justice seem to be at stake; being right seems to be important to chili aficionados. Chocolate cake lovers welcome more chocolate cake recipes—the more, the merrier—but chili lovers? Loyalty to one's own particular regional style is as unquestioning as loyalty to the local football team.

This contemporary flexing of the chili muscles appears all too often to be testosterone driven. However, what was apparently the very first chili contest was won by a Mrs. F. G. Ventura, at the Texas State Fair in 1952, and she held the title of "World Champion Chili Cook" for fifteen years. After that, chili competition deteriorated. In the August 1967 issue of *Holiday* magazine a writer named H. Allen Smith, who hailed from Illinois, declared that "no living man, and let us not even think of woman in this connection, no living man, I repeat, can put together a pot of chili as ambrosial . . . as the chili I make." The gauntlet was thrown down. Smith went on to say, "You may suspect, by now, that the chief ingredients of all chili are fiery envy, scalding jealousy, scorching contempt, and sizzling scorn. The quarreling that has gone on for generations over New England clam chowder versus Manhattan clam chowder . . . is but a minor spat alongside the raging feuds that have arisen out of chili recipes."

These raging feuds even reached the U.S. Senate, where, in 1974, Senator Barry Goldwater of Arizona mixed it up with Senator John Tower of Texas over the chili issue. Senators Henry Bellman of Oklahoma, Robert Taft of Ohio, and Joseph Montoya of New Mexico joined the fray too. Welcome to the silly chili wars, and they're not over yet.

WHY BEANS GIVE YOU GAS

Beans aren't the only culprits. Far from it. Peas, broccoli, cauliflower, cabbage, Brussels sprouts, onions, eggplant, celery, asparagus, peaches, apples, pears, whole grains, carbonated drinks, fruit drinks, milk, milk products (ice cream!), prunes, raisins, nuts, diet foods that contain sorbitol or xylitol, breads and cereals that contain lactose, and even popcorn can be guilty where flatulence is concerned.

Gas and its accompanying discomfort and embarrassing expulsion are, unfortunately, natural and unavoidable. When you eat, enzymes break down some of the food while it's in your stomach and small intestine. Nutrients are absorbed or stored, and all is well. But if, for example, there's a shortage or absence of certain enzymes, some of the food does not break down, and it makes its way to your large intestine in an undigested state. Bacteria in the large intestine go to work on the leftovers and in the process of gobbling they produce a variety of gases: hydrogen, carbon dioxide, nitrogen, methane, hydrogen sulfide.

The gases make you feel bloated and uncomfortable and, more to the point, they exit your body in a rush of wind. Farts. Most of the gases are odorless, but hydrogen sulfide isn't—and that's the one that causes the smell we associate with farting.

Proteins and fats don't cause much gas because they're generally absorbed before they reach the large intestine. But you can't eat a diet of just proteins and fats; you need a lot of those healthy foods on the list above, in spite of their gas-producing talents. So wrap your head around the certainty that farts are a part of life, and if you don't like it, wrap your head around trying one of the antiflatulence preparations.

15 WORLD-FAMOUS VEGETARIANS

Gandhi	Albert Einstein	Isaac Bashevis Singer
Susan B. Anthony	Jane Goodall	Leo Tolstoy
George Bernard Shaw	Charles Darwin	Leonardo da Vinci
Cesar Chavez	Vincent Van Gogh	Louisa May Alcott
Thomas Alva Edison	Mark Twain	Franz Kafka

SPOTTED DOG AND OTHER BRITISH ECCENTRICITIES

It's probably not fair to land on the Brits for their food-related oddities, but how can you resist making fun of a cuisine that includes something called spotted dog, especially when its alternative handle is spotted dick?

Americans are often charmed by the names the English give their national dishes and snacks, and then stunned by the real things. Bubble-and-squeak—cute, right? Maybe not, when you discover what it is: a fry-up of leftover mashed potatoes and cabbage or, worse, Brussels sprouts. Chip buttie: how adorable, but only if you're in the mood for two buttered slices of white bread sandwiched around French fries and tomato sauce. Toad-in-the-hole? Sausages baked in batter. Groaty dick pudding? Something with beef, leeks, and oat groats. And haggis? Don't ask (but see below).

Spotted dog (or dick, if you have the nerve) is *pudding*, and it's also *a pudding*. In England, pudding is both a general term for dessert (Q: What's for pudding? A: Treacle tart) and a term for a sweet cooked thing vaguely related to an American pudding. To make spotted dog, mix together a large amount of flour and either margarine or suet (suet!), add some salt, some sugar, and a bunch of currants or sultanas (raisins, to you); stir in water to make a dough. In case you haven't figured it out yet, the currants or raisins are the spots on the spotted dog. The doughy mixture is shaped into a cylinder, tied in a pudding cloth, and boiled for a couple of hours. Then, when the cook is sure the pudding is dead, it's turned out onto a dish and served with what the Brits call

WHAT ON EARTH IS... HAGGIS?

Prepare yourself. This is not a description (or a concoction) that sits well on American stomachs. Scottish stomachs, yes; American stomachs, no. Haggis is a traditional Scottish dish, and here's how it's made: The offal of a sheep (heart, lungs, liver, and so on) is boiled and minced. The mince is mixed with beef suet, onions, oatmeal, and seasonings, then stuffed into a sheep's stomach lining. The stomach is stitched closed, and the haggis is boiled again for several hours. It's often served with "neeps and tatties"—mashed turnips and creamed potatoes.

custard sauce. (The French, wags that they are, call it crème anglaise, and you just know they don't mean it kindly. *Au contraire*.)

If you're feeling peckish (Brit-speak for hungry) and you want a nosh (you know what a nosh is), the English have it covered. You could have a bickie or two (short for biscuits, which are cookies): digestive, Garibaldi, Twiglets, ginger nuts, or HobNobs. A handful of crisps (potato chips) in a variety of flavors, like beef, smoky bacon, or cheese-and-onion. A fairy cake (just an innocent cupcake), Jaffa cake, or a bar of Cadbury's choc. A couple of nice soft buns—fruit buns, baps, or Bath buns. An ice lolly, a slice of Victoria sponge, jam roly-poly, or a dish of sticky toffee pudding. Or if you're really desperate, spread some marmite (gooey flavored yeast extract, from a jar) on granary (a kind of brown bread), add some Cheshire cheese—and you've got a sarny (sandwich) to die for. Have mushy peas on the side.

> **TIDBIT:** Plum pudding is plumless. Once upon a time plum pudding might have contained plums, but nowadays the traditional British Christmas dessert is plumless. It's clueless, too, by American standards. We've never taken to this steamed (or worse yet, boiled) concoction of suet (you know, solid white beef fat), raisins, candied fruit, breadcrumbs, almonds, and spices. Can't imagine why we don't like it—and even smothering it with hard sauce won't change our minds.

10 FOOD PATHOGENS THAT CAUSE FOOD POISONING

Some of these bad bugs have longer official names, but these are the names you may recognize.

campylobacter	*Listeria*	*Clostridium botulinum*
salmonella	E. coli	hepatitis A
shigella	*Staphylococcus aureus*	hepatitis E
	Clostridium perfringens	

THE GREASE TRUCKS

Rutgers University in New Brunswick, New Jersey, is the home of a food phenomenon. In a parking lot on campus there's a fleet of open-sided trucks that serve awesomely awful sandwiches to a population of clamoring students. This has been going on for several decades without abatement (and possibly without improvement). The trucks are known as the Grease Trucks, and they have earned their titles.

The sandwiches are all built around a theme: fat. Each one is *called* "Fat" something-or-other (Fat Cat, Fat Mojo, Fat Romano, and so on), and they are *full* of fat, and they could certainly *make* you fat, too. Each sandwich is a combination of ingredients that screams "teenager," and has, in fact, been invented by one or more teenagers who happen to be students at Rutgers. The underlying concept is this: I want it all, I want it now, and I want it cheap. Instead of taking the form of a normal meal, the main course, side dishes, and condiments are glommed together inside a big hero roll—you get it all now cheap.

The original "Fat" sandwich was the Fat Cat: two cheeseburgers, mozzarella sticks, French fries, lettuce, tomatoes, mayonnaise, and ketchup. From there it only got worse. The Fat Koko: cheese steak, mozzarella sticks, French fries, marinara sauce, lettuce, and tomatoes. The Fat Romano: cheese steak, pork roll, French fries, eggs, lettuce, tomatoes, onions, mayonnaise, and ketchup. The Fat Darrell Especiale (you've read about it and heard about it): chicken fingers, mozzarella sticks, French fries, lettuce, tomatoes, onions, marinara sauce, and mayonnaise.

We can only hope the kids will outgrow their need for Fat Darrells by the time they graduate.

---

10 FOODS THAT CAN RAISE YOUR CHOLESTEROL LEVEL

egg yolks	coconut oil
organ meats	palm oil
fatty meats	palm kernel oil
lard	cocoa butter
full-fat dairy products	foods containing hydrogenated fats

A Few Food Stats—Believe Them or Not

Each year Average American eats
46 slices of pizza, more than a pound of honey,
10½ pounds of carrots, 27 pounds of cheese,
more than 14 quarts of ice cream, 75 pounds of chicken,
more than 7 pounds of grapes, about 15 pounds of sodium,
almost 18 pounds of turkey, and 4½ pounds of broccoli.

★

Average American will eat nowhere near the recommended
amount of fruits and veggies—only about four servings per
day, but that includes French fries and potato chips.

★

The Sugar Association claims that Average American eats only
1.6 ounces of sugar daily.

★

Average American will eat
at least one out of every six dinners away from home.

★

Fifty-four percent of Americans are convinced
that they're eating healthy diets and that there's
no reason to alter their eating habits.

★

Government figures assert that
two-thirds of Americans are either overweight or obese.

★

Thirty-three percent of American adults are on diets—
that's about 71 million people.

★

Ninety-five percent of all dieters will
regain their lost weight in one to five years.

★

Ten percent of America's disposable personal income
goes to—food!

HOW TO BEHAVE WHEN YOU'RE TAKEN OUT FOR DINNER

When someone takes you out for dinner, *you're a guest* and you must behave like one.

Turn off your cell phone and beeper and put them *away*. This is an ironclad rule, unless you're a doctor on call or your wife is going into labor at any minute, in which case maybe you shouldn't be out for dinner. You owe undivided attention to your host and peace and quiet to other diners.

Don't take it upon yourself to flag down the waitperson for any reason whatsoever (exception: your host is choking and you've forgotten how to perform the Heimlich maneuver). If you need something, like a glass of water, mention casually that you'd love a glass of water and trust that your host will see to your needs.

Don't waffle around for too long when you're ordering. Dithering is boring, especially when accompanied by commentary: Oh, I shouldn't have the lasagna, it's so fattening, I should have the grilled chicken with a salad, no, how about the fish, okay, I'll have the fettucine Alfredo with a side of gnocchi.

12 Risky Dinner-date Foods

Don't eat these on a first or second date. They're messy, out of control, likely to drop or drip into your lap—and guaranteed to humiliate you.

spaghetti with meatballs ★ spareribs ★ chicken Kiev ★ soup of any kind ★ mussels in broth ★ lobster ★ crisp tacos ★ anything covered with melted mozzarella ★ large cherry tomatoes ★ green salad with sloppy dressing ★ peas ★ rice

Don't drink too much. If you're nervous, you may think that an extra drinky-poo will help, but it won't. You'll just get tipsy (or drunk, heaven forfend) and make a fool of yourself and want to emigrate to Saskatchewan in the morning.

Don't get angry at the service, the food, or anything else. Aside from being the height of ungraciousness, your displeasure will make your host feel uncomfortable and, worse, as if he's an idiot with execrable taste in restaurants. On the other hand, if something is seriously wrong—like the chef left the veal out of the veal scaloppine or the milk for your tea is curdled—tell your host, with a deprecatory smile, so he can summon the waitperson and correct the mistake. Imagine how humiliated he'll feel if you clam up now but mention the problem two hours later.

Don't forget your manners, not that you ever would. Talking or laughing too loudly, chewing with your mouth open, picking your teeth, slurping—never. It's also very bad manners to disappear to the restroom for half an hour. This means you, ladies.

That's the "don't" side; here's the "do" side: Look good; you owe it to your host and to your reputation. Be a good companion. Make conversation. Be polite to the waitstaff. When the meal is over, thank your host sincerely. And do not ask for a doggy bag.

15 KINDS OF SUSHI

yellowtail	salmon	octopus
tuna	salmon roe	shrimp
tuna belly	fluke	flying fish roe
sea urchin	mackerel	snapper
squid	eel	clam

TROPICAL FRUITS

If you were running for Most Globally Popular Tropical Fruit, you'd definitely want to be a pineapple. If you couldn't be a pineapple, you'd want to be a mango, to take the prize for first runner-up. Second runner-up would be Miss Avocado, and third would be Miss Papaya. Your court would probably consist of Miss Lychee (or litchee, litchi, or leechee), Miss Durian, Miss Rambutan, Miss Guava, and Miss Passionfruit. There are bound to be surprises in any contest, but that's the most likely lineup according to recent statistics from the Food and Agriculture Organization of the United Nations.

Here's what else the FAO tells us: The most pineapples are grown in Thailand, the most mangoes in India, the most avocados in Mexico, and the most papayas in Brazil. The most pineapples are *exported from* Costa Rica, the most mangoes and papayas from Mexico, the most avocados from Chile. Now here's a shocker: the most pineapples, mangoes, and papayas are *imported to* the United States and the most avocados go to Europe.

Many types of the world's enormous assortment of tropical fruit won't make it to your local Food Emporium. When was the last time

---

AMAZING FOOD EVENT: 1893

Introduction of Juicy Fruit Gum

Apocryphal or completely true, the Juicy Fruit gum story is great: Twenty-nine-year-old William Wrigley, Jr., went to Chicago in 1891 with thirty-two dollars in his pocket, a talent for selling, and a flexible mind. When he sold Wrigley's soap to merchants and they preferred the free baking powder he offered them, Wrigley switched to selling baking powder. When the merchants liked the free chewing gum he included with the baking powder, Wrigley switched to selling chewing gum. Juicy Fruit appeared in 1893, with Wrigley's Spearmint hot on its heels. Juicy Fruit is the best-selling fruit gum in the United States today.

---

you had a glimpse of an ababai? A jackfruit? A langsat or a mangosteen or a salak? But more and more tropical fruits are showing up in ethnic markets and gourmet shops: tamarillo, sapote, cherimoya, carambola (star fruit), tamarind, sapodilla, prickly pear, mamey, pepino, and others. Even coconuts, plantains, and pomegranates can look pretty exotic if all your grocery usually carries are apples, bananas, and oranges.

FAVORITE TROPICAL FRUIT NAMES (OR NICKNAMES): vegetable brains, sherbet fruit, stinky fruit, dragon's eyes, velvet apple, elephant apple, macho banana, chocolate pudding fruit, Swiss cheese plant.

MUST OR MYTH:

Buy melons, peaches, nectarines, and plums only at the peak of ripeness.

This is a myth. Melons, peaches, nectarines, plums, and apricots, too, will ripen after picking. They won't necessarily get sweeter, but they will get softer and they will develop more flavor if you leave them at room temperature (in other words, out of the fridge). Keep a close eye on them so you can eat them when they've reached the ripeness you want. If you're not ready to eat them, refrigerate to hold them (for a few days) and let them come to room temp again for maximum flavor.

10 OF AMERICA'S MOST POPULAR FRUITS

apples	peaches	watermelon
bananas	pears	cherries
oranges	plums	grapes
	strawberries	

A MOMENT OR TWO WITH...

SMOOTHIES

A smoothie is:

a. a refreshing drink
b. a snack
c. a treat
d. a quick energy boost
e. a meal
f. a fun way to consume fruit
g. all of the above

All of the above, of course, at different moments. A smoothie is a blender-whirled drink made of fruit and something that can turn fruit into a liquid: ice, fruit juice, milk, soymilk, yogurt, frozen yogurt, ice cream, ice milk, sherbet. Smoothies mix up fresh and fast, and they can be enhanced with sweeteners, cocoa powder, vanilla, or other flavorings. Or they can be pumped up with vitamins, minerals, protein supplements, ginseng, herbs, echinacea, and other health food additions.

Smoothies haven't quite taken over the beverage market the way purveyors and franchisers hoped, but they've certainly become a part of the fast food galaxy. They've even begun to transcend what looked like an inherent problem: cold smoothies appeared to be a great idea for a hot day—but summer doesn't last all year. Somehow, though, we got used to the year-round smoothie, freshly made or bottled, especially when we buy wraps; smoothies and wraps just seem to go together. And the latest fad? Alcohol-spiked smoothies, a lot like frozen daiquiris and margaritas.

THE SUBLIME STRAWBERRY

Imagine a land where tasty little red berries grew wild, in abundance, ripe for the plucking, no cultivation needed. That was North America right into the nineteenth century. Wild strawberry patches abounded and very little deliberate planting occurred. By the mid-1800s, however, Americans wanted fresh strawberries even in the cities, and cultivation began in earnest. In the late 1800s, refrigerated railroad cars made it possible to ship the berries, among other fresh fruits and vegetables, all over the country.

Although every state in the union grows strawberries, California—with its warm days and cool nights—produces most of the berries we see in the markets year-round. Strawberries are harvested at peak, or so we're told, and do not ripen after picking. Don't bother leaving them out on the kitchen counter—they won't improve in color or flavor, which is pretty depressing since most boxes of strawberries contain at least a few half-ripe, half-green ones.

Buy boxed strawberries no more than a few days before you want to eat them. Look for deep red berries with their leaf caps still attached. Watch out for moldy, bruised, weepy, or crushed berries—they're spoiled or spoiling, and, if you find some, you should toss them out right away. Pop the boxed berries into the fridge unwashed; when you're ready to eat them, rinse gently but well, air dry, and wait until they're at room temperature. That's the best they'll ever be, and that isn't saying much if you've ever been lucky enough to taste local strawberries picked *really* ripe, delivered to your local farm stand or farmers' market, and sold within a day or two of harvesting.

FAVORITE STRAWBERRY FACT: Those itty-bitty black dots on the berry's skin are seeds, and there are about two hundred of them per berry.

THE JOY OF BRUNCH

Oh, bliss—it's Sunday morning and you can sleep late. You roll over and snuggle down into the blankets, mmm, warm and cozy, don't have to go to work. But wait! It's Sunday morning! Brunch! You promised to be at the Hotel Splendide (or the Café Dynamite or the Brasserie Très Chic) at—when? The ungodly hour of 11:30 A.M.?

Now, now, now, it's not so bad once you spend fifteen minutes under the shower and take a couple of aspirin. You can do this. Your (a) spouse-to-be; (b) parents; (c) close friends; (d) not-even-vaguely-close friends; (e) visiting cousin Elvira will be waiting with cheerful good-morning smiles (how do they manage that?) and bright conversation (oh, help), happy to see you. If only you can see them through that pesky fog in front of your eyes . . .

Who invented brunch, anyway? Must have been some devil determined to steal your entire Sunday, because after you scarf down the mimosas and the huevos rancheros (frittata, eggs Benedict, French toast), the side of home fries, a couple of sausages, biscuits with butter and jam, berries, and coffee, they're going to have to wheel you home on a gurney. And when you finally get home (assuming you do get home without a detour to the ER), you'll be useless for the rest of the day. All you'll be good for is a nap. And another nap. Oh, please, another nap.

Okay, get it together and put on some clothes. Without bending over too far, because if you bend over too far you'll black out. Someone told you that brunch has been around since the 1930s, which wouldn't surprise you at all since this morning you feel as if you've been around since the 1930s. How many brunches have you been to in your lifetime? More than you can count. One too many. If only you could skip today's.

But you can't, so you'd better get to the front door and open it. Slowly. Ah, fresh air. Sunshine. Blue sky. Hey, everything looks great out here, and suddenly you're hungry—for brunch.

Who consumes the most coffee in the world? Americans do. More than half the population (over the age of ten) drinks roughly three to four cups a day. That's a lot of coffee, all told, for a country that wasn't really in on the original craze. Coffee plants as we know them originated in Ethiopia, and brewed coffee made its way from Africa to the Middle East and Turkey, and then to Italy and France by the mid-1600s. The court of Louis XIV made coffee drinking fashionable, and the king sent a single coffee plant to the island of Martinique—which was then cultivated and, amazingly enough, eventually led to the planting of coffee throughout Central and South America.

The cool coffeehouses of the 1950s—beatniks, jazz, and espresso—were direct descendants of the coffeehouses that popped up in London, Paris, and New York way back in the late 1600s and early 1700s. Those earliest coffeehouses were hotbeds: English king Charles II tried unsuccessfully to shut them down in order to suppress the spread of liberal political ideas, and it's thought that the French Revolution was hatched over steaming cups of coffee in Parisian cafés. In Boston, after the Tea Party, drinking coffee instead of tea became an act of patriotism.

12 COFFEE-GROWING COUNTRIES

Brazil	Mexico	Venezuela
Ethiopia	Guatemala	Ecuador
Kenya	Costa Rica	Nicaragua
Colombia	Jamaica	Tanzania

10 Ways to Make Good Brownies Even Better

Add chopped nuts (walnuts, pecans, almonds, pistachios, macadamias, toasted hazelnuts, peanuts, or even cashews) to the batter.

Add chopped chocolate (milk, semisweet, or white) to the batter.

Top with chocolate or vanilla glaze.

Top with ice cream.

Add chopped dates and walnuts to the batter.

Add coarsely chopped Oreos to the batter.

Add coarsely chopped Peppermint Patties to the batter.

Spread the batter in a jelly-roll pan and bake for less time, to make crisp brownies.

Add chopped dried cherries to the batter.

Add a teaspoon of powdered instant coffee or instant espresso to the batter; scatter chocolate-covered coffee beans on top.

THE TAO OF BAGELS AND LOX

Plain, sesame, poppy seed, onion, or pumpernickel? Cream cheese, butter, both, or just a shmear? Lox, nova, or smoked salmon? Toasted or not? These are the deep, probing questions we must ask ourselves when we ponder the meaning of bagels and lox. If we are to achieve bagel-and-lox nirvana, we must choose wisely.

A bagel, until fairly recently, was a straightforward item. No egg, no milk, no garlic, no onion flakes, no raisins, no nothing but plain yeast dough made with water and sweetened with malt. The dough was hand-rolled into the correct shape and size (*not too big!*), then boiled in water and baked in an oven. It was a perfectly simple, delicious bread— crunchy on the outside, chewy on the inside—eaten mostly in the northeastern states.

Mr. Lender of Lender's Bagels changed all that. Once he came up with the notion of frozen bagels in 1962, bagels could be (and were) shipped all over the country, and bagels entered the national consciousness. And then came designer bagels: sourdough, oat bran, apple-cinnamon, pumpernickel-raisin, sun-dried tomato. Distant and possibly unwelcome relations of the original Eastern European Jewish food. As Ed Levine writes in *New York Eats*, "If God wanted us to make sun-dried tomato bagels, he would have put more Jews in Florence."

The rectangular block of cream cheese, it will surprise you to know, is an American invention of 1872, for which we can thank one

---

15 FOODS THAT ARE BETTER (OKAY, JUST AS GOOD) AS LEFTOVERS

hot and sour soup	chili	potato salad
split pea soup	beef stew	deviled eggs
gazpacho	baked ham	clam dip
fried chicken	fried rice	roasted veggies
meat loaf	roast turkey and stuffing	blintzes

Mr. Lawrence of New York State. But it was the Breakstone brothers, Isaac and Joseph, who commercialized cream cheese in 1920. For no known reason it immediately became the spread of choice for bagels, and in 1928 Kraft began selling it as "Philadelphia Brand." After that it was open season on cream cheese: now we find it mixed with chopped vegetables, chopped scallions, roasted red peppers, herbs, chopped pineapple, or other ingredients. Not to mention the "lite" versions and whipped versions.

Lox is a pretty simple matter: it's salmon (usually Pacific salmon) that's been cured in a mixture of salt, sugar, and spices. Nova is cured in that same salt-sugar brine, then cold-smoked to add a slightly smoked flavor. Smoked salmon (Scotch, Icelandic, Canadian, and others) is brined and then hot-smoked both for flavor and preservation. Where you buy your lox (or nova or smoked salmon) is probably as important as which kind you choose. Find a really reliable source or disappointment will dog you.

As for toasting your bagel or not, it's your choice. So is the kind of bagel, how much of which kind of cream cheese you slather on, and the type of salmon you opt for. Not to mention the extras: sliced tomato, cucumber, raw onion, capers. There's no right or wrong choice where the perfect bagel combo is concerned. Including whether or not to spread butter on the bagel before adding cream cheese. That's strictly between you, your taste buds, and your cholesterol level.

15 FOODS THAT ARE USUALLY DISAPPOINTING AS LEFTOVERS

pizza	toast	steamed veggies
pasta	fried shrimp	waffles
risotto	liver	popovers
ramen noodles	fish	fruit salad (especially with bananas or apples)
most Chinese food	half-finished convenience meals	
quesadillas		

TRUE TALES OF THE DINNER TABLE:
BONES

Jerome Kass, playwright

My father had a problem with his dentures. Three of the top teeth were broken; they were just about half the size of all the other teeth. He refused to have a new set of dentures made, on the grounds (possibly valid) that he couldn't afford them. So eating was an issue for him. He could chew only soft foods, and the only soft food he liked was hamburger, so every night except Sunday—every single night of the week and month and year from the time he was about thirty-five until he died at fifty-eight—my mother prepared six hamburgers in my father's particular way: chopped sirloin mixed with diced onion, a raw egg or two, about a cup of matzoh meal, and lots of salt and pepper, fried in Crisco. She offered him no vegetables, no salad, nothing to go with the meat, because he would ignore it if she did. The only other food he would eat with his hamburgers was soft white bread, Wonder bread or Silvercup, not necessarily because he loved it, but because he sincerely believed that unless you ate bread with a meal you were "noshing," not eating. He went so far as to insist that my sister and I eat bread with all our meals, the result of which was that we were both little blimps for as long as we lived at home.

My older sister was always on a diet, and she would eat only chicken or fish with vegetables—spinach or string beans exclusively, neither of which I was willing to eat. Nor would I eat fish because I was seriously afraid of fish bones, a paranoia inherited from my father, who was sure that he would choke on a bone and die if he ever ate fish. As for chicken, I agreed to eat it for Friday night dinner but not at any other time. And never prepared any way but roasted. Boiled chicken made me "nauseous." My enthusiasm was for steak, pan-broiled. Not the steak my mother would normally have bought—kosher steak—which I rejected because I insisted that it had worms in it. My mother assured me that the "worms" were not worms at all but gristle. But I wasn't buying it. I wanted "goyishe sirloin or filet mignon," and that's what I got four or five nights a week. Where vegetables were concerned, I would eat only carrots and/or peas. And I always demanded a

can opener	nutcracker	egg slicer
pepper grinder	apple corer	rotary cheese grater
mini food processor	cherry pitter	tea ball
mandoline	instant-read thermometer	box grater
salad spinner		potato masher

starch—mashed potatoes, French fries, or some form of pasta.

In other words, every dinnertime, six nights a week, my mother would prepare three different meals. She complained about the injustice of it over and over again, but she did it anyway.

On the seventh night, Sunday, like every other Jewish family in the Bronx, my mother, father, sister, and I went to one or another of the three Chinese restaurants in the neighborhood—where my father would order lobster Cantonese, my sister would order chicken chow mein, and I would order spare ribs and egg rolls.

You may wonder what my mother ate. Well, six nights a week, she would scrape my father's leftover hamburgers onto a plate, along with my sister's leftover chicken or fish and string beans and spinach and my leftover steak and carrots and/or peas and potatoes or pasta. On Sunday nights at the Chinese restaurant she would eat leftover lobster Cantonese along with leftover chicken chow mein and spare ribs and egg rolls.

If anyone asked her why she didn't prepare something for herself at home or order something separate for herself at the Chinese restaurant, she would respond, "It's fine. I like bones."

The Story of
THE SETTLEMENT COOKBOOK

Mrs. Simon Kander was not, reputedly, a warm and fuzzy person. She was, however, a formidable lady who got things done. In Milwaukee in 1896 she and a group of other Jewish women opened a settlement house for Eastern European Jewish immigrants, to teach them English and other useful skills that would assist them in assimilating into American society. Not least of these skills—at least in Lizzie Kander's opinion—was cooking.

In 1901 Mrs. Kander observed that in the cooking classes (some of which she taught herself) the high school girls were spending precious time copying down the recipes that the teacher wrote on the chalkboard. It occurred to Mrs. Kander that many hours could be saved and much more progress made if each girl were given a printed booklet

****

11 Great Cookbook Web Sites

Books-for-Cooks.com

ecookbooks.com (*Jessica's Biscuit*)

FoodBooks.com

vegweb.com
(*all vegetarian*)

cookbookswelove.com

gourmetguides.com

theGoodCook.com

abebooks.com

cookbookstore.com

amazon.com

BarnesandNoble.com

****

containing those recipes, along with instructions on various other household matters such as cleaning, stain removal, and building a fire. The settlement could sell the booklets, too, for a bit of income.

She applied to the Settlement Board (all men, of course) for eighteen dollars to fund the project. They turned her down, though they added—famously—that they would be happy to "share in any profits from your little venture."

Little venture? *The Way to a Man's Heart ... The Settlement Cook Book* was printed with the help of Mrs. K's friends and connections, and the 1901 edition was not a booklet after all; it came off the press at 174 pages. The first thousand copies sold out in about a year. The cookbook committee enlarged the book and printed fifteen hundred more. By 1910 it was doing so well that profits from the book were used to purchase land for a new settlement house and more cookbook profits were used to help build it.

In 1917 there was so much cookbook action that the ladies had to hire office help; in 1921 the committee incorporated as the Settlement Cook Book Company and agreed to take a twenty-cent royalty on each book. Mrs. Kander's "little venture" continued to yield money for all involved, and along the way the book became a classic. Many editions have been published, and over 2 million copies have been sold; in 1978 it was inducted into the James Beard Foundation's Cookbook Hall of Fame. The popularity of *The Settlement Cook Book* spanned most of the twentieth century, and many a young woman started married life with a couple of saucepans and a copy of the book.

From its inception *The Settlement Cook Book* was not just a book of recipes; it was a document of culture, a manual of what was considered proper, important, and useful for girls and women to know in the kitchen and the home. When an immigrant girl read Mrs. Kander's authoritative advice on what to serve for dinner or how to lay a table, she felt confident that she was on good solid American ground. And she was.

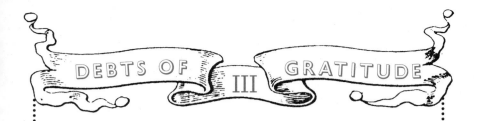

NICHOLAS APPERT (1749–1841) invented canning, roughly as we know it today. Napoléon was offering a twelve-thousand-franc prize to any inventor who came up with a new method of preserving food for his armies, and after years of experimenting Appert had it: glass jars sealed with wax. He won the prize.

Pharmacist **CHARLES ELMER HIRES** (1851–1937) launched commercial root beer at the U.S. Centennial Exposition in Philadelphia in 1876. It bubbled with natural ingredients like sassafras root, sarsaparilla, juniper, wintergreen, and other flavors. The Hires family began selling the first bottled root beer in 1893.

TERESSA BELLISSIMO gave us Buffalo chicken wings on a Friday night in October 1964, out of the kitchen of the Anchor Bar in Buffalo, New York. Teressa wanted to whip up a midnight snack for her son Dominic, the bartender, and his buddies, but not much was left in the larder. So she deep-fried some wings, brushed them with her special sauce, and served them with celery sticks and blue cheese dressing. The rest is history.

ALBERT KUMIN was the pastry chef at New York's Four Seasons restaurant in 1959 when he created the ultimate chocolate dessert: chocolate velvet cake, a moist, dense, rich, fudgy cake that—though it has many variations and many imitators—has rarely been surpassed. Chef Albert later became head pastry chef in the Carter White House.

10 Great Nonfiction Books about Food and Foodies

How to Cook a Wolf, M. F. K. Fisher

Clementine in the Kitchen, Samuel Chamberlain

Fast Food Nation: The Dark Side of the All-American Meal, Eric Schlosser

The Man Who Ate Everything: And Other Gastronomic Feats, Disputes, and Pleasurable Pursuits, Jeffrey Steingarten

Stuffed: Adventures of a Restaurant Family, Patricia Volk

The Gallery of Regrettable Food, James Lileks

The Soul of a Chef: The Journey toward Perfection, Michael Ruhlman

Appetite for Life: The Biography of Julia Child, Noel Riley Fitch

Between Bites: Memoirs of a Hungry Hedonist, James Villas

The Supper of the Lamb, Robert Farrar Capon

AMAZING FOOD EVENT: 1920

Invention of the Eskimo Pie

Christian Nelson was both a high school teacher and the owner of an ice cream shop in Onawa, Iowa. He must have had some sympathy for kids, because when a young customer had trouble deciding between an ice cream sandwich and a chocolate bar (the boy had only enough money for one or the other) Nelson went home and invented the Eskimo Pie, a chocolate-covered ice cream bar. It was originally called the I-Scream-Bar, but Nelson and his new partner, Russell Stover (the candy maker), renamed it, and by 1922 they were selling a million a day.

SECONDARY AMAZING FOOD EVENT: In 1923 Frank Epperson applied for a patent for his "Epsicle," soon to be renamed "Popsicle." The Roaring Twenties were hot times for ice cream.

IS THE CALORIE REALLY YOUR ENEMY?

A calorie is an innocent little unit of energy; technically speaking, it's the amount of energy (or heat) it takes to raise the temperature of one gram of water one degree Celsius. Zzzzz, your eyelids are drooping.

Okay, let's put it differently and plunk it right into the food arena where it belongs: In order to survive we need energy, and we get that energy from *food*, which is loaded with *calories*, which can convert to *energy*. Energy keeps your heart pumping, your digestion working, your legs moving, and so on. So far the calorie sounds like a pretty good friend, not an enemy. Food = calories = life.

Food is made up of carbohydrates, fats, and protein, each of which has a calorie count, of course. Carbs have four calories per gram, protein has four, and fat has a whopping nine. You "burn" those calories—or some of them—every day by means of your metabolism. Your metabolic processes break down the carbs, fats, and protein into a variety of molecules that travel the bloodstream to your cells, where they're either put to use on site or go on to become energy.

Different people need different amounts of calories. How many you need depends on your metabolism, how much physical activity you engage in, and how much energy your body uses to digest your food. If you take in fewer calories than you burn, you lose weight. If

20 LOW-CALORIE FOODS

mung beans	spinach	radishes
carrots	fennel	lemons
celery	tomatoes	grapefruit
lettuce	broccoli	watermelon
cabbage	Brussels sprouts	turnips
cucumbers	lentils	cauliflower
peppers		watercress

you take in more calories than you burn, you know what happens: you gain weight. If you're trying to lose weight, calories can start to seem like enemies.

CALORIE FACT: Thirty-five hundred *extra* calories (meaning 3,500 more than you actually need) taken in and not burned off are stored in your body as a pound of fat; 3,500 calories eaten and then burned off as energy (see above) equals maintenance—your weight stays the same; 3,500 unneeded calories burned off either by eating less or by exercising more means you'll ditch a pound.

10 HIGH-CALORIE FOODS

fish oil	goose fat	vegetable oil
lard	turkey fat	shortening
beef fat	duck fat	margarine
	chicken fat	

TIDBIT: Feeling glum? Try a plum. Indeed, fruits, vegetables, and whole grains—rich in complex carbohydrates—supply the brain with a steady dose of glucose, which has a calming effect and gives you extra power for problem solving and memory.

MEET...

REX STOUT (and Nero Wolfe)

Rex Stout (1886–1975) settled down to full-time writing in 1927 and published a few modestly successful novels. It wasn't until 1934, though, that he switched gears and produced the first Nero Wolfe mystery, *Fer-de-lance*. Stout ultimately wrote more than seventy mystery novels that starred the huge, grumpy, beer-drinking, reclusive (or agoraphobic, depending on your point of view) genius gourmet (or glutton, again depending on your POV) Wolfe, and his sidekick Archie Goodwin.

Nero Wolfe's obsessions are orchids, which he grows on the top floor of his brownstone in Manhattan, and edibles, which are prepared for him (and sometimes with him) by his cook, Fritz Brenner. Solving the cases that are literally brought to his door is just a means to an end: earning money to buy more orchids and more food.

The mysteries are great fun, but they're especially delicious to read if you're a foodie. As much as the stories are about murder and mayhem, they're equally about meals. And such meals! Breakfasts, lunches, snacks, and dinners that ooze with butter, cream, cheese, and eggs, homemade bread, biscuits, muffins, the very best meat and fowl, lobster, shrimp, and clams, the freshest fish and a whole lot of shad roe. Vegetables and salads pop up here and there, but the food Wolfe likes best is not green. Even sweet desserts get short shrift in favor of savory protein, fat, and carbohydrates.

Stout's seventy-second Wolfe mystery was published a month before his death, and a seventy-third was discovered and published posthumously.

COOKBOOK NOTE: The *Nero Wolfe Cookbook* is "by Rex Stout and the Editors of the Viking Press." Stout assures us on the "Thanks" page that his only contribution to the book is the excerpts from the Wolfe stories that precede each recipe. He thanks Michael S. Romano (yes, that Michael Romano, of Union Square Café fame, among many other honors) for testing half the recipes and writing first drafts of many of them. But the book claims 225 *original* recipes. Where did they come from? And what did the editors of the Viking Press have to do with it? It's a mystery. Where's Nero Wolfe when you need him?

71

TYPICAL MENUS

Weight Watchers, Then and Now

Ever since its 1963 inception, Weight Watchers—the brainchild of Queens, New York, housewife Jean Nidetch—has been a highly successful weight-loss program for hundreds of thousands of participants. Today it works on a point system; back then it involved a complicated menu plan that had women laboring long and hard to figure out what to eat and when to eat it. The Program was very specific, very dictatorial, very rigid, and it seemed to work wonders for some people who had hitherto never been able to control themselves.

There was a long list of outright no-no's (like cake, cookies, candy, pizza); that part was simple. But there was also a detailed list of yes-yeses that required constant checking, reiteration, calculation, and obedience. Take eggs, for example, back in the early 1970s: you could have four eggs each week, but only for breakfast or lunch—never for dinner; they could be cooked in the shell, poached, or scrambled without added fat; raw eggs were forbidden; you could use the yolks and whites separately, but you had to use them in the same meal. And that was just eggs. You had to eat at least five fish meals each week (lunch or dinner), but shellfish could make up only one of the five. You had to eat liver once a week. There were rules about vegetables, fruits, meats, cheeses, dietetic products (no-no's, except artificial sweeteners, sodas, and margarine), condiments, bread, cereal, fats—rules, rules, and more rules. Dieting became a way of life, and that, one assumes, was the point: you

---

10 MOST POPULAR WEIGHT-LOSS DIETS OF THE RECENT PAST

high-fat, low-carb	high-protein	blood-type-determined
high-carb	no-sugar	liver-cleansing
low-fat	enzyme-activated	single-food-per-meal
moderate-fat		

8 Wildly Caloric Desserts

1. entire box of filled chocolates

2. entire strawberry cheesecake

3. entire pan of brownies

4. quart of ice cream hiding at back of freezer

5. Aunt Tubby's prizewinning seven-layer cake with buttercream frosting

6. aerosol can of whipped cream

7. jar of butterscotch sauce

8. all the leftover Halloween (Easter, Christmas) candy

still got to be obsessed with food, but now you were obsessed with dieting, not overeating.

How different Weight Watchers is today, even aside from the new point system. Today you can go into one of the major fast food franchises and order a Weight Watchers meal—and a Weight Watchers dessert. No work for you at all. There's onion soup, grilled shrimp, grilled chicken, grilled fish (all served with salad and vegetables), cheesecake, layer cake. Points have been calculated for you; all you have to do is pay and eat. And then you can stop into your favorite supermarket and pick up WW food products for your next fifteen meals. Try not to eat them all at once.

POP QUIZ!

1. Which of the following is not a sausage?
   A. chorizo
   B. andouille
   C. banger
   D. chipolata
   E. cerveza

2. How many pairs of legs does a lobster have (including the big front claws)?
   A. 5
   B. 6
   C. 7
   D. 9
   E. 11

3. The guy at the next table asks for schlag on his sundae, so the waiter brings a dish of vanilla, chocolate, and strawberry ice cream topped with
   A. chopped walnuts
   B. fudge sauce
   C. whipped cream
   D. raspberry sauce
   E. crushed toffee

4. *True or false:* Bird's nest soup, from China, contains no bird's nest.

5. *True or false:* Bird's nest pudding, from New England, contains no bird's nest.

6. The hometown of the original Oreo cookie was
   A. Peoria, Illinois
   B. Medford, Oregon
   C. Bakersville, California
   D. New York, New York
   E. Boston, Massachusetts

7. *Name that cuisine:* Where would a buttie come from?

8. *True or false:* Lox is significantly different from smoked salmon.

9. Ti leaves are
   A. tea leaves, in the Indonesian spelling
   B. leaves used to wrap food before cooking, in Polynesia
   C. leaves used for making a nutritious soup, in Africa
   D. leaves used for purifying water, in Central America
   E. none of the above

Answers: 1. e; 2. a; 3. c; 4. false; 5. true (it's made of fruit, crust, and sauce); 6. d; 7. England (it's a slang term for a sandwich); 8. false, 9. b

CAJUN COOKING
AND CREOLE COOKING

Right away we're into a food debate: What's Cajun and what's Creole? Overlap is the problem. While there are some specifically Cajun dishes and some specifically Creole, there are blurry areas too.

Roughly speaking, Cajun is associated with country cooking, while Creole comes from the city—the steamy southern seaport of New Orleans, of course. Creoles claim descent from the early, supposedly aristocratic French settlers who arrived in southern Louisiana in the early 1700s and wanted to reproduce the food with which they'd been familiar in Europe. Creole cooking is usually described as more sophisticated, more traditionally French—but it also unmistakably folds in Spanish, African, German, and Italian influences. There's a lot of pasta and tomatoes in the Creole repertoire.

Around 1785 Cajuns—French Acadians—migrated from Canada to fertile central Louisiana, so French culinary thinking applied there, too, with input from American Indians and Germans. Cajuns pulled many of their ingredients from the surrounding rivers, bayous, swamps, and woods: crabs, crawfish, shrimp, fish, frogs, turtles, ducks, wild turkeys, squirrels, wild plants. They raised a lot of pigs (and used pork fat where Creole cooks might have chosen butter), made a lot of sausage (andouille, boudin, and head cheese, among others), grew beans, yams, tomatoes, and okra.

Before travel became easy between these two geographic and cultural territories, the difference between the two cuisines was surely more marked. But now? Hard to tell precisely which is which. Cajun cooks use plenty of herbs and tend to spice their food more heavily

8 VARIETIES OF WINTER SQUASH		
butternut	spaghetti	dumpling
acorn	kabocha	Hubbard
buttercup		delicata

kale	tomatillos	broccoli
collards	arugula	spinach
asparagus	watercress	spinach pasta
limes	string beans	green peppers
lime gelatin	peas	cucumbers

than Creole cooks, but not always. Both make major use of that definitive trio: chopped green peppers, onions, and celery. Both cuisines are into rice. Both use filé powder, the ground dried leaves of the sassafras tree, for thickening—a Choctaw culinary contribution. Both use another special thickener: brown roux, a mixture of flour and oil or pork fat, which is cooked over low heat for such a long time that it turns dark brown; it's the base of soups, sauces, and especially gumbo. Cajun cooks still like to put a lot of ingredients into one big pot; Creole cooks are more likely to serve separate dishes—but not always. It's confusing. Take this mini pop quiz and see if you know what's what.

WHICH IS CREOLE AND WHICH IS CAJUN?

1. gumbo
2. red beans and rice
3. crawfish étouffée
4. pralines
5. coush-coush
6. jambalaya
7. chef Paul Prudhomme

But the debate is far from over.

Answers: 1. Creole, 2. who knows?, 3. Cajun, 4. Creole, 5. Cajun, 6. both, 7. Cajun.

18 Basic Cooking Measurements

dash = a few drops

pinch = less than ⅛ teaspoon

3 teaspoons = 1 tablespoon

½ tablespoon = 1½ teaspoons

2 tablespoons = 1 fluid ounce

3 tablespoons = 1 jigger

¼ cup = 4 tablespoons; 2 fluid ounces

⅓ cup = 5 tablespoons + 1 teaspoon

½ cup = 8 tablespoons; 4 fluid ounces

⅔ cup = 10 tablespoons + 2 teaspoons

¾ cup = 12 tablespoons

1 cup = 16 tablespoons; 8 fluid ounces

½ pint = 1 cup

1 pint = 2 cups; 16 fluid ounces

1 quart = 4 cups; 2 pints; 32 fluid ounces

1 gallon = 16 cups; 8 pints; 4 quarts

1 liter = approximately 4 cups or 1 quart

kilogram = approximately 2 pounds

THOMAS JEFFERSON'S GARDENS

The accomplishments of Thomas Jefferson cause the mind to reel. Thinker, writer, politician, diplomat, architect, scientist—there seems to be no end to the breadth and depth of this extraordinary American's talents and interests. Not least of them was his passion for growing and eating food. It went far, far beyond the norm for most wealthy, educated men of his day.

Some of his enthusiasm for good food was acquired when he was minister to France, from 1784 to 1789; certainly his love of wine and viniculture blossomed there. Even before he went to France as a diplomat he hired a French chef to train his slave James Hemings in the art of French cookery, and when Jefferson went to France, Hemings accompanied him to study French cuisine. But the true measure of Jefferson's passion can be taken by studying his vegetable and fruit gardens at Monticello, which evolved over many years and engrossed him both as scientist and gourmet. Jefferson had many careers (often simultaneously), and gardening was unquestionably one of them.

The man was *everywhere*: he tracked the progress of his crops, cataloged the success of seed varieties, extrapolated garden wisdom from his own observations, studied the theories and advice of experts. The scientist in him was adventurous, eager to try new methods, eager to propagate not just plants but ideas about plants. He recorded in his Garden Book, precisely and exhaustively, the details of weather, yield, cultivation, fertilization, harvesting, and the conclusions drawn from his on-site observations. He sowed many species of many plants in order to eliminate the inferior and improve the superior. He experimented continually. He was ambitious. He aimed, always, for excellence.

Though Jefferson was not a doctrinaire vegetarian (he referred to meat as a condiment to his vegetables, used in small amounts or just for flavoring), the main part of his diet came from the enormous variety of vegetables and fruits he grew. The vegetable garden at Monticello was a thousand-foot-long, eighty-foot-wide terrace divided into twenty-four plots that overlooked two orchards, a vineyard, and his "berry squares" of figs, currants, gooseberries, and raspberries.

The sheer volume of Jefferson's garden output was astonishing, reportedly 250 varieties of vegetables. He grew peas, beans, carrots, beets, onions, lettuce, radishes, cucumbers, sea kale, cabbage, celery, artichokes, asparagus, cauliflower, squash, broccoli, salsify, peppers, eggplant, tomatoes, and okra, among other things. In addition to berries, his fruit crops included dozens of varieties of peaches, grapes, apples, pears, apricots, and plums. Some plants flourished, some did not, but Jefferson persisted; if one seed failed, he tried another—and another and another, until he either achieved the results he wanted or learned enough to know it was time to move on to the next experiment.

15 BASIC (DRIED) HERBS AND SPICES YOU REALLY OUGHT TO HAVE

. . . if you're planning to cook anything more interesting than oatmeal.

black pepper	thyme	cumin
basil	tarragon	chiles
oregano	rosemary	cinnamon
bay leaves	dill	ginger
sage	coriander	nutmeg

15 LESS-BASIC (DRIED) HERBS AND SPICES YOU MIGHT LIKE TO HAVE

. . . if you're really into cooking.

mustard powder	caraway seed	turmeric
marjoram	celery seed	cloves
chervil	paprika	allspice
parsley	saffron	cardamom
fennel seed	curry powder (a blend of herbs and spices)	mace

MEET...

GEORGE WASHINGTON CARVER

When you think G. W. Carver, you think "peanuts," but though Carver's study of the cultivation of peanuts and the uses of peanuts was critical to the recovery of agriculture in the South, Dr. Carver was a whole lot more than that. Botanist, chemist, researcher, humanitarian, he was an extraordinary man for his time and all time.

Carver was born in slavery in 1864, on the Missouri farm of Moses and Susan Carver. When he was an infant, he and his brother and his mother were abducted from the farm; his mother was gone forever, but the Carvers found George again and raised him until he was twelve. He spent those years observing and studying wild plants so ardently that people began to call him the "plant doctor." In spite of terrible segregation and race prejudice, he managed to achieve the education he needed: a bachelor of science degree and a master of science degree at what is now Iowa State University. He was then appointed the first African American faculty member at the Iowa State College of Agriculture and Mechanics.

In 1897 Booker T. Washington invited Carver to become the director of agriculture at Tuskegee Institute, and Tuskegee became his base until his death in 1943. At Tuskegee he developed the revolutionary crop rotation method that transformed southern agriculture. Southern soil was extremely depleted from many years of planting only cotton and tobacco, and farmers were sinking further and further into economic decline. Carver showed them that his system of crop alternation would change all that: if they planted soil-enriching crops such as peanuts, sweet potatoes, and soybeans for one year and cotton the next, the soil would recover and agriculture would thrive again—and it did.

Over the years Carver found many industrial and other uses for peanuts, pecans, soybeans, sweet potatoes, and other crops—inks, dyes, paints, stains, and synthetic rubber, for example. He shared his work and his ideas freely with all people; fame, fortune, and patents were never his goals. In 1940 he gave his life's savings to establish the Carver Research Foundation at Tuskegee, for agricultural study. Happily, he lived to see his work recognized and honored, and after his death, in 1953, his birthplace was declared a national monument.

⊞◆◆◆⊞

And Speaking of Food . . .

Jean Ritchie, Singing Family of the Cumberlands, 1955

You never saw such a bustle, seven or eight women in one little kitchen all cooking their special dishes. Ollie was the chicken-frying expert, and she was turning out dishpans full of it, brown and crispy-crusty. Nobody but Mom could make fitten dumplings, least to hear her tell it, and she was hot and happy over the big black iron pot on the back of the stove . . . Mallie was watching the oven where a big pone of corn bread and the long square pan full of biscuits were turning a tender gold. May fixed platters of deviled eggs and the wooden bread tray full of green sallit. Pots of nutty, meat-seasoned shucky beans stood already done in the warming closet, together with long pans of hot mealy yellow sweet taters baked in their own skins . . . I felt so hungry that I had the idea I could eat up every bit of all that loaded-down table full of vittles and still not want to quit.

FOOD FOR THE WHITE HOUSE

Imagine the bliss of having on staff a chef (and about twenty-five trained helpers) whose sole job it is to feed you, your family, and your guests whatever you want whenever you want it. That's what the president of the United States has.

Now look at it the other way around: You're an experienced and accomplished chef, which by definition means you're a leader and a decision maker, accustomed to ruling your kitchen with an iron hand. You agree (happily, we presume) to take the job of executive chef at the White House, and now you're subject to the requirements of the president, the first lady, the first children, the White House social secretary, the Social Office, the Office of Protocol of the Department of State, and heaven knows who else.

Your new battleground is called the Presidential Food Service, and the mission of the PFS is, according to the White House Web site in 2004, to "provide worldwide food service, security, and personal support to the President and First Family . . . provide gourmet meals and

❖❖

And Speaking of Food . . .

Marjorie Kinnan Rawlings, The Yearling, 1938

Jody heard nothing; saw nothing but his plate. He had never been so hungry in his life, and after a lean winter and slow spring, with food not much more plentiful for the Baxters than for their stock, his mother had cooked a supper good enough for the preacher. There were poke-greens with bits of white bacon buried in them; sand-buggers made of potato and onion and the cooter he had found crawling yesterday; sour orange biscuits and at his mother's elbow the sweet potato pone. He was torn between his desire for more biscuits and another sand-bugger and the knowledge, born of painful experience, that if he ate them, he would suddenly have no room for pone. The choice was plain.

support catered functions and Social Aide Dinners for visiting Heads-of-State . . . operate the White House Mess Executive dining rooms, provide a carryout service and . . . complete catering coordination to the White House complex . . . provide logistics coordination for White House Mess personnel and valet services for Presidential trips and events." This description might leave you scratching your head about what the PFS actually does and therefore what you, the executive chef, are expected to do.

"Grace under pressure" is a quality that should probably be listed prominently in your job description. So should an ability to speak nicely to the press. You'll have to be flexible and versatile, because you'll be called upon to produce everything from the simplest sandwiches to the most elaborate receptions and banquets. You'll have to manage a staff, stick to a budget, know all about American and international food, and have boundless energy and stamina. You'll cater to the food quirks, taboos, allergies, and sensibilities of every head of state who's feted at the White House, every bureaucrat, dignitary, politician, and pal of the president (and his family) who's invited for a meal. And you'll have to do it without having a single tantrum.

There will be endless menu planning, strict schedules, constant ordering of provisions, testing of the food for each and every major dinner, more testing if the dishes don't please the first lady, plus the ordinary daily meals to prepare. Mistakes will be unacceptable. Could this be a fun job or what?

Walter Scheib, White House chef during the Clinton terms and for one George W. Bush term, said in May 2003, "We are not a hotel or restaurant, we are a private home and our clientele is only four people [a reference to the Bushes]. Luckily, we know their likes and dislikes very well." Apparently not well enough, since he was fired at the beginning of President Bush's second term. First Lady Laura Bush and the new White House social secretary were no longer happy with eleven-year veteran Scheib. He was, he himself asserted, unable to "satisfy the First Lady's stylistic requirements."

10 Agricultural Facts about the States

★ Georgia is the nation's number one producer of peanuts, pecans, and peaches.

★ Hawaii is the only state that grows coffee—not to mention more than a third of the world's supply of pineapples.

★ Washington produces more apples than any other state.

★ California grows more than 300,000 tons of grapes annually and produces more than 17 million gallons of wine.

★ In 1997 Kansas produced 492.2 million bushels of wheat, enough to make 35.9 billion loaves of bread.

★ Maine grows 99 percent of the nation's blueberries.

★ North Carolina is the largest sweet potato producer in the United States.

★ More land is farmed in Texas than in any other state.

★ The first so-to-speak American potato was planted in 1719 in Londonderry Common Field, in what would eventually become New Hampshire.

★ Surprise! Vermont is the largest producer of maple syrup in the United States.

5 Food Facts about the States

★ New York has more than 18,000 dairy farms, which makes dairying the state's most important farming activity.

★ Most of the United States' salmon, halibut, crab, and herring come from Alaska.

★ More turkeys are raised in California than in any other state.

★ Nearly 90 percent of the nation's lobsters (about 40 million pounds) are caught off the coast of Maine.

★ Wisconsin produces more milk than any other state.

MY 'HOOD IS BAD FOR MY HEALTH

Pauline Gordon, teenager

Every afternoon my abuela (grandmother) walks down the squeaky steps leading to our kitchen. When she hops into that apron, I know it's my cue to run for cover. Making up her own recipes is how my abuela relieves her stress. She puts all her worries behind her when she takes on her mission: What's for dinner?

With a dash of this and a sprinkle of that her creations are ready. I admit that my abuela performs miracles. She stretches her budget by mixing leftovers with fresh foods, is obsessed with cooking pork in every meal, adds plenty of grease and oil—and people savor every last taste. I think it's disgusting.

I get angry and frustrated with this woman. Why is she so hard-headed? She talks about saving a dollar, but if we have enough money for Direct TV and HBO, I think we can afford some healthier, fresher food, instead of eating like it's hard times. My grandmother brings home ninety-nine-cent juice, sodas, and junk foods that taste like complete crap and have no nutritional value. Like many people in my neighborhood, my abuela comes from a really poor background. Putting food on the table was an everyday struggle in her family. Every bit of food was considered a blessing.

I think what we put in our bodies should be one of my family's biggest concerns. I began feeling conscious of how I eat last spring, when I started noticing how depressed and moody I was. At that time, my face was breaking out and my stomach was never agreeing with me. I would wake up nauseous, and get severe headaches that left me looking like an insane witch by the end of the day. I know what's healthy and what isn't, but I was constantly eating junk at fast food restaurants or running to the corner store for a pint of Häagen-Dazs every time I felt depressed.

Over the summer I joined a nutrition workshop. When I began reading the nutritional facts on the back of cartons, I started thinking about the vitamins, fat, and protein that each food has to offer. I stopped going to the corner store for candy every time I had spare change. Then we got to buy a week's worth of healthy food. I took my healthy week seriously. I drank tons more water and ate more veggies. I started using substitutes for sugar, like honey and fruits. Whenever I had an urgent craving for a sweet, crispy, layered cheese Danish, I settled for a granola bar or a tall glass of vanilla soymilk. Though healthy eating took an adjustment, I was feeling great! No more of that oily feeling I would get when I ate greasy foods. After an icy glass of soymilk, I felt like I could take on the world.

But eating healthy in my neighborhood—Brownsville—is a challenge. My neighborhood is grim, with worn-down and torn-looking houses and projects surrounded by nothing but fast food restaurants, Chinese take-outs, and fried chicken spots filled with miserable obese people. Sure, the food is cheap. There's a bargain everywhere you go. But you're only getting what you pay for—unhealthy processed and fried food. The Kentucky Fried Chicken place even gives out free sodas with every meal. Why can't they give out bottled water or juice for a change?

I know why people eat in those places. You can buy only junk if you're hungry without much in your wallet. As much as I want to stay healthy, I have to stretch five dollars to buy a meal. Sometimes I buy an Ensure and a banana nut muffin, or a veggie slice from the pizza store, and find myself hungry in an hour. I long for the taste of organic fruit on my tongue.

Eyes see, brain picks up data, stomach growls in response. With that I go to bed, another night of an unsatisfied stomach. I lie in bed wishing it would all go away: poverty, my neighborhood, my grandmother's cooking, my headache. Maybe I'm ungrateful or stubborn. (Why can't I just give in and eat unhealthy food like everyone else does? Hey, at least there's more on your plate.) But my anger bursts like a cannon scattering balls of depression. Why is my neighborhood such a threat to our health? Why are healthy foods out of reach of the poor?

10 Ways to Improve Basic Chicken Salad

If your basic mayonnaise-dressed chicken salad is dying of
boredom, add one of the following improvements.

chopped walnuts or pecans and chopped apple or pear

★

minced scallions (white and green parts) and crumbled bacon

★

chopped fresh basil and grated Parmesan cheese

★

chopped cornichons and a little Dijon mustard

★

chopped pitted kalamata olives and whole capers

★

mango chutney and a little curry powder

★

cubed avocado and minced jalapeños

★

minced cooked mushrooms and chopped flat-leaf parsley

★

tiny cubes of Jarlsberg cheese and snipped fresh chives

★

chopped dried apricots and whole currants

THE PILLSBURY BAKE-OFF

The year was 1949, and the place was the Waldorf-Astoria Hotel in New York City. World War II rationing was over, Rosie the Riveter was back in the kitchen, and TV was busily promoting the cozy stay-at-home mom. Pillsbury—or, more precisely, its ad agency—took notice of the postwar status of women and decided to celebrate the company's eightieth birthday with a national contest for amateur bakers, offering a grand prize of $50,000. That astronomical sum alone would have attracted attention, but the concept was also a perfect fit for the times. Women entered the competition in droves, and the Grand National Recipe and Baking Contest (quickly renamed the Pillsbury Bake-Off) was a runaway success. Pillsbury never looked back.

In the 1950s the only required Bake-Off ingredient was Pillsbury's flour, which tilted the entries toward made-from-scratch cakes, pies, quick breads, and yeast breads, with cute names such as Starlight Double-Delight Cake and Snappy Turtle Cookies. By the '60s, timesaving and convenience were major lifestyle issues, and the folks at Pillsbury got real: the contest wasn't just about dessert anymore; it encouraged recipes for heartier, easy-to-make food, and contestants were permitted to use cake mixes, frozen vegetables, processed cheese, and canned goods. In the '70s, the entries showed a marked international influence; in the '80s, they reflected affluence and an uptick in entertaining, as well as a swerve toward "healthy" eating; in the '90s, they emphasized ethnic cooking for a diverse America.

That wasn't the only diversity rolling out at the Bake-Off: in 1996 fourteen of the finalists were men. Kurt Wait won the grand prize with his recipe for Macadamia Fudge Torte.

---

6 NUTS USED MOST OFTEN IN COOKING

pecans	almonds	hazelnuts
walnuts	pine nuts (pignoli)	peanuts

GRANULATED WHITE SUGAR,
SUPERFINE SUGAR, CONFECTIONERS' SUGAR,
LIGHT BROWN SUGAR, AND DARK BROWN SUGAR?

Granulated white sugar is refined cane or beet sugar. When it's granulated even more, it's called superfine sugar or bar sugar, and it will dissolve quickly and easily even in cold liquids—very handy for making cocktails, iced tea and coffee, and meringues. Confectioners' sugar is also known as 10X (say "ten-ex") or powdered sugar because it's been ground to a powder; to keep it soft and prevent serious clumping, a little cornstarch is added during processing. Unfortunately, the sugar still clumps a bit and usually needs sifting before use, and it does impart a slightly cornstarchy taste to uncooked buttercream frostings, icings, and glazes. It's a trade-off.

Brown sugar is simply white sugar to which molasses has been added. Molasses is what gives it that characteristic warm, mellow flavor and moist, crumbly texture; light brown sugar has less molasses, dark brown sugar has more, and you can taste the difference.

4 Reliable Ways to Melt Chocolate

For all four methods, chop the chocolate before melting. And be super vigilant to avoid scorching. Chocolate is tricky.

1. in a heavy saucepan over very low heat, stirring constantly

2. in the top of a double boiler, over simmering water, stirring constantly

3. in a bowl in the oven, at 200°F, just until soft and stirrable

4. in a microwave-safe bowl or glass measuring cup in the microwave oven, at high power, for a minute or more; check as you go

BAKER'S POP QUIZ!

1. Sponge, in baking terms, is
   A. another name for angel food cake
   B. another name for cream puff pastry
   C. a thin layer of cake moistened with simple syrup
   D. a mixture of yeast, flour, and liquid
   E. a mixture of baking powder, flour, and liquid

2. Double-acting baking powder is one of the leavening agents bakers use frequently. How recently was it developed?
   A. 1867
   B. 1889
   C. 1905
   D. 1922
   E. 1932

3. Which of the following ingredients is not used to make nesselrode pie?
   A. chestnut puree
   B. candied fruits
   C. raisins
   D. chopped chocolate
   E. maraschino liqueur

4. Pound cake is so called because in the original recipe it
   A. was a stiff dough that required a short period of pounding
   B. was sold in the streets of London for one pound
   C. was a corruption of the old English "pownde" cake, a sweet bread baked in a loaf
   D. was so rich that it was thought to add a pound to the eater's weight
   E. was made with a pound each of flour, butter, sugar, and eggs

10 KINDS OF FLOUR

semolina	bread	rye
all-purpose white (bleached, unbleached)	cake (or pastry)	buckwheat
	self-rising	rice
	whole-wheat	corn

5. A quick bread is a bread that
   A. bakes for under thirty minutes
   B. requires no more than five ingredients
   C. is leavened only with baking powder or baking soda
   D. is made from a mix or from commercially prepared dough
   E. none of the above

6. When yeast ferments, it gives off
   A. carbon dioxide
   B. carbon monoxide
   C. hydrogen peroxide
   D. nitrogen peroxide
   E. ammonium bicarbonate

7. *True or false:* Store crisp cookies in an airtight container and chewy cookies in a container with a loose-fitting lid.

8. The common wisdom about making the best pie crust is that you need
   A. a marble countertop
   B. a seasoned rolling pin
   C. cool hands
   D. strong arms
   E. dough that has been thoroughly worked before rolling

9. *Name that cuisine:* In what country is jaggery used?

Answers: 1. d; 2. b; 3. d; 4. e; 5. c; 6. a; 7. false (the opposite is true—crisp cookies are best stored in a container with a loose-fitting lid and chewy ones in an airtight container); 8. c; 9. India (it's a kind of unrefined sugar)

****

12 *Web Sites for Bakers*

Kingarthurflour.com	betterbaking.com
wilton.com	bread.allrecipes.com
bettycrocker.com/baking	cake.allrecipes.com
joyofbaking.com	cookie.allrecipes.com
pastrywiz.com	pie.allrecipes.com
verybestbaking.com	kitchenkrafts.com

****

THE TALE OF THE TOLL HOUSE CHOCOLATE CHIP COOKIE

Serendipity is often the mother of invention, and for Ruth Wakefield, serendipity did the trick. Wakefield invented the first chocolate chip cookie—the cookie of cookies, the *ne plus ultra* of American cookiedom, the standard by which every other American cookie is still measured.

Ruth and Kenneth Wakefield owned the Toll House Inn, a lodge near Whitman, Massachusetts. The lodge had a restaurant, and the restaurant was famous for Mrs. Wakefield's cooking. She was no ordinary home cook: she had graduated in 1924 from the Framingham State Normal School Department of Household Arts, and she'd had a career as a dietician and lecturer on food. The apple fell on her head, as it were, one day when she ran out of baker's chocolate for her usual chocolate cookie recipe. Casting about for a substitute, she chopped up a bar of Nestlé's semisweet chocolate (reputedly given to her by the chocolate man himself, Andrew Nestlé), and added the bits to her

MUST OR MYTH:

For cookies and cakes, cream butter and sugar just until well blended.

Myth, for sure. Well blended isn't good enough. Creaming, by definition, means to beat until light (aerated), lighter in color, fluffy, and smooth. When you cream butter and sugar, plan to spend at least two or three minutes beating— and scraping down the bowl *often,* so every bit gets treated equally. The mixture is creamed properly when it's perfectly blended (no separation) and the sugar is no longer gritty. This takes patience, so relax, put on your headphones, and hang in there.

CREAMING TIP: A food processor can do just as good a job of creaming as an electric mixer. Same rules apply.

favorite Butter Drop Do cookie dough. What she'd hoped was that the bits would permeate the plain vanilla dough and yield a batch of chocolate cookies; what she got was a batch of butter cookies studded with oozy, melty, scrumptious pockets of pure chocolate. Bingo! A legend was born, and it was named the Toll House cookie.

And speaking of smart cookies, Ruth Wakefield was one: she went ahead and published her recipe, which became an instant hit, and in 1939 licensed the same recipe to Andrew Nestlé to print on his new product—Toll House Morsels, made specifically to be used in making Mrs. Wakefield's Toll House cookies. The best part of the deal? A lifetime supply of chocolate morsels for Ruth Graves Wakefield, mother of the chocolate chip cookie. She lived until 1977.

10 Easy Cookie Decorations

To decorate *before* baking (**BB**), paint the cookie with egg white and add decorations; to decorate *after* baking (**AB**), spread or paint with glaze and add decorations.

BB: colored sugar, sprinkles, or dots

BB: chopped or whole nuts

BB: raisins or currants

BB: dried cherries, strawberries, cranberries

BB: chopped nut brittle or toffee

BB or **AB:** glacé cherries

BB or **AB:** chocolate chips or sprinkles

AB: M&Ms or other small candies

AB: simple piping with store-bought icing

AB: chocolate-covered raisins or peanuts

BAKER'S CHECKLIST

★ mixing bowls

★ measuring cups (metal, glass)

★ measuring spoons

★ spatulas (rubber, metal)

★ wire whisks

★ pastry brushes

★ grater

★ baking pans:
cake pans (round, square, rectangular),
loaf pan,
ring pan,
bundt pan,
muffin tins,
jelly-roll pan

★ cookie sheets

★ wire racks for cooling

★ oven thermometer

★ timer

★ pastry bag and tips

★ cookie press

★ electric mixer

★ food processor

ADELLE DAVIS

Adelle Davis was a force to be reckoned with in the 1950s. Her most popular book, *Let's Eat Right to Keep Fit*, was published in 1954 and advanced a then-controversial theory of proper diet (her definition of proper diet) as the key to physical and emotional well-being. She advocated the regular (and sometimes extreme) use of vitamins and minerals (a subject the medical profession was uncomfortable with at that time), and to add fuel to the firestorm that broke out around her, she also claimed that diet could prevent or cure disease. She was an avid promoter of organic foods and of cooking methods that preserved the nutrients in those foods.

Davis wasn't entirely wrong, of course. We understand the importance of diet and good nutrition better today than we did back then (in part *because* of Adelle Davis), but many of her theories were and are far from proven. While some of her basic ideas about nutrition hold water, quite a few others either flat out don't or are in perpetual dispute among scientists and health professionals. Her followers—then and now—*believe*, and they dismiss criticism of her as reactionary prejudice; her critics are alarmed at what they perceive as the propagation of baseless (even dangerous) theories about nutrition.

Davis did have training in her field, and she did undoubtedly help many people to change their eating habits and have healthier lives. She certainly nailed doctors on their shocking lack of interest in and information about nutrition. But serious scientists have found much of her advice to be unsupported by solid research and many of her citations of experts to be incorrect, misquoted, or taken out of context.

It's easy to dismiss Adelle Davis as a food faddist—but just as easy to revere her as a pioneer in the cause of eating well for a healthier life. From our current point of view she appears to have been right in the broad view and wrong in the details. And the devil, as we know, is in the details.

QUAINT SALADS FROM THE NOT-TOO-DISTANT PAST

The 1956 edition of *Betty Crocker's Picture Cook Book*, a standard of the time, welcomes us to the salad chapter with this cheerful advice: "A Different Salad Every Day Makes Your Meals Healthful and Gay." There are thirteen salads displayed in the opening spread, and not one of them is a green one. Most use lettuce leaves as a base for other ingredients—artichokes, fruit extravaganzas, stuffed tomatoes, molded shapes, hard-boiled eggs, chicken—but it's clear that at midcentury, salad usually meant something more than tossed greens. Simple green salad was just a subset— a small one, at that—of a large and varied category that included some pretty strange combos.

Betty seemed to place high value on the quantity of ingredients used in a salad: the more, the better. Labor-intensive was good too, and she suggests setting up a Salad Center in the kitchen, stocked with staple ingredients and necessary utensils. According to Crocker, making a good salad was a seven-step procedure, and none of the steps were simple. There was a lot of choosing involved—of salad type, color, texture, form, flavor, dressing—and the unsuspecting housewife might well have felt unequal to the task. Remember, this was just the salad; that same housewife still had the main course, side dishes, and dessert to prepare at mealtime. Stress Central, '50s-style. See if you can get your head wrapped around one of these:

---

12 TASTY VEGETABLE SALADS

salade niçoise	Caesar salad	Greek salad
corn salad	German potato salad	insalata tricolore (arugula, radicchio, endive— coincidentally the colors of the Italian flag)
black bean salad	American potato salad	
three-bean salad	giardiniera (Italian marinated vegetable salad)	
cucumber salad		
cole slaw		

★ Hearty Macaroni Salad, for which you combine cooked macaroni, liver sausage, peas, Cheddar cheese, chopped celery, minced onion, parsley, and chopped green pepper, then dress with mayonnaise and serve on lettuce leaves.

★ 24-Hour Salad, for which you toss together (with a fruit dressing) canned cherries, canned pineapple, orange sections, and cut-up marshmallows, then stuff the mixture into lettuce cups and garnish with maraschino cherries and more oranges.

★ Winter Salad Bowl, for which you marinate grated raw parsnips, chopped onion, chopped celery, and chopped olives (with pimentos), then add torn-up lettuce and toss with mayonnaise.

★ Chicken-Almond Soufflé Salad, for which you make lime gelatin (using mayonnaise in place of some of the required water), freeze the mixture slightly, whip it to a fluff, then fold in cooked chicken, green grapes, and slivered almonds.

★ Mock Chicken Salad, which is made with cubes of cooked veal "when chicken is high and veal not so expensive."

Veal was cheaper than chicken? Now there's a glimpse into another world.

---

8 Cooking Projects to Start If You Have Nothing Better to Do

1. Make jam from seasonal fruit, preferably from a local farm stand.

2. Make ravioli.

3. Bake bread.

4. Bake three kinds of butter cookies.

5. Make lemon curd.

6. Make and freeze enough tomato sauce for eight meals.

7. Make and freeze enough pesto for eight pasta nights.

8. Make infused oils and vinegars.

TV DINNERS

In retrospect, the invention of the TV dinner in 1953 seems inevitable: you had to eat, preferably with all members of the family in attendance, but you didn't want to leave that fascinating box with its grainy gray images. Swanson saw a need and filled it—or did they?

According to colorful but unverifiable legend, it was the other way around. C. A. Swanson & Sons had 270 tons of leftover Thanksgiving turkey shuttling back and forth across the United States in refrigerated railroad cars because they had no other place to stash the birds. Not wanting to let them go to waste, Swanson exec Gerald Thomas (who died in July 2005) came up with the idea of the TV dinner, a spin on the (then) style of airline meals. Sound like a story too good to be true? Very possibly it is. More likely a slew of marketing, sales, research, and management people were involved in developing the new product.

The first TV dinners were packaged in tripartite aluminum trays, and each one contained turkey, stuffing, gravy, mashed potatoes, and peas. Turkey was (and still is) the favorite, but Swanson also made dinners whose main courses featured Salisbury steak, meat loaf, or fried chicken. The trays were shiny and clean-looking, and the sections were pretty similar to the sections of those baby dishes from which most American children had learned to eat their pablum and pureed green beans. The neatness of the little compartments was appealing too: Remember how you always hated it when, at a normal meal, the peas accidentally wandered over into the mashed potatoes or the meat

---

13 FOODS YOU MIGHT NOT HAVE THOUGHT OF GRILLING

peaches	broccoli florets	baby bok choy
fresh pineapple	leeks	radicchio
bananas	fennel	endive
plantains	small beets	wedges of precooked
asparagus	(precooked)	sweet potato

touched the vegetables? TV dinner trays took care of meandering food.

Though the meals were frozen, many buyers didn't yet own freezers, so the dinners were usually thawed and reheated on the day of purchase. The food itself spoke to some ubiquitous and possibly nostalgic notion of what good home cooking comprised: if Mom wasn't going to cook, this was the next best thing short of going out to a restaurant. The cozy comfort message may have been subliminal, but it got through. Instead of the five thousand TV dinners Swanson anticipated selling in the first year, they sold an awesome 10 million.

Over the decades Swanson expanded its line to include seventy-six frozen meal products, and the term *TV Dinner* was phased out along with that aluminum tray. The tray earned a place in the Smithsonian Institution in 1986, and nowadays all the meals are, of course, packaged in microwavable containers. TV dinners started as convenience foods promoting more leisure; frozen meals today seem to be convenience foods we can prepare in the few free moments of our unleisurely lives.

A Few American Food Moments from the 1950s

1950: Dunkin Donuts store opens; Jell-O apple gelatin comes on the market

1951: first Jack-in-the-Box, San Diego, California

1952: first Mr. Potato Head marketed; Cheez Whiz introduced

1953: White Rose Redi-Tea, first instant iced tea, appears; Jell-O instant pudding marketed nationally

1954: Swanson TV dinners sold at ninety-eight cents apiece

1955: Quaker brings out instant oatmeal

1956: Jif peanut butter born

1957: Special K introduced

1958: Sweet 'N Low introduced

KNOW YOUR PLACE SETTINGS

We usually think (or worry), when we sit down to eat at a dinner party or restaurant, that it's our responsibility to know which fork or spoon to use for which course. It is, to some degree, but it's even more the responsibility of a gracious host to make it easy for guests to figure that out. If the places have been set correctly and the guests know the One Basic Rule, all should go without a hitch. The O.B.R. is this: work your way in.

You know, of course, that the forks are on the left of your plate and the knives and spoons are on the right. You may also know that the dessert spoon and fork are either above your plate or given to you when dessert is served. Okay—ready, set, go. The first course arrives. If it's forkable (like salad or pâté), reach for the fork farthest away from your plate. If it's spoonable (like soup), use the spoon farthest away from your plate. When you're done eating, place the used fork on the diagonal on your plate; leave the used spoon in your soup plate or on the service plate on which the soup bowl is resting.

On to the next course: this is probably the main dish, so use the next fork (again, the one now farthest from your plate) and the big knife to the right of your plate. Now you're pretty much home free, as long as you remember to use the *small* knife (the one resting on your bread plate) to butter your bread. (And in case you didn't know, never butter the whole slice of bread or a big chunk of roll. Instead, break off a small piece, butter it with that small knife, and pop it into your mouth.) When you're finished eating the main course, place your used fork and knife *together* horizontally or diagonally across the middle of your dinner plate. Relax and wait for dessert.

Formal dinner parties are a more complicated matter, entailing a lot more silverware and glasses and odds and ends like salad knives and fish forks; to acquit yourself well at one of those could take some serious studying. But for most nice-but-not-too-formal dinners and restaurants, the above guidelines will see you through.

PLACE-SETTING TIP: Chances are that no one will even notice if you make a gaffe, and in the cosmic scheme of things, how much does it matter if you do?

A Few American Food Moments from the 1940s

1940: first McDonald's, San Bernardino, California; first Dairy Queen, Joliet, Illinois

1941: M&Ms hit the stores; first issue of *Gourmet* hits the stands; Cheerios introduced

1942: start of Dannon company; Kellogg's Raisin Bran appears in stores; K rations for the troops contain soluble coffee that will become postwar instant Maxwell House

1943: food rationing continues, including flour, fish, and canned goods

1944: Chiquita banana jingle first heard in the land

1946: General Foods introduces Minute Rice

1947: sugar rationing ends; Betty Crocker cake mix goes on the market; Reddi-Wip is introduced

1948: V-8 appears; Baskin-Robbins starts to form a chain in California

1949: first Pillsbury Bake-Off; first Sara Lee Cheese Cake

12 Main Dishes to Serve
When Your Boss Comes for Dinner

When much depends on dinner, play it safe. Stick to what you do well (if it's suitable), or cheat and order something from a really good take-out place. Serve the take-out on your own china, and no one will be the wiser. However, if you must cook, make . . .

- ★ your mother's (or grandmother's)
     most reliable roast chicken recipe

- ★ baked chicken

- ★ leg of lamb

- ★ baby lamb chops

- ★ grilled or broiled steak

- ★ grilled veal chops

- ★ pork roast

- ★ baked ham

- ★ cold poached salmon

- ★ sautéed shrimp or scallops

- ★ pasta primavera

- ★ pasta with seafood

12 Main Dishes to Serve
When Your New In-laws Come for Dinner

Unless your new in-laws are snooty, aim for homey, cozy, and yummy. If you don't cook, order great barbecued chicken or ribs from the best place in town and serve it on the heirloom platter they gave you for your wedding. If you *must* cook, make . . .

★ your mother's (or grandmother's)
   most reliable pot roast recipe

★ meat loaf

★ veal cutlets

★ braised pork chops

★ baked chicken legs

★ oven-fried chicken

★ roasted Cornish game hens

★ stir-fried shrimp or scallops

★ broiled fish fillets with flavored butter

★ pasta with a great bolognese sauce

★ lasagna

★ spaghetti carbonara

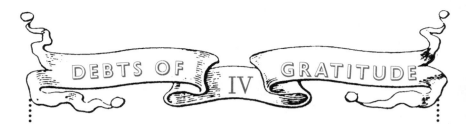

DEBTS OF GRATITUDE
IV

FREDERICK MAYTAG II and **ROBERT MAYTAG** (of the Maytag appliance dynasty) owned the Maytag Dairy Farms in Iowa. When they heard about Iowa State U's new process for making blue cheese, they got right onto it. The result, in 1941, was the delicious, tangy, crumbly-smooth blue-veined Maytag Blue—one of America's best cheeses.

MARJORIE KINNAN RAWLINGS (1896–1953) was the author of the 1939 Pulitzer Prize–winning novel *The Yearling*, but she was also a transplant to south Florida, the mistress of a seventy-two-acre orange grove, and a fine cook who learned everything there was to know about the local dishes. In 1942 she put it all into a wonderful cookbook called *Cross Creek Cookery*.

In 1908 New York tea merchant **THOMAS SULLIVAN** sent small handsewn silk bags of tea to his restaurant customers, a convenient way of delivering samples of his fine teas. To his surprise, instead of opening the bags and tipping the loose tea into waiting teapots, his customers popped the bags right into the pots. The bags were neat and easy to use, and the commercial tea bag was born.

RICHARD HELLMANN used his wife Nina's scrumptious homemade mayonnaise in the sandwiches and salads he made in the New York deli he opened in 1905. Customers clamored for Nina's mayo, so Richard started selling it to them by the scoop, then selling it to other stores, and finally, in 1913, he built a three-story factory in Queens and had a great success with Hellmann's Blue Ribbon Mayonnaise.

TEX-MEX COOKING

Tex-Mex is a regional American style of cooking, neither Texan nor Mexican, but a hybrid that refers culinarily to both. In the introduction to his book *Authentic Mexican*, Rick Bayless explains, "There have developed two independent systems of Mexican cooking. The first is from Mexico, and . . . it is the substantial, wide-ranging cuisine that should be allowed its unadulterated, honest name: Mexican. The second system is the Mexican-American one, and, in its many regional varieties, can be just as delicious. But its range is limited, and to my mind it forms part of the broader system of North American (or at least Southwest North American) cookery."

What Mr. Bayless seems to be saying is that both types of cooking are delicious; one just happens to encompass a broader range than the other. The broader one is Mexican; the more limited one is Tex-Mex. Both good. Just different. Too bad that the proponents of each had to get so huffy about it.

The line was drawn in the sand in 1972, when Diana Kennedy published *The Cuisines of Mexico* and put her culinary foot down about what was really Mexican food and what wasn't. High and low cooking from the interior of Mexico was real; Americanized, adapted, invented Mexican-style dishes from northern Mexico and south and west Texas were not. Insulted as the border Tejanos were, she had a point. On the other hand, she was a Brit who'd never lived in Tex-Mex country, and

10 PEPPERS HOT ENOUGH TO SET YOU ON FIRE

According to the standard heat index (computed in Scoville units, named in honor of the man who took on the job no one else wanted to do), these are ten of the hottest peppers on earth. Approach with caution. Or not.

habanero	chiltepin	Tabasco
Scotch bonnet	santaka	cayenne
Thai	piquín	aji
	dundicut	

7 Basic Ingredients for Salsa Roja

ripe tomatoes (uncooked or roasted)	green chiles (jalapeños or serranos)	cilantro
white onion	garlic	fresh lime juice
		salt

why pick on Tex-Mex? North Americans had adapted Chinese food and Italian food to regional tastes, and no one had landed on those revisionist (or invented) dishes like a ton of bricks. It didn't seem fair, especially because folks loved their Tex-Mex food from California to Houston to Chicago and down into northern Mexico, too. So what if nachos, margaritas, flour tortillas, fajitas, crisp tacos, crisp chalupas, chile con queso, chimichangas, and chile con carne were not to be found in the interior of Mexico? They tasted *good*.

Why, one wonders, does this *guerrita* between Mexican and Tex-Mex have to be a matter of either/or? Why can't deeply authentic Mexican food in all its rich variety coexist peacefully with its less exacting, more accessible, often quite satisfying Tex-Mex cousins? Aren't there days when you want a Fig Newton and other days when only a chocolate éclair will do?

One of my close friends often reminds me that you can't make people eat what they don't want to eat—and you can't stop them from eating what they *do* want to eat. It might be more noble to hold out for a perfectly authentic *pato en pipián rojo*, but if you're dying for a chicken chalupa you'll be heading for your local Tex-Mex café *muy pronto*.

6 BASIC INGREDIENTS FOR SALSA VERDE

tomatillos	green chiles (jalapeños or serranos)	cilantro
white onion		salt
garlic		

ALL ABOUT TORTILLAS

If you know Spanish cooking, you're familiar with the Spanish tortilla, which is a round, flat egg-and-potato dish that resembles an unfolded omelet. When Cortés and his Spanish soldiers invaded Mexico in 1519 they found the indigenous people eating round corn-flour flatbreads, and it seemed logical to the Spanish to call these breads tortillas too. Today we buy factory-made corn or flour tortillas, usually sealed in plastic packets of eight or ten or more. Some are good, some are awful, but none compares to the freshly handmade and baked tortillas still to be found in some parts of Mexico.

Making tortillas by hand from scratch takes time, energy, practice, and good ingredients. The basic method is this: Boil some white corn with slaked lime (or wood ashes) and let it steep overnight. In the morning discard both the liquid and the skins floating on its surface and wash the skinned corn kernels. Grind the corn on a *metate*, a stone grinding tool, and keep grinding (adding small amounts of water continuously) until you have a pliable dough that's not too dry and not too sticky. Break off a piece of dough, quickly pat it into a thin round, and place it on a hot griddle for up to a minute on each side.

This description makes the process sound reasonably simple, and it is, except that it takes a lifetime of experience to know just how much to grind the corn, how much water to add to keep the dough from either crumbling or getting gloppy, and especially how to pat the dough into a very thin, very even, very round layer. Try it—you'll see how hard it is.

Alternatives are available if you still want to have a go: buy masa harina instead of treating and grinding the corn yourself, and use a tortilla press instead of shaping the tortillas by hand. Or find the best brand of ready-mades in your area and heat them up.

BANANAS AND PLANTAINS

This you're not going to believe: the banana plant—the one that looks like a giant house-eating palm tree—is a perennial herb of the lily family. Hard to imagine a banana having any kinship with an herb or a lily, but it does. Each plant produces one bunch of bananas about every fifteen months; each bunch comprises several "hands" of about a dozen "fingers" (okay, bananas). Bananas are available in quantity year-round, and a good thing they are because the banana is America's hands-down favorite fruit; we eat millions each year. Makes sense: properly ripe bananas are sweet, neat, and full of tryptophan—a protein that converts to serotonin and makes us feel good. (Depressed? Eat a banana, it might help.) They're high in fiber, rich in iron, and loaded with potassium; they neutralize acid, soothe queasiness, satisfy that sweet tooth, and can bring on a bit of drowsiness. Sort of the all-purpose portable snack.

Plantains (*plátanos*, in Spanish) are also called "cooking bananas" because they're just not eaten raw. They look a lot like plain old bananas, except that they're larger and longer, with thicker, tougher skins. When the skin is green, which it often is in the store, it's murder to peel the skin cleanly from the flesh. No matter—slit the skin lengthwise, yank it off, and boil or fry the plantain as if it were a potato, a starchy, comfortingly mild accompaniment to spicy foods. You can even skip the peeling step and bake the plantain right in its skin.

As the plantain ripens over a few days, the skin gradually darkens to black, and the flesh gets sweeter and more tender, even spongy—and a lot easier to peel, too. Stash in the fridge for up to a few days to stop ripening.

When you're eating in a Latin American restaurant, ask for *plátanos maduros* if you want soft, sweet slices of sautéed plantain. If you want firm, crisp, unsweet slices, ask for *tostones*.

FOOD OF THE AZTECS

When we speak of Aztec food, as we often do, we generally mean what was eaten at the time of the emperor Montezuma (or, more correctly, Moctezuma II), when the Spaniard Hernán Cortés and his small band of soldiers invaded Mexico in 1519. The Spaniards documented their conquest of the Aztec capital Tenochtitlán (later Mexico City) in great detail. That documentation included detailed reports about food, so we know what upper-class and royal Aztecs ate because the Spaniards who wrote the journals weren't hobnobbing with the peasants.

We do know that the poorest people in Montezuma's society sub-sisted on corn, beans, and tortillas, as they continued to do in Mexico after the Spanish conquest and right up into more modern times. Corn (or maize) was hugely important to the Aztecs, and it was eaten in many forms: atole, a porridge flavored with chiles or fruit; tortillas; pozole, a stew using whole kernels of corn; corn on the cob; and tamales plain or stuffed with beans, chiles, or meat when it was avail-able. However, that information is hardly a complete description of what was available to eat in Montezuma's world.

Though the Aztecs had been a nomadic tribe in the Valley of Mexico, in the fifteenth century they vanquished the peoples sur-rounding the valley and established a stable culture whose center was Tenochtitlán. The society was dominated by the merchant, military, reli-gious, and noble classes. They liked to eat well, and stability made it possible to cultivate produce in an organized way, to domesticate ani-mals and fowl for food, and to bring fish and shellfish in from nearby waters and from the coastal areas.

It was a culture that leaned more toward the vegetarian than the carnivorous, but the Aztecs also ate wild deer and rabbits, wild birds such as quail and pigeon, iguanas, and many kinds of insects. They grew and ate tomatoes and tomatillos; avocados (yes, guacamole was an Aztec invention); several varieties of squash; nopal, which is prickly pear cactus; jícama; manioc; many kinds of beans; onions; sweet pota-toes; peanuts; and fruits such as mamey, cherimoya, zapote, guava, cus-tard apples, pineapple, and papaya. The Aztecs had chiles of all kinds for flavoring, and epazote leaves were their most important herb. They

lemons	yellow peppers	lemon gelatin
yellow squash	sweet corn	yellow plums
mustard	corn muffins	omelets
curry (sometimes)	lemon pudding	yellow cake
Cheddar cheese	lemon sorbet	saffron rice

ground chia seeds and amaranth seeds for flour, and used the amaranth leaves as greens, too. Vanilla, extracted from the pods of a species of orchid, was highly prized, and used to flavor chocolate, which was equally prized.

Which brings us to chocolate: the Aztecs loved chocolate, once they got used to it and learned to grind the roasted cacao beans for making beverages. The most common chocolate drink contained ground chocolate and finely ground corn flour flavored with vanilla or honey or chiles. So important was chocolate drinking that the Aztecs made exquisite little cups for the purpose, and it is said that Montezuma drank fifty cups of chocolate each day both for pleasure and to give him strength. Unfortunately, fifty cups of chocolate a day didn't save Montezuma from destruction: he was murdered either by the Spaniards or by his own people—which group is not quite clear—and the mighty Aztec empire came to an end. Among the many treasures the Spaniards took away from Mexico was . . . chocolate.

AMERICAN INDIAN FOODS

Long before Europeans arrived on this continent, American Indian peoples hunted, gathered, raised, and prepared a huge variety of foods. Take, for instance, the extensive menu of the native peoples of the Southwest. It included deer, bear, coyote, bobcats, gophers, mice, voles, rabbits, antelope, elk, and many more animals; ants, grasshoppers, and other insects; nuts, seeds, and a great variety of roots; wild plants (such as garlic and carrots); wild berries (such as raspberries and currants); fish from lakes and streams; and migrating birds. Food was a constant concern, and these peoples were experts in finding it and extracting every morsel of energy and utility from it. Waste was not an option.

Just as we now have foods that most of us eat (like pizza) and foods that are regional (like po'boy sandwiches), native peoples had both regional specialties and foods-in-common. What each tribe ate depended, of course, on area, climate, season, and tradition; hunters had their kind of food, harvesters had another. On the Great Plains the native peoples hunted buffalo; on the northwest coast salmon abounded; in the Southeast there were crabs, wild geese, and wild turkeys. But the most important *agricultural* contribution of American Indians—and the one they had most in common with one another—was corn.

All over North and South America corn was cultivated and modified to suit particular growing conditions. Seeds were carefully selected, preserved, and planted, often in hills with beans and squash. So nutritionally crucial was this trio of corn, beans, and squash that they were called the Three Sisters, and rituals and legends attended them.

Combining these three was an act of agricultural genius: the bean vine twines around the sturdy cornstalk, a natural beanpole; the broad leaves of the squash keep the ground both moist for the corn's shallow roots and protects from encroaching weeds or other plants; the bean plant replaces nitrogen in the soil (corn needs a lot of nitrogen). Even better, the food value is high because the amino acids in corn and beans work together to produce complete protein in the human body. The metaphor of the Three Sisters was a powerful one in cultures in which survival depended on working together in harmony.

10 Foods Named After Cities

Philly cheese steak

Boston cream pie

Boston baked beans

New York steak (or Kansas City steak)

New York cheesecake

Manhattan clam chowder

Smithfield ham

Philadelphia sticky buns

New Bedford pudding

Buffalo chicken wings

Strictly American:
12 Foods That Sound Foreign but Aren't

chop suey

veal parmigiana

English muffins

Turkish taffy

Swiss steak

vichyssoise

egg foo yong

Russian dressing

clams posillipo

French toast

London broil

German chocolate cake

WHAT ON EARTH IS...

Before modern methods, the safe preservation of food (especially protein-rich nutritious food) was an ongoing problem for nomadic peoples, travelers, and families needing to store sustenance for the winter. When fresh food from the field, garden, orchard, woods, mountain, and river ran out or was beyond reach, preserved food kept people alive.

American Indians, trappers, explorers, settlers, and herders all made jerky: salted, air-dried strips of lean meat that were lightweight and nourishing and lasted almost indefinitely. Jerky could be made from beef, venison, buffalo, elk, antelope, or whatever animal was available. Some liked it cut thin, others preferred thick strips; smoking the meat was popular too. Jerky could be chewed by itself or added to soup or stew. American Indians had a distinctive technique of adding dried berries and melted fat to their dried meat to make a paste—pemmican—that was shaped into small cakes and eaten out of hand or added to soups.

Today jerky is made commercially with serious dehydrators and smokers (you can do a home version too, if you're so inclined), and though some hikers and backpackers still use it as food, mostly we just snack on it and remember the days of the Oregon Trail.

8 Great Things to Make with Stale Bread

1. small salad croutons

2. large garlic-and-herb- or grated-cheese-topped
soup croutons (great with onion soup)

3. bread pudding (with lots of brown sugar)

4. panzanella (Italian bread salad made with fresh tomatoes)

5. French toast

6. cinnamon toast

7. Welsh rarebit

8. a trail of breadcrumbs in the woods,
so you can find your way back home

WHAT DOES "ORGANIC FARMING" MEAN?

Methods of organic farming vary, of course, according to individual farmers, climate, crops, and local laws, but the principles most organic farmers hold in common are the same: no use of synthetic fertilizers or pesticides; no genetically modified organisms (GMOs); protection of the soil from erosion and loss of nutrients; biodiversity (growing not just one, but a variety of crops); and, for livestock and poultry, no antibiotics or hormones, and access to outdoor grazing.

Organic farmers rely heavily on green manure and composting for their fertilizer needs, with low use of commercial fertilizers. A particular kind of pest control is important too: using beneficial predatory insects to keep the problem pests under control; planting "companion crops" (such as corn, beans, and squash) that discourage insect pests; rotating crops; and simply accepting a certain amount of pest damage.

Most organic farms are independently operated on a relatively small scale, unlike conventional farms that are operated on a huge scale by major food corporations. Organic farms sell mostly to local food co-ops, farmers' markets, high-end specialized supermarket chains (such as Whole Foods), and smaller high-end food shops. Giant agribusiness sells nationwide to supermarkets and other wholesale operations.

It's unlikely that today's organic farms could ever provide sufficient food for a nation, but it's equally unlikely that conventional agribusiness farms will be motivated to solve their own (and therefore *our*) problems, such as soil depletion; natural resource depletion; pollution of soil, water, and air; danger from certain chemical pesticides; and the social instability that results from putting family farms out of business. (And there are problems that both types of farming share: hygienic or unhygienic handling of food, for instance, and the contamination of foods by biological toxins.) Like it or not, organic farms are in a constant struggle to remain viable.

20 Basic Nonperishable Foods Every Well-stocked Pantry Should Have

★ sugar

★ salt

★ flour

★ spices and herbs
(see the list on page 79 for basics)

★ olive oil

★ vegetable oil (safflower or canola, for example)

★ vinegars
(balsamic, red wine, white wine, and so on)

★ pasta

★ rice

★ canned stock
(chicken, beef, vegetable)

★ crackers, cookies, chips

★ canned tuna, sardines, beans, and other favorite proteins

★ canned tomatoes (whole, chopped, paste)

★ jams, jellies, preserves

★ honey, maple syrup

★ backup condiments (mustard, mayonnaise,
ketchup—unopened, of course)

★ tea, instant coffee

★ beverages (bottled water, juice, soda, and so on)

★ bottled sauces, salad dressings

★ cereals

Technically speaking—that is, according to the U.S. Department of Agriculture—a chicken is free-range if it has access to the outdoors. In other words, even conventionally raised chickens, if they can go out of the coop and into a yard, may be labeled free-range. The definition has nothing to do with the actual amount of time a chicken stays outdoors, how clean the yard is, if the yard is fenced in, how crowded the conditions are, what the chicken eats, or whether it's given hormones or antibiotics. And the term does not necessarily imply anything about the flavor, texture, or freshness of a chicken, either.

The problem is that a lot of people attach more meaning to the term *free-range* than it deserves: they assume it means organic or that the chickens are strutting around outdoors, basking in the sunshine and fresh air, and plumping up on green grass. Some free-range chickens are; some aren't. Read the labels carefully if you want the true story.

CHICKEN FACT: According to a study done in 2004 by the Agricultural Research Service of the USDA, approximately the same percentage (about 25 percent) of free-range chickens and conventionally raised chickens tested positive for salmonella.

TIDBIT: Generally speaking, *vegetarians* do not eat meat, fish, or poultry. However, you've probably met more than a few people who call themselves vegetarians who do eat fish and shellfish, and some who eat poultry. *Vegans* are strict vegetarians who also refrain from eating animal by-products (such as eggs, dairy products, and honey) and don't even use animal by-products (such as leather, silk, fur, and certain soaps and cosmetics). *Fruitarians* eat only raw fruits, seeds, and nuts.

19 *Specialty-food Web Sites*

TheCMCCompany.com (*Asian, Mexican, and other foods*)

bobsredmill.com (*whole-grain and organic products*)

penzeys.com (*fantastic herbs and spices*)

orientalpantry.com (*Asian foods of all kinds*)

http://www.beryls.com (*cake and pastry supplies from abroad*)

ethnicgrocer.com (*world foods*)

flyingnoodle.com (*pasta, sauce, and more*)

gracewoodgroves.com (*citrus fruits, tomatoes*)

KaribaFarms.com (*dried fruits and vegetables*)

EBFarm.com (*organic fruits and vegetables*)

cajungrocer.com (*everything for Cajun cooking*)

bakerscandc.com (*cake and candy-making supplies*)

sweetc.com (*baking and candy-making;
formerly the beloved Maid of Scandinavia*)

walnutacres.com (*organic everything*)

americanspice.com (*spices, condiments*)

formaggiokitchen.com (*Italian specialties and more*)

www.harney.com (*tea!*)

specialteas.com (*more tea!*)

http://www.katysmokehouse.com (*smoked seafood*)

THE REAL LIFE OF BEES

Can you think of two natural (unprocessed) foods, consumed by humans, that are produced *specifically* as food? One is milk. The other is honey. Milk and honey—has a nice ring to it, don't you think? Milk (human or animal) is produced for the sole purpose of nourishing the young. Honey is produced for the sole purpose of feeding the bees.

Bees have been doing the honey thing for more than 150 million years, and they've gotten pretty good at it. Like all living creatures, they try to ensure their own survival, in this case by collecting nectar from flowers when flowers are in bloom, converting it into the high-energy bee food we call honey, and storing it in beeswax honeycombs against the times of the year when flowers are unavailable. If they have to they'll travel many thousands of miles and visit many thousands of flowers to collect the amount of nectar they need.

It's the source of the nectar that determines the taste and color of the honey. Pale honeys are usually mild in flavor; darker ones are usually stronger. Clover, sage, alfalfa, and orange blossom are common types of honey, but there are lots more: acacia, tulip-tree, tupelo, wild-flower, buckwheat, eucalyptus, linden, thyme, raspberry, spearmint, manzanita, and others. You can buy honey in three forms: in the comb (which is totally edible); chunk-style (a combination of liquid honey and chunks of waxy comb); and plain old liquid, extracted from the comb and usually pasteurized to keep it from crystallizing.

BEE FACT: If you were a bee with a hankering for a round-the-world trip, you'd need about an ounce of honey to give you enough energy to fuel your journey.

14 REPUTEDLY APHRODISIAC FOODS (BUT DON'T COUNT ON THEM)

chocolate	artichokes	celery and cucumbers
oysters	asparagus	sweet potatoes
chiles	dates and figs	fennel
beef	garlic and onions	apricots and pomegranates
curry	nuts	

Priscilla Goodmanners Tells It Like It Is:
THE EDIBLE HOST(ESS) GIFT

Taking a small offering when you're invited to an informal dinner party is just the nice thing to do. I'm not talking about the thing you bring when you've asked the host if there's anything you can bring. If you do that, chances are he or she will say, Sure, bring wine, and then you'll ask what kind of wine would work with dinner, and he or she will tell you what's needed, and that's what you'll bring. That's not exactly a host(ess) gift; it's a sort of we're-all-in-this-together contribution.

A host(ess) gift can, indeed, be wine. But accompany the wine with a remark: "Tiffany and I thought you and Jennifer would enjoy this on another night." That way the host(ess), who may be serving only reds when you've brought white, won't feel obligated to open your wine tonight. You can do the same thing with a bottle of champagne or an interesting liqueur.

Instead of alcohol, consider these edible possibilities: a small box of really, really good chocolate; glacé fruits; maple sugar candy; marzipan; a tin of great pistachios; a tin of great cocoa powder; fancy preserves; exotic fruit; a sampler of unusual spices or herbs; panforte or panettone; butter cookies from the best bakery in town; macaroons; gourmet brownies; chocolate-covered nuts or coffee beans; nut brittle; a tin of shortbread; glacé chestnuts; caviar; amazing olive oil; white truffle oil; a tin of pâté; a jar of good olives, a jar of tapenade, and a jar of sun-dried tomatoes; a selection of fancy peppercorns; a selection of fancy teas or coffees; thin after-dinner mints.

11 FOODS POPULARIZED AT THE 1904 ST. LOUIS WORLD'S FAIR

hamburgers	iced tea	peanut butter
ice cream cones	Dr Pepper	scones
hot dogs	cotton candy	black olives
lemonade	grapefruit	

TELL ME ABOUT...

COTTON CANDY

This definitely isn't rocket science: all you need is sugar and a machine, and you've got cotton candy. The sugar is melted to liquid, then spun in the cotton candy machine. As it spins, the liquid is forced through teeny holes into the center of the machine, forming thousands of sugar filaments that cool instantly and can be collected onto a stick or a cardboard cone. Wasn't it great to watch the cotton candy guy swirling the cone around and around inside the machine with just the right light touch to make a gigantic cloud of fluffy cotton candy especially for you?

National Cotton Candy Day is December 7. Bad choice. That's the date that F.D.R. assured us would "live in infamy" after the bombing of Pearl Harbor in World War II.

FAVORITE COTTON CANDY FACT: Until 1920 cotton candy was called fairy floss.

SUNDAES AND MALTEDS:
The History of the Soda Fountain

Ah, the romance of the soda fountain: the gleaming glassware, the shiny silver spouts, the malted milk mixer that looked like a rocket ship, the frosty ice cream bins, the huge mirror behind the smiling soda jerk in his crisp white shirt.

A curious confluence of conditions produced those legendary soda fountains. For one thing, nineteenth-century Americans were a little obsessed with the supposedly healthful benefits of bubbly mineral water (dubbed "soda water"). Only the rich could actually afford to visit and drink from the natural mineral springs scattered across the country; poor folks were out of the loop. But in 1832 the invention of a technique for carbonation—the conversion of still water to bubbly by the addition of carbon dioxide—made soda water available to the masses. It was sold in drug stores, and soon smart pharmacists began adding flavoring to the plain soda. Big improvement. By 1898 we had ginger ale, root beer, Dr Pepper, Coca-Cola, and Pepsi-Cola, among others.

Meanwhile, ice cream had taken America by storm. High and low, young and old, Americans were hanging out in droves in pretty little ice cream parlors. True, ice cream was something you could have made at home, but making the stuff was hard work, and it was much more fun to dress up, go downtown, and meet your friends and family at the Ice Cream Shoppe.

Here's where it starts to get confusing. There was soda water mania and ice cream mania. There was soda water available in drugstores and ice cream available in ice cream parlors—but some ice cream parlors served ice cream sodas, and some drugstores served plain ice cream. Could the dedicated, full-service soda fountain, where *all of it and more* was available, be far behind? It wasn't. Soda fountains popped up in drugstores and independently, too, sporting impressive equipment and offering new and exciting concoctions: molded ice cream, ice cream sundaes, ice cream cones, banana splits, malteds, milkshakes, ice cream sodas, frappes, floats, coolers. They offered the friendly soda jerk as well, showing off his skills by creating just the luscious combination you craved *while you watched*. And maybe, if you were a pretty girl, adding that extra scoop of vanilla or that extra squirt of chocolate syrup to your favorite soda fountain treat.

Soda fountains became institutions in small towns and big cities alike. They were refuges on hot summer days, treats on Sunday afternoons, approved places for first (and second) dates. Soon they began to sell pastries, pie, sandwiches, and other food, and presto-change-o, they became lunch counters. During Prohibition soda fountains were havens of temperance, innocent gathering places. During the Great Depression they struggled, but 1940s Hollywood films gave them a boost, and in World War II the soda fountain was portrayed as another piece of Home for which the soldiers and sailors longed.

Nothing lasts. As technology advanced in the 1950s, prepacked ice cream became ever more available in groceries and, eventually, in supermarkets. The ice cream man with his refrigerator truck and his bell began to deliver ice cream sandwiches, ice cream bars, Popsicles, and frozen custard right to your very own street. Soda fountains disappeared one by one, and—sadly—few remain.

10 Easy Cupcake Decorations

★ sweetened shredded coconut

★ white or semisweet chocolate chips

★ candy corn, M&Ms, redhots, or other brightly colored small candies

★ animal crackers

★ simple piping with store-bought icing

★ chocolate-dipped strawberry

★ paper parasol

★ gumdrops

★ silver dragées

★ candied violets

What's the Difference between ...

ICES, GRANITA, SHERBET, SORBET,
ICE CREAM, ICE MILK, GELATO,
AND FROZEN YOGURT?

Pay attention and this will be easy: Ices are made of sweetened fruit juice or fruit syrup and water. Granita is Italian fruit ice, except that there's also wine-flavored and coffee-flavored granita. Sherbet is fruit ice too, except sometimes—when it contains milk, egg whites, or gelatin. *Sorbet* is the French word for sherbet, and it's just like sherbet—except that it's never made with milk. And oh, yes, sometimes sorbets are on the savory side (like tomato) or herb-enhanced (like with thyme), when they're used as palate cleansers between courses of a fancy meal. Got that so far?

Ice cream contains (along with sweetening and flavor and maybe some chunky stuff) cream and some variety of milk, to the tune of 10 percent (or more) milk fat. Ice milk is a lot like ice cream, except that it has less milk fat. Gelato (or gelati, if you're having more than one) is Italian ice cream, denser and richer than its American cousin because there's not as much air in it.

Frozen yogurt is frozen yogurt, with sweetening and flavor added.

TIDBIT: The soda jerk was not a soda nerd. Okay, he might have been a nerd, too, but that's not what his title meant. "Jerk" did not refer to his personality, but to his hand motions. In fact, he was also called the soda jerker, which makes the whole thing a lot clearer: in the days of soda fountains, the young man behind the marble counter had to jerk the handle of the soda spigot in order to fill the tall soda glasses.

HIGH TEA AND ELEVENSES

High tea, the elaborate three-course late-afternoon affair that Americans think of as quintessentially British, has pretty much gone the way of the Raj. Not that any Brit skips the afternoon cuppa (possibly with a bit of nosh to accompany it), but true high tea is now an event mostly for special occasions, ladies of leisure, and tourists.

High tea is a sequence of tea sandwiches, scones (and perhaps crumpets), and assorted small pastries, cakes, and sweets. The thin crustless sandwiches might contain fillings of watercress, smoked salmon, cucumber, ham, tiny shrimp, egg mayonnaise (egg salad), or chicken mayonnaise. The raisin-studded scones are small and freshly baked, and served with Devonshire clotted cream and fruit preserves (and sometimes with lemon curd, too). The assortment of sweets might include tiny fruit tarts, trifle, cream puffs, petits fours, crème caramel, or ripe strawberries. And the tea? Darjeeling, Assam, Earl Grey, Lapsang souchong, jasmine, mint, chamomile, with several more choices if none of these suits. The tea is always steeped in the leaf (loose) in a fine china teapot kept hot and filled. Teabags are unwelcome at high tea.

A MOMENT OR TWO WITH...

HOT CROSS BUNS

As Good Friday approaches, bakery windows fill up with tempting pyramids of hot cross buns, the sweet yeast bread that's traditionally eaten all through the season of Lent—and *only* during Lent. Each bun is shot through with raisins and candied fruit, and decorated with a white icing cross painted across the golden brown top.

Eating sweet yeast cakes on Good Friday is a medieval English custom dating back at least to the sixteenth or seventeenth century; a knife-slash cross on the top of the bread was the precedent to the sweet icing cross, which may have become common only in the early eighteenth century. You can almost hear the street vendors singing, "Hot cross buns! Hot cross buns! One a penny, two a penny, hot cross buns!"

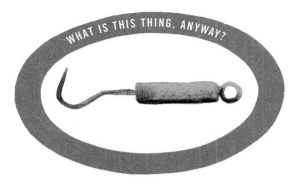

It's a butter curler. If you're into that sort of nicety, pull it along the top of a slab of butter and voilà! Nifty little curls.

There's another ruffle on the tea story—something called a "cream tea." This ritual originated in Devon, in the southwest of England, where they make the famous Devonshire clotted cream you always get with high teas and without which there would be no cream teas. Clotted cream is simply a very thick unsweetened cream. To make it, rich milk is heated gently until a thick layer of cream forms on the surface; when the cream is cool, it's spooned off and refrigerated. A cream tea is less elaborate than a high tea: scones topped with clotted cream and fruit preserves, served with pots and pots of steaming tea. You can have cream teas all over England these days, not just in Devon, but whether you'll get homemade clotted cream or something out of a jar *anywhere* is in serious question.

The English drink tea all the time, morning, noon, and night, at breakfast, lunch, and dinner, and they also punctuate the day with the odd cup of tea. The mid-morning tea break has been dubbed elevenses, referring to the hour of eleven A.M., and it's like our requisite mid-morning coffee break. Tucked in between a light modern breakfast (the traditional heavy-duty English breakfast having also pretty much gone the way of the Raj) and a light modern lunch, a cup of tea and a biscuit or two—a biscuit to a Brit is a cookie to a Yank—perks up the flagging spirit and revs up the flagging worker.

IN THE BAG

Naomi Touger and Molly Touger, sisters

Despite her hour-and-a-half commute, our mother made dinner most nights when we were kids. She was an amazing cook. On an ordinary Tuesday she'd make lamb with hollandaise sauce or chicken paprikash with sour cream on egg noodles. She'd arrive home from work and before she could take off her coat we'd come rushing from whatever corner we'd been in and bellow Mo-om, what's for dinner? She'd be holding a grocery bag, and we would know that whatever was in it was what we'd be eating. More often than not, it was not what we wanted. If it was fish, we would groan and flop to the floor and have a dramatic fit.

Still, we ate what she gave us, even the fish. There would be no alternate kids' meal, no cut-up chicken pieces and macaroni and cheese. Not eating was not an option. As a result, we quickly developed sophisticated palates. We were not proud of this. As the children of Jewish academics in Irish working-class Boston, this was yet another thing that made us stick out. We particularly hated leftovers. Whatever our mother made the night before ended up in our lunch wrapped in waxed paper. It was horribly upsetting to unwrap a pork chop when the kid across from you was eating peanut butter and grape jelly on Wonder bread.

Despite all of this, we appreciated—in fact loved—the food. When we liked something, we told her so. Our father led the ritual. We would each take a taste and then everyone would "ooh" and "mmm," and exclaim at how delicious. Even when we were at our crappiest stages developmentally, we appreciated a good meal. Then we would dig in and our appreciation would last until we started yelling at each other for making mouth noises or teasing our father for getting a corn kernel stuck in his eyebrow or being otherwise mortifying. We got sent away from the table if we were being too unpleasant. The next night we'd do it all over again.

Now that we're grownups, we revere our mother's cooking, both the process and the product. We live in New York, work late, and usually the last thing we want to do upon arriving home is cook. When we do, we cook the foods from our childhood. But preparing familiar foods is not the same thing as having them made for you.

When we tell our mother that we're coming home for the weekend, she asks us what we'd like to eat. We tell her and she goes to the grocery store and she buys it and when we come home, it's like the best of childhood. The thing that's in her grocery bag is always the thing that we hope it will be. At the table, the oohing and mmming doesn't degenerate except into jokes and a game where we try to make our mother laugh until she pees. We eat until we're full and then our father leans in to inspect our plates, carefully, to see if there's one smackaroo of meat left to nibble on. And on the train ride back to New York, we happily eat our leftovers.

A MOMENT OR TWO WITH...

LATTE

You know you love it, but what exactly *is* a latte? It's espresso with a lot of frothy steamed milk, served in a tallish glass or paper cup. The espresso can be caffeinated or decaf, the milk can be whole or skim, you can sweeten it if you like, and you can powder it with cinnamon or chocolate.

Once upon a time adult Americans just drank coffee, plain old coffee. Then there was decaf coffee, then espresso, then cappuccino, then flavored coffees, then decaf espresso, then decaf cappuccino, then decaf flavored coffees, and then latte. And double latte. And decaf latte. Then mocha, white chocolate mocha, Frappuccino, shakes with coffee, coffee drinks with ice cream—a menu of coffee treats that rivals the sandwich menu at any deli. The coffee-treat thing is so popular that even Dunkin' Donuts and the other fast food spots are jumping on the bandwagon.

COFFEE NOTE: It's not just for adults anymore. Teenagers are the new market for snazzy coffee drinks, and not the decaf versions, either. After all, if you've been raised on caffeinated sodas, what's a little caffeine in your coffee? It's not illegal. Yet.

13 Foods Most Kids Hate
(Temporarily, We Hope)

1. anything you insist is Good for Them

★

2. anything they haven't tried before

★

3. anything on any diet their parents are on

★

4. rare, bloody meat

★

5. lumpy mashed potatoes

★

6. most fresh green vegetables

★

7. most fresh fruits

★

8. anything you try to slip past them by calling it
Cutie Fruity Yummy Roll-ups

★

9. anything bitter

★

10. anything soggy

★

11. tuna or chicken salad with something unexpected
(like chopped celery) in it

★

12. burgers without buns

★

13. soupy yogurt

13 Foods Most Kids Love
(Until They Hit the Next Phase)

1. anything made of potatoes, especially potato chips

★

2. anything rolled in a flour tortilla

★

3. anything stuffed in a pita bread

★

4. frozen pizza

★

5. ramen noodles

★

6. things with crisp names, like Pop Tarts or Hot Pockets

★

7. juice boxes

★

8. packaged mac and cheese

★

9. instant pudding

★

10. grapes

★

11. anything deep-fried

★

12. anything camouflaged with melted cheese

★

13. anything they've eaten
seventeen thousand times before

The True Saga of
BOSTON BAKED BEANS

There are three parts to the question of Boston baked beans: their origin, their ingredients, and whether Boston can legitimately claim them. The only thing not in dispute is why the beans were baked at all: religious necessity came face-to-face with nutritional requirements, and baked beans were the result.

The strict Puritan settlers of Massachusetts were not permitted to cook from sunset on Saturday through sunset on Sunday, their Sabbath day. But since they had to eat to keep up their strength for prayer, the wives adapted a hearty bean dish that could be set in the home oven or communal oven on Saturday, eaten on Saturday night, and eaten again on Sunday morning and afternoon. This, you'll notice, smacks of the ancient Orthodox Jewish custom of putting food in the oven on Friday before sunset, to be consumed on Friday night and all day Saturday (the Jewish Sabbath), when labor of any sort was forbidden. And what do you know—a baked bean dish called *skanah* was traditional to Jews of Spain and North Africa, from whence it could have been transported to New England by a seafaring gourmet.

The usual attribution for the original dish of baked beans lies closer to home. Dried beans were staple to the Iroquois, Penobscot, and

---

18 TRADITIONALLY NORTHEASTERN FOODS

Maine lobster	succotash	Boston cream pie
maple sugar candy	johnnycakes	hero sandwich
clam fritters	Anadama bread	New York cheesecake
clam chowder	Boston brown bread	egg cream
Yankee pot roast	Boston baked beans	Long Island duckling
Cape Cod turkey (baked cod)	New England boiled dinner	bagels, lox, and cream cheese

Narragansetts of the area that became New England; they made a mixture of beans, bear fat, and maple syrup, which was then baked in animal skins that were placed in cooking pits. The colonists could easily have altered the recipe to taste, using their more familiar molasses and pork fat.

Do Boston baked beans really come from Beantown? Not according to the good people of Beverly, Massachusetts. They insist that it was all a mistake. In 1890, to mark the twenty-fifth anniversary of the end of the Civil War, veterans gathered in Boston for a gigantic convention. The Beverly Pottery created several thousand small bean pots, marked "Beverly Pottery," as gifts for the visiting soldiers—who took them home and told one and all that the bean pots came from Boston. Lucky Boston has been known ever since as Beantown, home of Boston baked beans, and Beverly has never really recovered from the shock.

TIDBIT: Picture a thirty-foot-high tidal wave of molasses tearing along the streets of Boston at the rate of thirty miles per hour, destroying property and killing twenty-one innocent people. It seems almost impossible to believe, but that's what happened in 1919 when a molasses storage tank broke and 2 million gallons of thick, sticky, gooey molasses burst free. The catastrophe came to be called the Great Molasses Flood.

THE SHAKER TABLE

Shakers, or "Shaking Quakers," were members of a dissenting group of English Quakers who were known and persecuted for the ecstatic dancing, shaking, and shouting that dominated their religious services. In 1774 eight followers and their leader, Mother Ann Lee, fled England and established a settlement in New York State. Their worship was exuberant, but in all other ways their lives were defined by simplicity, steadiness, hard work, utility, self-sufficiency, and economy, as well as integrity and communality. At their height, in the 1840s, there were nearly six thousand Shakers living in eighteen villages in eight states; unfortunately, their commitment to celibacy ultimately resulted in a dwindling membership. Shakers did not leave a legacy of members, but they certainly left a legacy of amazing architecture, crafts, and furniture.

Shaker food was plain, made with uncomplicated ingredients, but generally heavier and richer than many of us would dare to eat today. The produce and livestock they raised fed the community; they treated their land and animals with respect and care. Excess foodstuffs were sold to the public, and Shakers also packaged and sold seeds that were known to be of high quality and completely reliable.

The community members ate together (at separate tables for men and women), so great quantities of food had to be set out three times a day. Shakers approached cooking in a methodical—even analytical—way, recording their recipes systematically, carefully noting measurements, timing, oven temperatures. Recipes were passed down within the communities and shared with outsiders as well. Since speed and efficiency in food preparation were necessary and valued, the Shakers invented timesaving utensils and appliances—the apple corer and the apple parer, for instance, and a revolving oven that allowed them to bake sixty pies at a clip. Meals were preceded by silent prayers and eaten at long tables set with simple plates and no adornments. Food was never wasted; what wasn't eaten to the last crumb was used in the next meal.

SOME TYPICAL SHAKER DISHES: brown bread; potato bread; biscuits of all sorts; homemade cottage cheese; apple cider pie; oatmeal pie; lemon pie (also rhubarb, pumpkin, cranberry, and mincemeat pies); dried apple cake; quince pudding; ambrosia cake; maple sugar cake;

crullers; pound cake; egg croquettes; corn pudding; corn soup; tomato fritters; lentil loaf; beet salad (also cucumber, corn, carrot, and cabbage salads); potatoes all sorts of ways; parsnip stew; fish and eggs; creamed oysters; salmon loaf; codfish balls; fish chowder; chicken pot pie; roasted wild turkey; veal loaf; baked tongue; roasted venison; meat dumplings; scrapple; hog's head cheese; pickles, relishes, and ketchups of all sorts.

10 Great Children's Books about Food or Eating

How to Eat Like a Child, Delia Ephron

Strega Nona, Tomie de Paola

Chocolate Fever, Robert Kimmel Smith

In the Night Kitchen, Maurice Sendak

Cactus Soup, Eric A. Kimmel

Stone Soup, Jon J Muth

Cloudy with a Chance of Meatballs, Judi Barrett

If You Give a Mouse a Cookie, Laura Joffe Numeroff

A Little Bit of Soul Food and ¡Hola! Jalapeño, Amy Wilson Sanger

Food for Thought, Saxton Freymann

20 Possibilities for Serving an Army of Guests

★ pots of chili

★ whole baked ham

★ whole roasted turkey

★ baked chicken wings and legs

★ pot roast with vegetables

★ spareribs

★ enchiladas

★ hearty soup

★ macaroni and cheese

★ spaghetti with sauce

★ lasagna

★ red beans and rice

★ baked beans

★ corn pudding

★ oven-roasted vegetables

★ green salad

★ cole slaw

★ loaf or tube cake

★ sheet cake

★ bar or drop cookies

20 Nonperishable Snacks That Can Save Your Bacon When Unexpected Guests Drop In

★ tortilla chips and bottled salsa

★ mixed nuts

★ pistachios

★ tamari almonds

★ tins of smoked mussels or oysters

★ jar of tapenade

★ jar of sun-dried tomato paste (not ordinary tomato paste)

★ tin of pâté

★ jar of marinated artichokes

★ jar of roasted peppers

★ jar of caponata

★ jars of olives (be sure they're good ones!)

★ tin of cheese straws

★ interesting crackers

★ tin of shortbread

★ tin of macaroons

★ fancy packaged cookies

★ glacé fruits

★ tin of fine chocolates

★ tin of nut brittle

WHAT TO USE INSTEAD OF SALT

When a dish has the blahs, the saltshaker is the first thing you're likely to reach for. Fine, but there are alternatives. What you're looking for is brightness and additional flavor, and you want to enhance the existing flavors in your food too. (Cookies and cakes made without a pinch of salt will taste flat and not quite right. Remember Aunt Ethel's too-sweet, characterless pound cake? She forgot to add a quarter teaspoon of salt.)

With lackluster savory dishes, a dash of good vinegar or fresh lemon or lime juice may do the trick—meat, fish, vegetables, and grains will often perk up nicely. Freshly ground black pepper can help; so can lemon zest. Fresh or dried herbs (appropriate to the food in question) will add interest, and so will minced garlic, onions, or shallots. Hot-and-spicy works too: try minced fresh jalapeños or other hot peppers, powdered dried chiles, red pepper flakes, cayenne, paprika, powdered Chinese mustard (reconstituted to a paste, with a little water), wasabi (ditto), or freshly grated horseradish.

If you reach for the condiments (such as Dijon mustard, ketchup, or Worcestershire sauce) you'll get results—but be aware that they all contain salt, defeating any lower-salt purpose you might have.

What's the Difference between . . .

ORDINARY SALT, IODIZED SALT, KOSHER SALT, AND SEA SALT?

Ordinary fine-grained table salt is mined mostly from dried salt lakes, then refined and treated with anticaking additives that help it pour easily from container and saltshaker. Iodized salt is that same table salt with a kick of iodine added to compensate for any potential insufficiency of iodine in our diets. Both are used in the kitchen as well as on the table, but some cooks prefer the coarser texture and clearer flavor of additive-free, iodine-free kosher salt. Sea salt results, logically, from the evaporation of seawater, either by sun-baking or kiln-drying. It tastes different from ordinary salt and it's more expensive, which lends it a certain cachet.

****

16 Great Web Sites for Info about Common Foods

aeb.org *(American Egg Board)*

porkpeople.com *(from Ontario, Canada)*

txbeef.org *(beef, of course)*

fish4fun.com

usapple.org

www.usarice.com

aboutseafood.com *(seafood of all sorts)*

aboutproduce.com

ChocolateInfo.com *(from the Chocolate Information Center)*

www.dominosugar.com

ilovecheese.com.

www.wheatfoods.org

breadworld.com *(from Fleischman's Yeast)*

eatchicken.com *(from the National Chicken Council)*

whymilk.com *(Milk Processor Education Program)*

carrotmuseum.com *(lots of fun)*

5 Web Sites about Less Common Food Topics

californiafigs.com

keylime.com

nutritiouslygourmet.com *(about organic foods)*

mushroomhunter.com

homecanning.com

****

PENNY CANDY AND OTHER NECESSITIES:

The Legacy of the General Store

In my working-class neighborhood, in 1950s small-town New Jersey, there was an odd institution we called "Gap's," as in "Let's go to Gap's for bubble gum." Mrs. Gap had converted the dim, antimacassared front parlor of her house into a very basic sort of general store that served a five-block radius of families.

We suburban children were utterly unfamiliar with the concept of the rural general store—we just knew that at Gap's, if you had a penny, you could buy Bazooka bubble gum, a Tootsie Roll, a Mary Jane, or a good-sized strip of candy buttons. For a penny or two more, you could have a Baby Ruth, a Mars bar, a little box of malt balls, a Sugar Daddy, or a packet of Pez. On a sluggishly hot August day, going to Gap's fended off childish boredom for as long as it took to walk the three blocks, find a shade tree, and slurp the sweetness out of our penny purchases. On a snowy December day, Mom might send one of us up to Gap's for flour, sugar, or salt, to save herself a slippery car trip to Main Street.

A MOMENT OR TWO WITH...

MARSHMALLOWS

The original marshmallow candy was made from the roots of a plant called a marshmallow (or marsh mallow). French confectioners in the 1880s sweetened the pulp of the marshmallow, whipped it up, and molded it to make the candy. It was a time- and labor-intensive method, and the confectioners couldn't keep up with demand until a faster system was devised and gelatin replaced mallow root. Marshmallows as we know them today are usually made of sugar, corn syrup, gelatin, modified cornstarch, and flavoring, and they're extruded rather than molded. According to Kraft Foods, Americans buy 90 million pounds of marshmallows every year. That's a lot of s'mores.

Invention of Granulated Sugar

Sugarcane had long been used to make molasses, but it wasn't until Louisiana gentleman farmer Etienne de Bore figured out a method for crystallizing the sugar syrup and turning the crystals into granulated sugar that sugarcane became a hugely successful crop. De Bore pulled this off in 1795 and sold his 1796 crop for a whopping twelve thousand dollars. His accomplishment literally revolutionized Louisiana's agriculture industry, converting it from the unprofitable production of indigo to the profitable production of sugar.

Gap's Store was a great-granddaughter of the rural American general store, the difference being that Gap's stocked nothing but basics and penny candy, and an authentic late-nineteenth-century general store stocked everything, including basics and penny candy. Aside from the dozens and dozens of nonfood items that a good general store carried, farmers and townspeople alike could find all the food staples they needed, bought in bulk by the store owner and sold in manageable quantities to the customers: coffee, flour, sugar, molasses, canned peaches, vinegar, salt, pickles, and crackers in barrels.

Farm people brought butter, eggs, and chickens to barter for whatever they needed, from seeds to calico to harness, kerosene, candles, boots, blades, needles, thread, and long underwear. And for a hard-earned nickel a child could buy a slew of one-for-a-penny, two-for-a-penny, or three-for-a-penny candies: peppermint sticks, horehound drops, gumdrops, chewing gum, jawbreakers, lemon drops, maple sugar candy, molasses cuts, anise drops, puff candy, rock candy.

Unlike Gap's, which was spooky, weird, faintly sinister, and made you want to stay there for as short a time as possible, the country general store was a magnet, a gathering place as essential to every community as fresh air and water.

WHY MARINATE?

Why, indeed? If you usually do it to tenderize your meat, don't bother. Marinating does not tenderize food. It doesn't penetrate deeply, it doesn't change the texture, it doesn't do much of anything except flavor the surface. In fact, leaving an acidic marinade on a piece of meat or fish for a long time will start to alter the surface texture to something unpleasantly mushy.

If you love the idea of marination, make a marinade, put it in a covered bowl, plastic container, or heavy-duty plastic bag with your meat, chicken, or fish, and stick the whole thing in the fridge for an hour. You'll feel good and it does no harm.

What could do harm, though, is cross-contamination during basting. You may use the uncooked marinade that was in the bowl (or container or bag) for basting, but you must stop basting with it at least fifteen minutes before the end of the cooking period, to allow time for any lurking bacteria to be killed off. If you were smart enough to reserve some of the marinade before combining it with the raw food, you can use that for basting when the meat, chicken, or fish is almost done. Delicious.

12 Perfectly Nice Savory Garnishes

sprigs of curly or flat-leaf parsley

snipped chives ★ sprigs of fresh rosemary

chiffonade of any dark green leafy vegetable

thin slices of the green part of a scallion

pickle fans ★ radish flowers ★ carrot curls

confetti of yellow, red, and green bell peppers

red or yellow cherry tomatoes, whole or halved

sliced olives ★ capers or caper berries

10 POPULAR CONDIMENTS

salsa	pickle relish	grated horseradish
ketchup	chutney	tartar sauce
mustard	chili sauce	honey mustard
	hot pepper sauce	

10 POPULAR CUTS OF BEEF

rib-eye steak	short ribs	skirt steak
T-bone steak	porterhouse steak	rump roast
sirloin steak	London broil	brisket
	rib roast	

WHAT IS THIS THING, ANYWAY?

It's a meatballer, but why anyone needs a meatballer is a deep question.
Damp palms have always worked fine . . .

POP QUIZ!

1. Which of the following is not an artificial sweetener?
   A. aspartame
   B. cyclamate
   C. mannitol
   D. olestra
   E. saccharin

2. Sweetbreads are the calf's
   A. lung
   B. heart
   C. kidney
   D. pancreas
   E. brain

3. Sumptuary laws imposed limits on culinary extravagance, from ancient Rome to sixteenth-century France and England. What did those laws attempt to control?
   A. the length of the menu—the number of courses permitted at a meal
   B. the purse-strings—how much money could be spent to feed each dinner guest
   C. the kitchen and the larder—the food being offered to guests, to be sure nothing banned was being served
   D. the social system—which classes could eat which foods
   E. all of the above

4. *True or false:* Prosciutto is eaten raw.

5. Rocket is
   A. chocolate candy with marsh-mallows and nuts
   B. salad greens
   C. fizzy lemonade
   D. a freshwater fish
   E. a variety of leek

6. Your best friend's wife asks you to mix her a gimlet. What do you reach for?
   A. gin and Rose's Lime Juice
   B. gin and Grand Marnier
   C. gin and dry vermouth
   D. gin and sweet vermouth
   E. gin and angostura bitters

7. If you're eating humble pie, you're scarfing down
   A. a colonial American pot pie made of leftover chicken and vegetables
   B. an old English dish made of deer entrails and spices
   C. pecan pie without the pecans
   D. New England fruit pie without the crust
   E. none of the above

8. *Name that cuisine:* What country do cornichons come from originally?

Answers: 1. d; 2. d; 3. e; 4. true (it's cured, but uncooked); 5. b; 6. a; 7. b; 8. France (they're very small tart pickles)

142

THE EXQUISITE SHRIMP

Next to canned tuna, shrimp are America's favorite seafood, and small wonder. They're versatile (in a variety of cuisines), they cook fast, and (so far) they're abundant. If you can get fresh shrimp, that's the way to go, but frozen shrimp are far more available and perfectly delicious; defrost them in the fridge overnight or in a bowl of cold water just before using. Don't buy frozen shrimp that have been thawed unless you can get them from a fish market you trust, since you have no way of knowing how long ago that thaw took place.

Shrimp come in many sizes with oxymoronic names (colossal, jumbo, extra-large, large, and medium) and a couple that make sense: small and miniature. Since shrimp size is unregulated, no one knows exactly how big a colossal shrimp actually is—are there eight to the pound? Ten to the pound? That's a pretty big shrimp. You're probably better off with any size that yields about fifteen to twenty per pound, but the size you choose will ultimately be governed by availability, price, appearance, and the requirements of your recipe. Shells should be free of black spots, any yellow tint, and grit. Sniff, too—shrimp should smell rather saltwatery and not at all unpleasant.

Removing the shells is easy (basically you just yank them off or use one of those clever shrimp-shelling gadgets), but then there's deveining—removing that long dark slimy veinlike thing that lurks under the surface of the back of each shrimp. It's a tedious and time-consuming task, and it creeps out a lot of ordinarily unsqueamish cooks. Nonetheless, you have to cope with The Vein because the idea of eating it creeps out a lot of eaters. It is, after all, the shrimp's intestinal tract, and eating the intestinal tract of anything isn't a pleasing notion if you stop to think about it, which you shouldn't.

So the task of deveining usually has to be done by *someone*. Maybe not you, but *someone*. Happily, any good fishmonger will offer cleaned shrimp (shelled and deveined) right alongside the other ones. Remember, though, that aside from aesthetic considerations, there's no harm in eating The Vein, and you can get used to almost anything.

10 Ways to Improve Basic Tuna Salad

Add zing to mayonnaise-dressed tuna salad by mixing in one of the following combos:

★ chopped celery and a sprinkling of celery seed

★ chopped pitted green olives and tomatoes

★ minced red onion and chopped seeded cucumbers

★ cooked or canned white beans, diced red pepper, and chopped fresh herbs

★ chopped hard-cooked eggs and chopped fresh dill

★ crumbled feta cheese and croutons

★ cubed boiled potatoes and sliced, pitted kalamata olives

★ chopped coriander, chopped pickled jalapeños, and a squeeze of lime

★ grated Cheddar cheese and grated carrots

★ chopped roasted red pepper and whole capers

WHAT ON EARTH IS...

A SOFT-SHELL CRAB

A soft-shell crab is not, contrary to some popular opinion, a distinct species; it's an ordinary blue crab caught in between stages of development: just after it has shed one hard outer shell and just before it grows a newer and even harder one. There's a window of only a few days during which the entire crab is edible, and not just edible—delicious. Peak season for fresh soft-shells is June and July, but you can find them from April to mid-September. Once soft-shell crabs (also called "peelers") are plucked from the water they're either shipped live to your fishmonger for you to indulge in right away, or cleaned and frozen for year-round consumption.

KNOW YOUR KNIVES

The hysteria and angst that surrounds choosing and sharpening a bunch of kitchen knives astonishes me. A knife is just a tool: buy the best you can realistically afford (even if it's a Chef Yokel paring knife), keep it in as good condition as you have time and energy for (including sharpening it), and use it. When you grow out of that tool, buy a better one.

Like all tools, knives run the gamut. Expensive isn't always best (one of my favorite knives came from the local housewares emporium, and it has a plastic handle), but it can be. Think about these criteria: Does the handle fit cozily in your palm? If it's a fancy knife, is it nicely weighted and balanced? Is there a comfortable ratio between handle and blade? Is the handle firmly attached to the blade?

That blade is important. High-carbon stainless-steel knives will hold a cutting edge for a good while, and they won't rust or discolor,

10 Interesting Foods to Mail-order on the Web

1. dried tomatoes and capers in olive oil (www.gustiamo.com)

2. freeze-dried, dehydrated, ready-to-eat foods for camping (aa-foods.com)

3. Australian barbecue sauce (AussieProducts.com)

4. dairy-free, gluten-free, all-natural chocolate (nspiredfoods.com)

5. duck bacon, duck fat, and so on (dartagnan.com)

6. roasted raspberry chipotle sauce (jelly.com)

7. red rice, black rice, purple rice (indianharvest.com)

8. fruit purees (perfectpuree.com)

9. Tamaya blue corn, red corn hominy (cookingpost.com)

10. truffles—the mushroom kind, not the chocolate kind (urbanitruffles.com)

either. Get yourself an eight-inch chef's knife in carbon stainless steel, and you'll be a happy cook. You'll also want a sturdy bread knife with a long serrated blade, a couple of good paring knives, and a boning knife with a narrow pointed blade. I promise that you'll also wind up with a few odds and ends (like my knife from the emporium) and you'll be surprised at which ones will become your favorites. (And if your favorite turns out to be that bone-handled steak knife you found at the thrift shop, no apologies are necessary.)

Then there's the issue of sharpening. The Knife Police want you to use a sharpening steel. They threaten that if you use a cheapo sharpener that grinds away at the knife blade, your knife will eventually grind away into nothing. *Eventually* is the operative word. If my knife blade is shot in ten years, I'll either buy a new knife or stop cooking. Life is too short for worrying excessively about shrinking knife blades. The point is that knives must be sharp (see below), and whatever sharpener you can get yourself to use regularly is the right one for you—sharpening steel, cheapo gizmo, electric sharpener, sharpening stone, or even the local professional knife sharpener.

KNIFE NOTE: Keep those blades sharp. No one quite believes that the sharpest knife is the safest knife until she's slicing or chopping with a dull one, and it slips. OUCH! You know the rest of the story, the one that involves multiple stitches. In future that lady should sharpen her knives so the blades will cut where they're supposed to cut. Sharp knives may seem a little scary, but the more you use them, the more confident you'll become and the less scary they'll seem.

---

11 COMPLETELY UNRUINABLE FOODS

summer tomatoes	baked potatoes	bread and butter
summer peaches	chocolate	stew
ripe avocados	ice cream	raisins
mac and cheese		olives

CUTTING BOARDS

Wood and plastic are your two basic cutting board choices. You may like wood because it looks good in your kitchen or plastic because it seems neater, or you may have a couple of each because that's what you got at your wedding shower. (And of course you avoid ceramic or other very hard cutting surfaces because they dull your knives in a flash.) You probably have a couple of sizes, too: small for cutting limes for your gin-and-tonics, medium for cutting bread or vegetables, large for cubing meat or dissecting chicken.

Aesthetics are nice, but the real issue is safety. The experts have gone back and forth, back and forth on the relative safety of wood versus plastic. Frankly, it's moot. Food-borne pathogens (bad bugs) can attach to, collect in, and generally inhabit the tiny and not-so-tiny nicks and grooves your knife makes in either kind of board, and unless you scrub that board really well after each use, you could get sick. The problem is cross-contamination: bacteria that dig into your cutting board during one session of chopping or slicing can hang around for a long time and contaminate the next food you cut on that same cutting board. And if that food happens to be, say, a piece of cheese or a slice of tomato that you pop into your mouth without benefit of cooking, you could be in for trouble.

Raw meat, poultry, and seafood are the worst potential culprits in the bug department. If you use your cutting board for one of these, when you're finished using it you must scrub it (and your knife and

11 COMPLETELY RUINABLE FOODS

soufflé (flat)	beets (undercooked)	toasted marshmallows (charred)
pie crust (soggy)	pasta (mushy)	eggplant (soggy, mushy, undercooked, overcooked, tough, rubbery, charred)
oatmeal (lumpy)	steak (tough)	
asparagus (overcooked)	fried eggs (rubbery)	
	roast turkey (dry)	

your hands) with hot, soapy water. Rinse it well and let it air-dry in the dish rack before you use it for any other food. And don't, for heaven's sake, dry the cutting board with the dishtowel you used for wiping raw chicken juice off your fingers. Talk about cross-contamination: from the raw chicken to your fingers to the dishtowel to the cutting board to the next food you cut on the board. Whew. Sound fussy and overly cautious? Maybe, but one bout of food poisoning will erase your doubts forever. Why risk it?

CUTTING BOARD TIPS: If you're really smart, you'll have a cutting board you use only for raw meat, poultry, and seafood, another for vegetables and fruits, and a third for bread. All cutting boards eventually get worn out and full of unscrubbable ruts and grooves; ditch them and buy new ones.

MUST OR MYTH:

Let grilled or roasted meats rest for ten to twenty minutes before carving or cutting.

This is not exactly a must, because nothing dangerous will happen if you don't, but it's a very good idea. Meat continues cooking even after you remove it from the heat source, so allowing it to rest for ten to twenty minutes gives the internal temperature and moistness time to even out. The fibers will relax and reabsorb some of the juices, making the meat tenderer, juicier, and easier to carve.

TALES FROM THE 'HOOD:
MASTERING MAC 'N' CHEESE

D'nashia Jenkins, teenager

"You want macaroni and cheese so much, you get in there and make it," Mom said. She was tired from work and didn't feel like making my favorite dinner. I love baked macaroni and cheese well done with lots of sharp Cheddar cheese and paprika. My mom would make it every two weeks on Sunday.

"OK, let's go," I said. "But how do I make it?" I was excited about making it myself, but nervous about messing it up.

My first macaroni and cheese didn't taste exactly like my mom's, but it was delicious. Mom thought it was good, "but there wasn't enough milk."

The next time I made it, I started to experiment. I kept almost everything she taught me the same but used different ingredients, like sazón (an orange Spanish seasoning that gives the food color and flavor). And while I put shredded cheese on the first layer and mixed it around, for my second layer I sliced the cheese and put the rest of the cheese on top.

I got some of my ideas for experimenting from watching other people make macaroni. My aunts and friends had their own ways to make it. I wanted my own flavor and style. I found the perfect way to do it when I was fifteen. I use Lawry seasoning for the noodles and put black pepper in a bowl with milk and two eggs, and stir it together. I pour this on top of the macaroni after layering it. Then when the macaroni is almost done, I take the top off the pan and let it cook to make sure the cheese melts all the way.

Now that you know how I make my famous macaroni and cheese, you can try and master it, but it will never taste like mine. One thing I learned when watching people cook, and trying to do the same thing myself, is that you can never get your food to taste exactly like someone else's—even if you know their secret ingredients.

VEGETABLE STIR-FRIES FOR LAZIES

There are five basic stir-fry tricks for lazies, all of which will make a lazy person happy and a busy person-in-a-hurry even happier.

★ If you want to make a meal out of a vegetable stir-fry, plan to rehydrate and serve that leftover rice from the Chinese take-out, and pick up a roasted chicken on the way home from work.

★ Your stir-fry should include no more than four vegetables. More than that will turn it into a characterless mush.

★ Buy raw vegetables that are already stemmed, peeled, cut, *prepared for cooking*. But do rinse them and pat them dry at home.

★ If your veggies are dense (carrots, broccoli, chunks of zucchini) precook them in the microwave oven, in a loosely covered bowl of water, just until tender.

****

13 Great Web Sites for Kitchen and Dining Supplies

www.cookwares.com

crateandbarrel.com

cookscorner.com

chefscatalog.com

chefstore.com

bridgekitchenware.com

shop.bakerscatalogue.com

KitchenKrafts.com

nextdaygourmet.com

potterybarn.com

cutlery.com (*more than just cutlery*)

surlatable.com

Williams-Sonoma.com

****

★ If you have the energy, chop some garlic and ginger and keep it handy for the last step. Do this *before* you start stir-frying.

While the microwave is doing its magic, heat your wok or big (preferably nonstick) skillet over medium-high heat until very hot; add some peanut or neutral oil and swirl it around; add any not-so-dense vegetables such as chopped onions, sliced red pepper, asparagus tips, shredded cabbage, Chinese broccoli or bok choy, sliced mushrooms, or corn kernels; give it all a thirty-second stir.

Turn down the heat while you quickly drain the microwaved vegetables and add them to the wok or skillet. If you've got chopped garlic and ginger, add that, too. Put the heat back up and keep stirring and tossing the mixture until it's cooked the way you like it. At the last, add some soy sauce, tamari, oyster sauce, or any prepared stir-fry sauce and stir for another fifteen seconds.

If you're really lazy, eat from the wok. If not, tilt your vegetables out into a nice bowl and serve with reheated rice and hot chicken.

TIDBIT: Tempeh, the fermented high-protein soybean product that many vegetarians love, has been a staple food in Indonesia for over two millennia. The Dutch took it to Europe after they colonized Indonesia, and it made its firm, chewy, nutty-tasting way to the United States fairly recently, in the twentieth century. It's considered by its advocates to be versatile because, they claim, it absorbs other flavors easily.

10 Interesting Vegetables

salsify

cardoon

purple broccoli

Jerusalem artichoke

Chinese long beans

kohlrabi

nopales (or cactus paddles, pads, or leaves)

chayote (or mirliton)

bitter melon

taro

A MOMENT OR TWO WITH...

TOFU

Tofu, or bean curd, is what you get when you curdle or coagulate soymilk. When coagulant is added to soymilk, the soymilk separates into curds and whey. The solidish curds float to the top of the liquid whey, and they're skimmed off and placed in a cheesecloth-lined form to drain. A lid goes onto the form, a weight goes onto the lid, and the curds sit for a few hours to become—tofu. The firmness of the tofu depends on how much liquid is allowed to drain off.

Freshly made tofu may be stored briefly in cold water and then eaten right away, since it's highly perishable. Commercially prepared tofu is often packed and sealed in water in plastic containers for a longer refrigerated shelf life of several weeks. Other tofu is vacuum-packed with no water at all for many months of unrefrigerated shelf life.

20 Show-biz Vegetarians

★

Brad Pitt

Richard Gere

Joanne Woodward and Paul Newman
(two for the price of one)

Billy Idol

Bob Dylan

Joan Baez

Elvis Costello

Meat Loaf (yes!)

k.d. lang

Sinead O'Connor

Lenny Kravitz

Kim Basinger

Phylicia Rashad

Danny DeVito

Ashley Judd

Shania Twain

Paul McCartney

Natalie Portman

Boy George

Mary Tyler Moore

★

mini hot dogs and hamburgers

mini pizzas or pizza bagels

chicken fingers

tacos with all the fixings

four-cheese mac and cheese

vegetarian lasagna

submarine sandwiches

Caesar salad

French fries

egg rolls, crisp wontons

chips and dips

New York soft pretzels

cookies and candy

ice cream sundaes

And Speaking of Food . . .

Mary and Russel Wright, *Guide to Easier Living*, 1950

The kitchen is the one place in the home where the fact that the American woman does her own housework has been honestly faced. In the kitchen the combined genius of architects, engineers, designers, home economists, and manufacturers has dramatically lightened women's work and has provided one of the great technological contributions to home life in centuries—an American achievement as typical, and as impressive, as American skyscrapers, highways, and jazz.

WHAT TO EAT AT A BAR MITZVAH, PART II:
GROWNUPS' FOOD

smoked fish (lox, whitefish, and so on)

pickled herring

sushi

spanakopita

quiche

hummus

baba ghanoush

knishes

latkes

Greek salad

roasted vegetables

fillet of salmon

sliced fillet of beef

rack of lamb or baby lamb chops

duck breast

carved meat from a carving station

soufflé

crème brûlée

chocolate torte

layer cake

STEW ON THE CEILING

or, The Story of the Pressure Cooker

A pressure cooker is, conceptually, a simple tool. Imagine this: You're simmering a pot of stew in a nice broth, with a well-fitting lid covering the pot. Heat builds up, the liquid boils, and there's so much heat and steam that the lid pops right off the pot. To keep the lid from popping off again, you shift it a teeny bit off center so there's a narrow slit for steam to escape. Now the steam can vent, the lid will stay in place, and your stew cooks nicely. There's only one problem: the escaping *steam* is actually escaping *broth* that's being converted to vapor as the stew cooks, so when you return to your pot an hour later, there's no broth left and the meat is looking very dry and sad.

You should have gone back to the kitchen a couple of times to add more liquid—or you could have cooked the stew (or pot roast, soup, chili, or whatever) in a pressure cooker.

A pressure cooker is a heavy pot with a tightly locking lid; the lid is lined with a rubber gasket and topped with a safety valve. Here's how it works: Food and liquid go into the pot; the lid is locked on to seal in ingredients, air, and steam (the rubber gasket ensures that); the pot goes onto the heat source; and the heat goes on under the pot. Now the fun begins. Steam forms inside the pot, which builds up *a lot* of pressure—but the pressure can't escape because the lid is locked in place! Help! It's going to explode! But wait, there's a safety valve. The valve relieves and regulates the internal pressure so your food cooks perfectly, and in a shorter time than it would in an ordinary stovetop or oven situation. Whew. Pretty neat.

Pressure cookers had a very specific purpose before and during World War II: They made it possible to can low-acid foods without risk of food poisoning. For farm wives and the cultivators of Victory Gardens, pressure canning was the way to get the most out of their homegrown produce: fruits and vegetables could be picked at the peak of ripeness and preserved for the winter. After 1945, cooks were still hot to use pressure cookers, but the first rash of postwar models were cumbersome, complicated, and not always reliable. In fact, some of them were time bombs waiting to explode—and explode they did. The valves failed, the lids burst off, and boiling hot contents flew all over the place. Stew shot up to the ceiling. Tomato sauce spattered the walls. Beans blasted from one end of the kitchen to the other. Consumers backed off fast. Why risk death and destruction?

Pressure cooker sales declined, and by the time the bad manufacturers were weeded out and completely safe new cookers were designed (primarily in Europe and Asia), a couple of American generations had learned to live without them. It wasn't until the early 1990s that European pressure cooker manufacturers inched their way back into the hearts and minds of American cooks with smart advertising and the promise of hearty, nutritious, money-saving, old-fashioned American food prepared under pressure.

The irony of the return of the pressure cooker is that it's neither particularly time-saving nor particularly easy to use. You must follow the manufacturer's rules, cut food into evenly sized pieces, time the process, watch the valve, clean the rubber gasket and rub it with oil after each use. You need steamer racks, special dishes, an accurate timer. And the pot is heavy, hard to sling around, and inconvenient to clean. So why bother? Well, there's the taste of the food—delicious. And maybe it's a little like some people feel about their new Corvettes: a great toy but not for everyday use.

8 MOST-HATED KITCHEN CHORES

cleaning the oven

cleaning the refrigerator

scouring the sink

scouring the crusted-on gook in the broiler pan

mopping the floor

cleaning the pantry shelves

emptying the dishwasher

cleaning up after dinner

WHY WE USE FORKS

Why *do* we use forks? There appears to have been no compelling reason for the adoption of forks *as eating utensils* except for a gradual change in manners that took place in Europe over several hundred years of the Middle Ages and the Renaissance.

Forks with two long, widely separated tines had been used as tools for steadying meat during carving and for spearing food from the common bowl, though not for conveying food to the mouth. Knives were much more important as eating utensils, but knives carried a lot of baggage: knives were weapons. Since weapons could potentially be lethal in social situations, rules (or taboos) were imposed on the way knives were used at table, or, to put it another way, the codification of non-

Priscilla Goodmanners Tells It Like It Is:

HOW TO EAT SOUP

Soup would get very complicated if you took the Etiquette Snobs seriously. They'd have you spooning it up counterintuitively: *away* from you. Really, when was the last time—outside of a high-class episode of Masterpiece Theatre—you saw anyone spooning *away* instead of *toward*? And what about Sip from the Side of the Spoon, another ironclad rule of the E.S.'s? Everyone I know (and I know some well-mannered ladies and gentlemen) sips from the tip, and no harm done.

The important points are these: don't overfill the spoon; don't drip; don't shove the entire spoon into your mouth; don't pick up your bowl and tilt the last few drops of soup down your throat (except with a two-handled consommé cup). And oh, yes, one more thing: no slurping.

threatening ways to wield a knife at table was the new table etiquette. The use of knives slowly became restricted to cutting things that really needed a sharp blade; it was, for example, taboo to cut soft foods with a knife or to pick up a knife during a course that didn't require it.

As the knife lost power, there began to be social room for the introduction of the fork. The appearance of this strange new utensil among the upper classes (and only the upper classes) was at first met with hostility and ridicule. The fork was irreligious, since God had given men perfectly good fingers to use for eating. The fork was foppish, affected, unnecessary. But gradually the position reversed. One by one the nations of Europe—first Italy, then France and Germany, and finally England—adopted the fork. Using a fork became the done thing and, more important, it grew an extra pair of tines and became more like our familiar four-tined utensil. Now a diner could actually get a whole forkful of food all the way to his or her mouth without touching the food or losing it between the old-fashioned pair of tines.

Other eating habits were changing concurrently. The acceptance of forks didn't happen in a vacuum: the elaborate process of carving several kinds of meat had moved from the dining table back to the kitchen, out of sight of diners; individual plates (instead of a common bowl) appeared by the sixteenth century; using the fingers as eating utensils took on negative value, became "uncivilized" and "barbaric"; knives at table were demoted even further from weaponry (sometimes by law, sometimes by fashion) when their sharp, pointed tips were blunted or rounded, as we know them today.

With the total acceptance of the fork came the impulse to expand into other eating utensils. Before they knew it, from the sixteenth century onward, diners became entangled in a progressively more complicated web of soup spoons, sugar spoons, serving spoons, oyster forks, fish forks, salad forks, fruit knives, and butter knives from which we have barely extricated ourselves today.

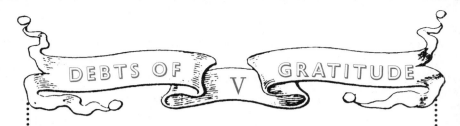

CHEF BOYARDEE (1898–1985), of canned ravioli fame, was born Hector Boiardi, and he was indeed a chef. After working in a lot of fancy hotel kitchens, he opened his own Italian restaurant in Cleveland, Ohio. Customers adored his spaghetti sauce, so he began selling it to them in milk bottles. He started a sauce factory down the block, added pasta and cheese to go with the sauce—and pretty soon the business went national.

NATHAN HANDWERKER (1892–1974) was the Nathan of Nathan's Famous, a walk-up hot dog stand that became an institution on the Coney Island boardwalk in New York City, dating from 1916. Handwerker sold his dogs for a mere nickel, and it took some aggressive marketing to get customers to have confidence in a cheap food. When buyers finally did succumb, Nathan's dogs were on the way to becoming icons of hot-dog-dom. The company still sells over a million every year.

LUTHER BURBANK (1849–1926) was an American horticulturist who, at Burbank's Experiment Farms in Santa Rosa, California, developed dozens and dozens of new varieties of fruits and vegetables, including 113 kinds of plums and prunes, ten kinds of berries, and the freestone peach.

EARL SILAS TUPPER (1907–1983) was in love with invention—and in love with plastics. Tupper first came up with a method for purifying the icky polyethylene slag from which most plastic products had been made, and then came up with a watertight, airtight lid for the containers he made from his purified slag. Result: the Tupperware we all know and love. And we can thank a smart lady named Brownie Wise for coming up with the Tupperware Home Parties that delivered Tupperware right to Mama's door.

15 Classic Italian Pasta Sauces

bolognese	amatriciana
puttanesca	Alfredo
marinara	pesto
tonnato	siciliana
carbonara	boscaiola
pomodoro	arrabbiata
vongole	carrettiera
aglio e olio	

12 Foreign Foods Americans Love

Danish blue cheese	Peking duck
paella	sashimi
tiramisù	Swedish meatballs
croissants	tacos
éclairs	frankfurters
couscous	Belgian waffles

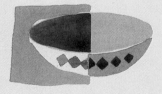

TALES OF THE LEGENDARY MICHELIN RED GUIDE

The Michelin *Guide Rouge*—the Red Guide—is the ultra-prestigious arbiter of restaurants in France, Italy, and England, among other places. "Stars," the people at Michelin tell us, "are only awarded for the food on the plate." Or, to put it another way, "Comfort and décor are not taken into account when stars are awarded." This is not to imply that the Red Guide has nothing to say about comfort and décor. It does. But where food evaluation *à la française* is concerned, food is the only thing that counts.

The guide has four major missions when it evaluates: to make anonymous restaurant visits by inspectors who know food and are paid only by Michelin; to include a wide selection of restaurants, in order to accommodate a variety of readers; to maintain the independence of its inspectors, which means they pay their own restaurant bills and no fee is levied for inclusion in the guide; and to update these restaurant evaluations constantly. Furthermore, the guide insists it has no "personal slant or attitude" and keeps above the fray of food trends and popularity contests.

TELL ME ABOUT...

PIZZA

Don't try to convince a Neapolitan that pizza doesn't have its origins in Naples. *Non è possibile!* But long before Naples got into the act, flat bread topped with oil and spices was common to ancient Babylonians, Egyptians, and other Middle Eastern cultures. Pizza as we know it today arrived in the States with Italian immigrants around 1900 and became popular in New York and Chicago after World War II because the returning GI's had learned to love it in Italy. The basic tomato-mozzarella-basil pizza—the margherita—was invented in 1889 in honor of Queen Margherita, wife of King Umberto I, on the occasion of a visit to sunny Napoli. Did you catch that red, white, and green theme? That's right, they're the colors of the Italian flag.

12 OUT-OF-THE-ORDINARY PIZZA TOPPINGS

bacon and eggs	herring	ham (or Canadian bacon) and pineapple
mashed potatoes	sardines, tuna, or mackerel	chicken or vegetable curry
eel or squid (a favorite in Japan)	grilled lamb	cheese, onions, and beef (a Dutch favorite)
potatoes and corned beef (another Japanese offering)	tandoori or barbe-cued chicken	
	shrimp and pineapple	

Logic suggests that if the Michelin inspectors find the food exceptional at a particular restaurant, other restaurants will mimic it. *Voilà!* A trend! So how can the inspectors be in the fray and also above it? They can try, but by its very nature—that of commenting on what *is*—the Red Guide makes an impact on what will *be*. To deny this, however charmingly, seems silly. Which establishments will survive, thrive, or disappear is inevitably influenced by the Red Guide, precisely because it does its job so thoroughly.

In France, where food looms larger than large, the Michelin Red Guide is often sucked into culinary controversy and *scandale*: a stressed-out chef eschews his one-star rating, a three-star chef commits suicide, a former employee has the temerity to break the Red Guide's code of silence. The following bit of French petulance sizzled on the company Web site (michelin.com) in 2005:

> Every year a certain food writer tries to get hold of our star list, by whatever means possible, so that he can announce the changes to the restaurateurs himself and even publish the details in the newspaper which employs him, before the guide is published. This is deeply disruptive and completely unprofessional behavior, made all the worse when he spreads false rumours about the star awards.

An American might consider it amusing or at least ironic that a gigantic tire-and-publishing empire would go after one obstreperous journalist, but it's doubtful you'd think so if you were French. The French—and the Red Guide—take these things very, very seriously.

LOVE APPLES OR (IF YOU PREFER) TOMATOES

There seems to have been a lot of fear hovering around tomatoes when they first made their appearance in Europe, presumably because tomatoes are members of the deadly nightshade family. Not all nightshades are dangerous—eggplant is a nightshade too—but somehow tomatoes took on the sinister reputation of being poisonous. My own theory is that the tomato's other rep—as an aphrodisiac—was the real reason for the mistrust: eat a tomato and run amok like a love-crazed teenager. That's scary.

Of course, Central and South Americans had been eating tomatoes and behaving normally for quite a long time before the exploring Spaniards mustered enough courage to take tomatoes back to Spain in the sixteenth century. And it was another couple of centuries before North Americans even grew tomatoes in their home gardens, much less ate them raw. It wasn't until the early twentieth century that tomatoes

---

10 SUPER-SIMPLE THINGS TO DO WITH SUMMER TOMATOES

1. Slice thickly; sprinkle lightly with sugar, salt, and pepper.

2. Slice; sprinkle with sliced pickled jalapeños, fresh coriander, and lime juice.

3. Slice; top with croutons, goat cheese, and a touch of vinaigrette.

4. Slice; top with fresh mozzarella, fresh basil, and a drizzle of balsamic vinegar.

5. Slice; serve with anchovies, roasted peppers, and olives.

6. Dice; toss with cucumbers, parsley, red onion, and crumbled feta cheese.

7. Scoop out; stuff with couscous, pine nuts, and chopped fresh dill.

8. Make salsa.

9. Make fresh tomato sauce.

10. Make a savory tomato tart.

were accepted in the United States as the perfect delights they are. Or were. Or can be.

Today we pick and choose among globe, beefsteak, plum (or Roma), cherry, pear, hydroponic, low-acid, yellow, orange, green, and heirloom tomatoes of varying quality and flavor year in, year out. But it is not romanticizing to say that eating a juicy tomato in or very near the sunny garden from which it was picked only seconds before is a more than heady experience—and may even qualify as aphrodisiacal.

TOMATO TIPS: With red tomatoes, the deeper the color, the tastier the tomato. Choose tomatoes that are heavy in relation to their size, feel resilient when you press them, and have a sweet scent. If you want to lose the juice and seeds, cut in half across the equator and squeeze each half gently. Don't cook tomatoes in an aluminum pot—the acid in the tomatoes will react with the aluminum, which will give your food an unhappy flavor and isn't too good for your health, either.

MUST OR MYTH:

Never refrigerate a tomato.

Never is a long time and a strong word. An *unripe* tomato should *never* be refrigerated because it won't ripen if it is. But if your tomato is looking ripe and you want to hold it for another day or two, go ahead and refrigerate it. Yes, it will lose some flavor, but at least you'll have a ripe tomato instead of a rotten tomato. When you're ready to eat it, let it come to room temperature, for maximum flavor and juiciness.

OLIVES

Here are some olives to avoid: olives picked right off the tree (too bitter); olives from a can (bad flavor); olives from a supermarket jar (boring, though there are now some fancy, better-tasting jarred olives available from gourmet stores and gourmet catalogs).

Most of the best olives come from Italy, Spain, Greece, Morocco, and Turkey; California has a big annual crop, but—sorry to say—those olives tend to end up in cans and jars and can't hold a candle to the better Mediterranean varieties. So buy in bulk from a reliable market where there's a nice selection of imported olives for you to choose from, and a rapid turnover, too.

Unripe olives are green, and fully ripe ones are black, and there are stages in between as well. Unripe green olives must be cured before they're edible. Some methods of curing leave them green, others turn them black—or purple or yellow or brown or red. Ripe black olives are processed too, and—well, it gets confusing, and we haven't even touched on issues of pitting or not, wrinkled versus smooth skin, stuffing with almonds or pimentos or anchovies, or marinating in spices or herbs. Your best strategy is simply to taste, taste, taste to find the olives you like. There are dozens of varieties; among the more commonly encountered:

- ★ alphonso: dark purple, tart, tender flesh
- ★ cerignola: very large, somewhat sweet
- ★ gaeta: small, black or dark purple, with smooth or wrinkled skins (depending on the curing process)
- ★ kalamata: dark purple or black, tender, salty, often pitted
- ★ Ligurian: small, black
- ★ manzanilla (or Spanish): green, often stuffed with almonds or pimentos
- ★ Moroccan cured: medium-sized, wrinkled, salty
- ★ niçoise: very small, purple to black, delicate flavor
- ★ picholine: small, green, often marinated in herbs
- ★ Sicilian: large, tangy, firm, often marinated with herbs or stuffed with hot pepper

What to Put on an Antipasto Platter
(American-style)

olives

Italian cheeses
(fontina, mozzarella, Parmesan, provolone)

marinated mushrooms, artichokes

roasted red peppers

marinated carrots and cauliflowerets

cherry tomatoes, pickled peppers

prosciutto, mortadella, salami

anchovy fillets, tuna in olive oil

baked clams

fresh figs, melon

What's the Difference between ...

VIRGIN OLIVE OIL, EXTRA-VIRGIN
OLIVE OIL, AND PLAIN OLD OLIVE OIL?

You're either a virgin or you're not, right? Wrong. If you're olive oil, you can be *extra* virgin. Good trick. What this means is that the first cold pressing of the olives produces an oil—*extra-virgin* olive oil—that is deliciously fruity and elegant (and expensive), with a very low acid level. The second cold pressing yields *virgin* olive oil, with a slightly higher acid level. Plain old olive oil (sometimes called pure olive oil) is a blend of virgin or extra-virgin and refined olive oil. They all have their uses.

GARLIC NATION

Improbable as it may seem, there was a time in America when a minority who did eat garlic was stigmatized, denigrated, and scorned by a majority who didn't. Garlic was, in much of the first half of the twentieth century, considered to be *ethnic*. Low-class. Down-market. Today Americans of every situation and origin eat nearly two pounds of garlic per capita per year and love it.

The most common types of garlic available to us are American garlic (papery white skin, strong flavor), Mexican and Italian garlic (lavender or pinkish skins, milder flavor), and so-called elephant garlic, which, though impressive in size, is neither a true garlic nor very garlicky.

Whole garlic breaks easily into cloves—actually called *bulbils*, a term that should delight any word lover—but the trick is separating each smooth clove from its stickily form-fitting skin. Here's how I do it: Cut off the stem end of the clove. Now grasp the clove with a thumb and forefinger at each end and twist gently in opposite directions; torque is what you're aiming for. The skin will loosen, break, and fall right off. *Voilà*: a pristine clove of garlic.

TELL ME ABOUT...

PESTO

Grazie a Liguria per pesto! Liguria is the province of Italy near Genoa, around the Gulf of Genoa, and we have to send a huge thank you to the Ligurians for coming up with that rich and delicious sauce made of basil leaves, pine nuts, garlic, cheese, and olive oil.

Basil is the classic pesto, but new variations keep emerging—parsley pesto is a favorite, and so is a mixture of green herbs. Walnuts are sometimes substituted for pine nuts, and the cheese can be Parmigiano-Reggiano, Pecorino Sardo, Pecorino Toscano, grana padano, or any other tasty, full-flavored grating cheese. Traditionally, Italians pound the ingredients together with mortar and pestle, but Americans generally do the job in a food processor and it works very nicely.

Chopping, mincing, pressing, or crushing the peeled clove will release essential oils and make the flavor sharper and more pungent. This is what you want in many dishes. On the other hand, roasting a couple of dozen peeled cloves in a small ovenproof bowl of olive oil or baking them in chicken broth will yield ambrosia: soft, sweet, mild garlic nuggets that you can mash together with a little salt and spread on bread. Or don't even bother with the mashing—just drop a couple onto a chunk of crusty baguette, flatten them a bit with your knife, sprinkle with salt, and fall in love.

Larousse Gastronomique defines a "point of garlic" as the small amount of garlic that can be held on the point of a knife, rather like angels on the head of a pin. How could that possibly be enough?

GARLIC TIPS: Squeeze that bulb of garlic before you buy it: it should be firm (not soft), plump, dry, mold-free, unshriveled, and unsprouted. If it has a green spike growing out of the end, don't even think of taking it home.

WHAT IS THIS THING, ANYWAY?

It's a mezzaluna (say "*metsa-LOO-na*"), and it means, in Italian, half moon. You may call it a crescent cutter if you prefer, and you may chop or mince with it, by hanging on to the wooden handles and rocking the curved blade from side to side (on your cutting board, naturally).

WHICH PASTA IS WHICH?

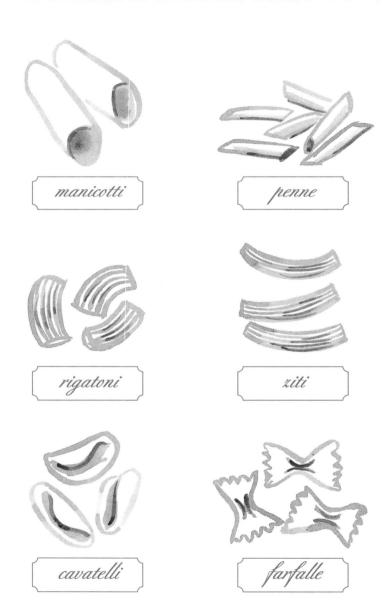

manicotti

penne

rigatoni

ziti

cavatelli

farfalle

fusilli

gemelli

radiatore

ditalini

orzo

OKTOBERFEST

In October 1810 Bavarian crown prince Ludwig married Princess Therese of Saxony-Hildburghausen, and all of Munich came out to celebrate the event on the fields in front of the city gates. The festivities were capped off with horse races, and a year later they decided to do the horse races again and to add an agricultural show, too. Over the years the festival grew into an extravaganza of music and dancing, carnival rides, costumes, floats, huge amounts of food, and oceans of beer, with millions of people flocking to the fun.

Oktoberfest caught on in America, too—hey, we'll use any excuse to throw a gigantic party, especially if it involves beer. North, south, east, and west, there are Oktoberfests all over the country in September and October: La Crosse, Wisconsin; Stowe, Vermont; Galveston, Texas; Fremont, Washington; Doylestown, Pennsylvania; Sandy, Oregon; Campbell, California; Zinzinnatti, Ohio (renamed for the occasion); and even in Harvard Square in Cambridge, Massachusetts. There are polka and waltz contests, brass bands, folk music, arts and crafts, carousels, juggling, puppet shows, parades, and lots more.

What do we eat at Oktoberfest? Try some of these: roasted chicken, bratwurst and many other kinds of sausage, barbecue, Bavarian pretzels,

---

TIDBIT: Anheuser-Busch, the largest brewer of beer in the world, began as a partnership between the older Eberhard Anheuser and the younger Adolphus Busch. Well, actually Adolphus fell in love with Anheuser's daughter Lily (and, amazingly, Adolphus's brother Ulrich fell for Lily's big sister Anna) and married her in 1861. Four years later, Busch's brewing supply company merged with Anheuser's beer company and Anheuser-Busch began its steady climb to the top. Today A-B ("where making friends is our business") does a lot more than brewing—not least of which is adventure park entertainment.

sauerkraut, Limburger cheese, potato pancakes, German potato salad, pickles, pickled pigs' feet, strudel, plum cake, cream puffs, cookies, marzipan. What do we drink at Oktoberfest? Wine, water, soda—and did we mention BEER?

BAVARIAN OKTOBERFEST FACTS: According to the Munich Tourist Office, in 1999, 6.5 million visitors to the Fest ate over 600,000 chickens, 150,000 pairs of sausage, and 62,000 pork knuckles. They downed 6 million liters of beer, 31,000 liters of wine, and 198,000 cups of coffee and tea.

10 KINDS OF GERMAN SAUSAGE

bratwurst	bockwurst	blutwurst
braunschweiger	knackwurst	schlachtwurst
mettwurst	Thueringer	weisswurst
	leberwurst	

14 KINDS OF NON-GERMAN SAUSAGE

pepperoni	chorizo	loukanika
kielbasa	saucisson	cotechino
andouille	chipolata	mortadella
banger	Toulouse	blood (or black) pudding
Chinese duck sausage	luganega	

10 KINDS OF ITALIAN CURED MEAT

Genoa salami	Felino salami	Calabrese
coppa	cacciatorino	sopressata
Milano salami	finocchiona	capocollo
	campagnolo salami	

What you eat with your fingers when you're at home with the drapes closed is your own business. Here I'm talking about dinner parties and restaurants of all kinds, and that's my business because I might be eating with you, and I definitely *don't* want to see you lift a gravy-dripping pork chop to your mouth with your bare hands.

On the other hand, I *do* want to see you eat a barbecued chicken wing or pork rib with your fingers (which you then wipe on a napkin; finger-lickin' good doesn't mean you get to lick your fingers). Ditto with not-too-huge pieces of fried chicken, shrimp with shells, and whole shrimp that are served with dipping sauce.

Some ethnic foods are finger-friendly: tacos, for instance, and spring rolls. Hamburgers, hot dogs, corn on the cob, French fries, potato chips, and pickles are finger foods; no surprise there. Large sandwiches (like heros or subs or muffulettas) should be cut into smaller pieces, and then they're finger foods; any sandwich smothered or sitting in gravy is not.

Artichokes—well, they're hard enough to eat with your fingers, much less a fork and knife. So are cherry tomatoes (assuming

5 Great Mystery Novels about Food

any mystery in the Nero Wolfe series by Rex Stout (see page 71)

Someone Is Killing the Great Chefs of Europe, Nan Lyons

The Cooking School Murders, Virginia Rich

Dying for Chocolate, Diane Mott Davidson

Bread on Arrival, Lou Jane Temple

they're not part of a salad, which *always* requires a fork), so choose small ones you can pop whole into your mouth; bite carefully— they spurt. Unsauced asparagus is finger-approved; dip the tip in any proffered sauce and don't wave the stalk around. Aside from looking weird, it's dangerous: the sauce may flick onto someone or something. Raw veggies (remember crudités?) can be eaten with the fingers, and the same no-flailing rule applies.

Bread, rolls, and large biscuits are eaten with your fingers: break off a small piece, butter it (yes, with your butter knife), and put it into your mouth. Regular cookies (crisp or moist), bar cookies (including brownies), and small dry cakes are finger foods. If the sweet is unwieldy or crumbly, break off small pieces rather than bringing the whole thing to your mouth.

It would be ridiculous to try to eat cherries, strawberries, and smallish fruits (such as Italian prune plums) with anything but your fingers. (Other fruits, such as peaches, apples, oranges, are usually served with fruit knives, and that's a topic for another day.) Bananas, the quintessential finger food, aren't usually served at dinner parties or in restaurants, so no worries there.

And in case you were waiting for official sanction, crisp bacon, mussels in their shells, and small frogs' legs can all be eaten with the fingers.

5 More Great Mystery Novels about Food

The Butter Did It, Phyllis Richman

Appetite for Murder, Cecille Lamalle

The Mint Julep Murders, Carolyn G. Hart

Devil's Food, Anthony Bruno

Eat, Drink, and Be Buried, Peter King

POP QUIZ!

1. Which of these is *not* a hefty oversized sandwich?
   A. sub
   B. hero
   C. grinder
   D. hoagie
   E. panzanella

2. Dashi is
   A. another name for the curds created when milk coagulates and separates
   B. a kind of crab
   C. Japanese soup stock
   D. a variety of taro root
   E. a colloquial term for the kitchen helper in a diner

3. *True or false:* Sara Lee is a real person.

4. Another name for those chocolate or multicolored sprinkles you get on your ice cream cone is
   A. jimmies
   B. jujubes
   C. jackies
   D. confetti
   E. none of the above

5. What is ergot?
   A. a unit of heat used in measuring oven temperature
   B. French for "snail"
   C. lettuce with frilly leaves and a slightly bitter taste, best used in combination with milder greens
   D. a fungus disease of rye that, when eaten by humans in contaminated bread, brings on madness and death
   E. a wild herb with a pungent flavor, used frequently in Latin American cooking

6. If your mom hands you a three-item shopping list and tells you to head for the bodega, where should you go?
   A. the bakery
   B. the butcher
   C. the fruit stand
   D. the liquor store
   E. the corner grocery store

7. If you were in the mood for a tangy relish with your meal, you'd ask for
   A. picadillo
   B. piccalilli
   C. pilaf
   D. pipikaula
   E. piccata

8. *Name that cuisine:* What country gave us zabaglione?

Answers: 1. e; 2. c; 3. true; 4. a; 5. d; 6. e; 7. b; 8. Italy (it's a frothy, eggy dessert)

176

BREAKFAST AROUND THE WORLD

Rise and shine—and what's for breakfast? Americans generally go for the usual toast, eggs, cereal, pancakes, fruit, fruit juice, milk, hot coffee or tea. But that's just America. Breakfast is not monolithic. In the north of India, for instance, most folks start the day with tea and bread; in the south of India, it's coffee and something made with rice (such as pancakes or noodles). In Pakistan they like a thick, sweet semolina dish and some crisp puri breads.

Egyptians eat ful (or fool or fuul), a fava bean stew that includes lentils, tomatoes, garlic, and lots of spices, and may be served with an egg and some pita bread. Israelis on kibbutzes go for yogurt with cucumbers and tomatoes, and fresh fruit. In Syria and Lebanon you might eat flatbread rolled with labnah (yogurt cheese) and possibly olives, tomatoes, and mint leaves. In Greece breakfast is, traditionally, thick, sweet coffee with fresh bread, olives, and good cheese; untraditionally it's bacon and eggs, pastry and fruit, and yogurt. Some Turks keep it simple with fresh bread with butter and honey, and tea, Turkish coffee, or a yogurt drink.

In Japan the traditional breakfast is miso soup and rice, and pickled plums, too (though more and more Japanese people are eating eggs and sausages and drinking coffee these days). In China, depending on

---

And Speaking of Food . . .

A. A. Milne, Winnie-the-Pooh, 1926

"When you wake up in the morning, Pooh," said Piglet at last, "what's the first thing you say to yourself?"

"What's for breakfast?" said Pooh. "What do you say, Piglet?"

"I say, I wonder what's going to happen exciting today?" said Piglet.

Pooh nodded thoughtfully.

"It's the same thing," he said.

which part of that huge country you're in, you'll eat dim sum—those little steamed, deep-fried, or boiled snacks of endless variety—or noodles or sticky rice or a rice gruel called congee. In Korea the traditional breakfast is a rich, meat-based soup, or a miso soup with tofu, fish, and hot peppers. All over Southeast Asia people breakfast on rice, noodle soups, curry, or sticky rice, along with fresh fruit—foods that are not very different from the foods they eat during the rest of the day.

In South America breakfast is milky coffee and pan dulce—sweet bread. Sweet coffee with milk and also chocolate beverages are common in Mexico and Central America, with tortillas, eggs, sweet bread, fresh fruit, and fried plantains. In Costa Rica they eat rice and beans, sometimes with eggs. In Jamaica breakfast might be bully beef (a kind of hash), johnnycakes, a vegetable called callaloo, and boiled green bananas. Another Caribbean breakfast is callaloo and salt fish, with yams, boiled bananas, or boiled dumplings. In Cuba we're back to milky coffee, this time with toast and perhaps ham and eggs.

12 Delicious Savory Omelet Fillings

1. Cheddar cheese, chopped scallions

2. mélange of sautéed mushrooms

3. chopped fresh tomatoes, sautéed onions, fresh herbs

4. salsa, avocado, chopped fresh cilantro

5. Canadian bacon, sliced fresh tomatoes

6. blue cheese, sautéed pear slices

7. sliced cooked sausage, roasted red peppers

8. smoked salmon, sour cream, fresh dill

9. salmon caviar, sour cream, capers

10. ham, minced bell peppers, minced onions

11. chopped cooked asparagus, grated Parmesan cheese

12. Gruyère cheese, bacon, minced fresh parsley

Russians mostly drink strong tea and eat bread, eggs, sausages, and pickles, with cereal for the children. The French, Belgians, and Italians love their coffee, with freshly baked croissants or rolls. The Swedes love their "hard bread" with fish-egg spread or, alternatively, cereal with slightly sour milk. England is getting over its obsession with the "Full English Breakfast" of eggs, bacon, sausage, tomatoes, and mushrooms (with soggy toast) and now leans toward cereal or croissants or even American-style muffins. In Australia old habits die hard: the English-style breakfast is popular (and so is toast topped with baked beans), and they're still slathering their buttered toast with a concoction called Vegemite—a salty spread made of brewer's yeast and malt extracts that come straight from beer making. And that's what's for breakfast in a few parts of the world.

10 POPULAR COOKBOOKS
of the 1970s and 1980s

1970: Hazel Meyer's Freezer Cookbook

1976: The Taste of Country Cooking, Edna Lewis

1977: The Moosewood Cookbook, Mollie Katzen

1978: The Quick and Easy Cookbook, Joan Savin

1979: La Methode, Jacques Pepin

1981: Maida Heatter's Book of Great Cookies

1982: Chez Panisse Menu Cookbook, Alice Waters

1982: The Silver Palate Cookbook, Julee Rosso and Sheila Lukins

1987: Authentic Mexican, Rick Bayless and Deann Groen Bayless

1989: The New Basics, Julee Rosso and Sheila Lukins

DOES ANYONE ELSE THINK THESE CEREAL NAMES ARE A LITTLE STRANGE?

Fruity Freakies	Malted Shreddies	Quisp
Corn Crackos	Crispy Critters	Quake
Froot Loops	Count Chocula	Quangaroos
Wackies	Frankenberry	Cocoa Pebbles
Fruit Brute	Sir Grapefellow	Fruity Pebbles
Kaboom	Dinky Donuts	Moon Stones
	Boo Berry	

TELL ME ABOUT...

SHREDDED WHEAT

Shredded wheat biscuits appeared in 1893 when Henry Perky invented the biscuit and the machine that made the biscuit, *with the intention of selling the machine.* He didn't care about making money from the shredded wheat—he wanted to cash in on the machine and let other people make the biscuits. Didn't happen. People loved the biscuits, so Mr. Perky changed course and began taking the biscuit business seriously. It grew and grew, moving from Boston to Worcester, Massachusetts, to Niagara Falls, New York. In 1928 the National Biscuit Company bought the company and kept it until 1993, when Nabisco sold it to Kraft-General Foods, which markets shredded wheat under the Post brand.

FAVORITE HENRY PERKY FACT: The factory he opened in Niagara Falls was, apparently, a modern marvel of a workplace. It was called the "Palace of Light," and it was constructed of thirteen thousand panes of glass, tiled in white, well-lit, air-conditioned, and equipped with amenities for the cereal-making employees. This was years before there were requirements for clean *food* workplaces. Mr. Perky was a progressive thinker and a good marketer, too, because his palace turned out to be a great tourist attraction. It was in operation until 1954.

SNAP, CRACKLE, AND POP
The Story of Rice Krispies

By the time Kellogg's rolled out Rice Krispies in 1928, the company was already in the marketplace with Corn Flakes (1907), Bran Flakes (1915), and All Bran (1916). Rice Krispies was their first puffed cereal. It was (and is) made by expanding rice kernels with superheated steam, creating the brittle weblike structure of each little krispy. When you pour milk on the krispies, those thin rice walls rupture with a sound you can hear: they snap, they crackle, they pop.

Those magic words—*snap, crackle,* and *pop*—first appeared on the cereal box in 1932, and the cartoon characters Snap, Crackle, and Pop followed in 1933. They were Kellogg's first icons, and they've lasted the longest. The Snap, Crackle, and Pop images have evolved over the decades, but the basic nature of their *hats* never changes: Snap has a baker's hat; Crackle has a red-and-white stocking cap; Pop wears what Kellogg's calls a military hat. Kids loved the big-eyed, apple-cheeked boys with their distinct personalities, and that sold a lot of cereal.

So did Rice Krispy Squares or, as they were also called, Rice Krispy Treats. If ever a product and a recipe came together like a match made in heaven, it was Rice Krispies and Rice Krispy Squares. Simple, cheap, easy-to-make, a cheerful mom-and-kid activity, the perfect combination of crunch, sweetness, and chewiness—the snack was destined to become an institution. Horrible adaptations have cropped up over the years (using, for instance, brown rice and black-strap molasses) but the original is still the champ. Tell the truth: have you ever met anyone who turned down a real Rice Krispy Square?

Granola has a reputation for being a "health food," whatever that may mean, and it came into popularity back in the earthy 1960s. It's a combination of toasted whole grains (mostly oats) bound together into crunchy little nuggets by a sweetener such as honey or corn syrup; often it includes nuts and dried fruits. There are lots of flavored granolas too—French vanilla almond, blueberry, strawberry, pumpkin spice, and so on. Modern granola has vague roots in a pair of nineteenth-century American cereals called granula and granola, but it's a much closer relative of the European breakfast food called muesli.

Muesli is what health food fans ate for breakfast long before granola came along—toasted grains (especially rolled oats), nuts, bran, wheat germ, seeds, raisins and other dried fruits, brown sugar. Fresh seasonal fruits such as chopped apples, bananas, oranges, or berries are added, along with milk and yogurt. There are many variations on muesli, depending on which country it comes from and which family is eating it.

10 Perfect Pancake Toppers

real (real!) maple syrup

honey

berry sauce

diced fresh fruit

sautéed fresh fruit slices (apples, pears, or peaches)

fruit butter

lemon curd

vanilla or fruit yogurt

cinnamon sugar

sweetened, softly whipped cream

✳✳✳

16 Great Recipe Web Sites for Everyday Use

eat.epicurious.com

familyfun.go.com/family/Cookbook/

Kraftfoods.com

recipelink.com

recipecenter.com

almanac.com/food

LandOLakes.com (*good baking info, too*)

cyber-kitchen.com

mealsforyou.com

meals.com

foodgeeks.com

FoodTV.com

seasoned.com

tasteofhome.com

wholefoods.com

recipezaar.com

✳✳✳

BUTTERMILK
AND WHAT TO DO WITH IT

The cultured buttermilk you buy today is a mere reference to the fresh buttermilk of yesterday. *That* buttermilk was the liquid left in the churn after the butter had formed and been removed. (In fact, the only bits of butter in that naturally low-fat liquid were the specks that escaped skimming.) Our buttermilk is low-fat, nonfat, or whole milk to which lactic-acid bacteria has been added in order to thicken it and give it that characteristic old-fashioned buttermilk tang.

Chilled buttermilk is good to drink just as it is (but be sure to shake the carton before you pour) or with a little sugar or sugar substitute stirred in. Coat pieces of chicken, fish, or seafood in buttermilk before dipping in flour or breadcrumbs when you're deep-frying, oven-frying, or baking. Try it for making creamy salad dressing, too, in place of

yogurt or sour cream. And buttermilk pancakes and waffles—terrific.

Best of all, though, is buttermilk baking: biscuits, muffins, scones, quick breads, cookies, layer cakes, tube cakes, cobblers, soda bread, shortcake. *Reliable* recipes that include buttermilk in the ingredients yield products that are moist, tender, and flavorful, since they've been tested (one hopes) and the balance of acid to alkali has been worked out. That's the tricky part of baking with buttermilk—balancing acid and alkali so the leavening process works properly.

If you want to venture out on your own, here's the rule of thumb for substituting buttermilk for milk in a baking recipe: for each cup of buttermilk used in place of regular milk, *reduce* the amount of baking powder by 2 teaspoons and *add* ½ teaspoon baking soda.

17 FOODS THAT FREEZE REALLY BADLY

cabbage	yogurt	sour cream
watercress	icing made from egg whites	boiled potatoes
cucumbers		mayonnaise or creamy salad dressings
raw tomatoes	cream or custard fillings	
lettuce	milk sauces	gelatin
raw apples	gravies and sauces thickened with flour or cornstarch	fried food (except French fries or fried onion rings)
cooked egg whites		

TELL ME ABOUT...

YOGURT

Yogurt is a pretty simple food: it's milk that's been cultured with a few specific varieties of good bacteria with slightly scary-sounding handles (*Lactobacillus bulgaricus, Streptococcus thermophilus,* and *Lactobacillus acidophilus*, to name the most common) and allowed to ferment and curdle to form a thickish, creamyish, tangyish white semisolid (or semiliquid, depending on how long you let the curdling process go on). Nowadays we have our choice of regular yogurt, made from whole milk, with the highest level of milk fat; lowfat yogurt, made from lowfat or part-skim milk; and nonfat yogurt, made from skim milk, with the lowest level of milk fat.

The general consensus is that yogurt containing live and active cultures is the most nutritious and does the most for your digestive and immune systems; it also seems to be digestible by lactose-intolerant people, because the live and active cultures break down the lactose in milk. Yogurts labeled "heat-treated" won't deliver the benefits of these cultures, since the heat destroys them. Freezing seems to knock out the good bacteria too, so no bennies from your favorite frozen yogurt. And forget about yogurt-covered pretzels or candies—they're for fun, not for health.

COOL WHIP, COFFEE-MATE, AND OTHER FOOD ANALOGUES

Cool Whip Whipped Topping is not fake: it's real Cool Whip. Ditto for Coffee-mate, Tofurky, Smart Dogs, Sweet 'N Low, Egg Beaters, margarine, and a host of other analogues. By FDA standards they're not imitations, either. The Food and Drug Administration says, "A food that imitates another food is misbranded unless its label bears . . . the word 'imitation' and immediately thereafter the name of the food imitated."

So even though it's white, creamy, fluffy, and used as a substitute for whipped cream, Cool Whip can't be construed to be an imitation of whipped cream because it makes no claims to be anything but whipped topping. It's an analogue, not an imitation. If you choose to infer that it's the equivalent of whipped cream, that's between you and your taste buds. There's no reason not to eat it, unless you happen to prefer something that tastes like what it's supposed to taste like: whipped cream.

Analogues do have upsides. Coffee-mate, the nondairy creamer, is a boon to offices lacking refrigerators and to lactose-intolerant hot beverage drinkers. Some people actually like it. Tofurky, a vegetarian turkey alternative, is a salve to the consciences of the meat-free, though you'd think by now they'd have resigned themselves to eating fish on Thanksgiving Day. Smart Dogs has an ingredients list that includes nothing the least bit hot-doggy: water, soy protein isolate, wheat gluten, evaporated cane juice, salt, yeast extract, and nine others, and it has no nitrites or MSG, either. Pink-packeted Sweet 'N Low (like the blue-

WHAT ON EARTH IS...

Basically, crème fraîche (pronounced "krem fresh") is cultured heavy cream—heavy cream that's been thickened with a fermenting agent. Sounds a little clinical for this scrumptiously rich, smooth, tangy topping that's usually about as dense as sour cream. Use it the way you'd use sour cream or unsweetened whipped cream (try a dollop on hot or cold tomato soup, for instance, or on hot apple pie) or sweeten it slightly and spoon it onto fruit, pie, cobblers, cakes, and other desserts. Add it to hot sauces, too; it won't curdle.

packeted Equal and the yellow-packeted Splenda) is indispensable if you're pretending to diet. Egg Beaters are egg whites that are pumped up with nutrients lost when the yolks are eliminated, but at least they have no cholesterol. There must be a reason for the existence of the butter-analogue margarine (also known as table spread, a truly bizarre term), but it's no longer very clear what that might be.

The marketplace is flooded with analogues, and more appear all the time. How long will it be before you forget what real whipped cream tastes like? It might not be long at all.

10 Fresh Fruits and Their (Potential) Cheese Partners

apples: *sharp Cheddar, Asiago, Gruyère, Stilton, Gouda*

pears: *Camembert, Brie, Gorgonzola, Taleggio, Roquefort*

grapes: *Havarti, Camembert, feta, provolone*

figs: *goat cheese, feta, Gorgonzola, mozzarella, ricotta salata*

peaches: *Edam, Monterey Jack, Maytag Blue, Saga Blue, Blue Castello*

plums: *Brie, Camembert, Havarti, Monterey Jack, Cheshire*

strawberries: *mascarpone, Camembert, Brie, goat cheese*

cherries: *Gorgonzola, Brie, Saint André, mascarpone, Roquefort*

apricots: *Emmenthaler, Edam, Maytag Blue, Roquefort*

melons: *mascarpone, Brie, goat cheese, Saga Blue, Gorgonzola dolce*

FOOD TABOOS

The Ponape islanders won't eat turtle meat or immature coconuts, Ethiopian Christians won't eat camel, and North Americans won't eat slugs. Food taboos vary enormously from group to group, culture to culture, country to country; what's taboo in yours may very well not be taboo in someone else's, or vice versa. You love a steak hot off the barby, while your vegetarian next-door neighbor may refuse even to touch meat: he has a taboo against food he regards as unhealthy. Your uncle in China may relish a nicely prepared dog, but you recoil at the notion of Fido in the frying pan: in the West there's a taboo against eating animals regarded as pets. We have an unfortunately narrow-minded tendency to believe that our own food taboos make sense while other people's food taboos are silly or horrifying.

Food taboos come about for cultural, religious, economic, and ecological reasons, but not always for the reasons we assume. For instance, you've probably heard the religious taboo against pork explained by the old trichinosis threat: pigs might be infested with trichinae and pass them along to pork-eating humans. It's true that pigs can be infested with trichinae, but there's no scientific evidence to demonstrate that at

---

AMAZING FOOD EVENT: 1890s

It's Not Coke, It's ... Pepsi

Sometime in the 1890s a pharmacist named Caleb D. Bradham invented a carbonated drink, as many pharmacists did back then. His customers loved it and called it "Brad's drink," but Bradham called it Pepsi-Cola. The "Pepsi" part referred to pepsin, a digestive aid that Bradham used in his drink and exploited in his advertising; the "Cola" part was a piggyback on the already popular Coca-Cola. Bradham had business troubles galore, and by 1923 the first Pepsi-Cola Corporation went bankrupt. So did the second one, but the third company to promote Pepsi hit the jackpot.

the time most pork taboos were established (thousands of years ago) anyone had any concept of trichinosis, much less how it was transmitted. If people didn't know about trichinosis, how could it have been the basis of a taboo?

Taste and newness can also influence the existence of food taboos, and those taboos (unlike religious taboos against certain foods) sometimes evolve over time. What may seem alien and dangerous and therefore unacceptable—like tomatoes, when they were first introduced to Europeans—can gradually achieve acceptance as people become accustomed to the flavor and convinced of the safety of eating the forbidden food. The traditional taboo against a suspicious food can eventually transform into exactly its opposite. And what a good thing that is. Just imagine life without tomatoes.

YOU WILL MEET
A HANDSOME STRANGER
The Story of Fortune Cookies

You do know, don't you, that Chinese fortune cookies aren't remotely Chinese? We're not sure what their exact provenance is, but we're sure it *wasn't* China and it *was* the United States. The history of the cookies is all over the place: no one seems to be able to pin it down.

The genesis of the fortune cookie is often attributed to the Chinese workers who helped lay the railways in the nineteenth century. They had no traditional moon cakes for the Moon Festival, so they tucked cheery messages into ordinary biscuits instead. Maybe. Possibly fortune cookies were invented by a Japanese-American, Makoto Hagiwara, to serve in his teahouse in San Francisco in 1914. Or not. Perhaps they were the post–World War I invention of David Jung, owner of the Hong Kong Noodle Company in Los Angeles, to hand out to homeless unem-

---

WHAT TO EAT AT A CHINESE NEW YEAR CELEBRATION

yau gwok (deep-fried dumplings)

jiaozi (boiled dumplings)

tang yuan (sweet rice dumplings)

whole chicken (cooked and served with head, feet, and tail)

whole fish (with head and tail)

long noodles (long and uncut, for long life)

jai (vegetarian dish including lotus seed,
ginkgo nuts, seaweed, and dried bean curd)

yu sang (New Year salad of striped bass,
daikon radish, carrots, ginger, and more)

spring rolls

jin dui (deep-fried cookies made with sweet potato dough)

---

ployed people to cheer them up. Or perhaps they weren't.

What we do know is that by the 1930s there were fortune cookie factories where the cookies were shaped by hand, and they continued to be shaped by hand until (probably) 1964, when Edward Louie, San Francisco owner of the Lotus Fortune Cookie Company, came up with a machine that did the folding.

Who writes the messages that wind up on those itty-bitty strips of paper? Sorry, don't know too much about that, either. But you can't help wondering: if the history of the cookies is so unknowable, how reliable could their predictions of the future be?

Traditional Christmas Foods from around the World

Within each country there are, of course, many regional specialties; this is just a festive sampling.

GERMANY: stollen; glühwein; lebkuchen

FRANCE: buckwheat cakes; chestnuts and turkey; oysters; foie gras; bûche de Noël

ITALY: panforte; panettone; pandoro; torrone

FINLAND: casserole of macaroni, rutabaga, carrots, potatoes, and ham or turkey

PORTUGAL: bacalhau with boiled potatoes

SPAIN: chestnut soup; turkey with truffles; turrón

AUSTRIA: braised carp; roast goose; cheese crêpes with apricot sauce

DENMARK: roast goose; vanilla wreath and pepper-nut cookies; chocolate-covered marzipan

UNITED KINGDOM: plum pudding; iced Christmas cake

POLAND: red borscht with pierogis; herring; carp

What's the Difference between . . .

BAKING POTATOES, ALL-PURPOSE POTATOES, NEW POTATOES, AND BOILING POTATOES?

Baking potatoes (called Idaho or russet) are the starchiest kind; they flake into tender chunks when they're cooked, so they mash well, too. All-purpose potatoes (usually called eastern) are the next starchiest: they're neither starchy enough to be perfect for baking, nor low-starch enough to be perfect for boiling. They straddle the fence, good enough but not great for either purpose.

"New potatoes" generally refers to those small, thin-skinned red or pale brown potatoes we see in the spring—the first of the new crop. (Technically speaking, though, any potatoes that are harvested and sent straight to market are, in fact, "new" potatoes, as distinct from most other potatoes, which are stored and sent to market during the rest of the year.) Whole new potatoes are firm and waxy, great for boiling and for roasting. Left in the ground, these "new" potatoes get larger, of course, but their skins stay thin and they hold their texture—still perfect for boiling and roasting. So that's what boiling potatoes are: the thin-skinned red or brown ones that aren't Idahos, russets, or easterns.

AMAZING FOOD EVENT: 1962

Instant Mashed Potato Flakes

Canadian research scientist Dr. Edward Asselbergs invented instant mashed potato flakes while he was working for the Department of Agriculture in Ottawa. His dehydration process was patented and used worldwide to produce protein-fortified foods and convenience foods.

SECONDARY AMAZING FOOD EVENT: Steven Spielberg allegedly used white potato flakes in place of real snow in the movie *Close Encounters of the Third Kind.*

TRUE TALES OF THE DINNER TABLE:
CULINARY ANHEDONIA

Barry Hoffman, writer

When my mother told me that all the food on my plate was "delicious," I believed her. Food, she said, never got any better than this. She never said, "Food is love." She didn't have to. I knew she loved me. What I didn't understand at the time was that the people who love you are often driven by demons you can't see. In my mother's case, her demon was demonstrable: she hated cooking.

In the years before Betty Friedan and the advent of feminism, making dinner was the top line of any mother's resume. Cleaning the house came next, of course, but you didn't really have to do that every day; you could even hire another person to do it for you once a week. Breakfast, lunch, and dinner for three children and a husband were, on the other hand, unrelenting tasks. They were your primary responsibility. They had to happen on time. Worse yet, everyone had an opinion. The situation cried out for rigorous controls.

My mother's solution to the problem was not the universal one. Other people do not serve the same seven dishes on the same seven days. My mother did. Our eating schedule wasn't merely predictable—it was inevitable. Today, whenever conversation turns to eating habits and home cooking, and I recall my mother's culinary anhedonia, people say, "What do you mean? It never changed?" I can still easily recite the dish I was served each dinner of each day of every week of every year of my life at home.

Monday was always Meat Day. This was a hamburger (with Hamburger Helper after it was invented) or meat loaf (with a cooked egg in the middle) or, when Dad's income started to improve, a steak. Tuesday was Breaded Veal Cutlet Day. Served with mashed potatoes and Del Monte green beans. Wednesday was Spaghetti Day (Prince, Ronzoni, or even Chef Boyardee out of a can on occasion). Thursday, when my father worked late at the shoe store, was Creamed Tuna on Toast Day. A can of Bumble Bee white tuna, a can of Campbell's mushroom soup, a can of Del Monte green (actually, pallid umber) peas, stirred together and poured over toasted Wonder bread. Friday we had boiled chicken, which Mom described as Chicken That Falls Off the Bone. Saturday my mother and father always went out dancing or to a party or to a restaurant, leaving us with a babysitter; Saturday was Hot Dog and Bean Casserole Day. Sunday we went out for dinner, but always to the same places for the same things: pizza at Pellicci's or the Open Door, or Cantonese food at Sai Wu's.

Mom's dislike for cooking didn't end with preparation. She was the fastest eater I have ever seen. She wanted to get the meal over with. As soon as she finished she ordered the table cleared, whether you were done or not. Many times I finished my meal standing at the kitchen counter, shoveling the last morsels into my mouth as my dish was put under the running water.

Why was she the way she was? Cooking, after all, is fun. You can be original. You can surprise and satisfy the people you love. You can learn and grow. It is an arena for imagination. How could food be anything but love? It had to do, of course, with the times. Frozen foods and cans and women's magazines made convenience the first order of an orderly household. In my mother's case, however, it also had to do with her own mother.

My grandmother was the cook in the restaurant she ran with my grandfather. They worked from five in the morning until ten at night. She cooked, he sat at the register talking to customers and being—as she called him with withering sarcasm even a seven-year-old could appreciate—"the big boss." They fought, cursed, and swore at each other constantly. My mother waited tables at the restaurant all through her high school years and after. If her family ate at home, it was food they brought back from the restaurant. Her mother never taught her to cook, and I don't think she ever got over that baptism in the cauldrons of cooking.

So in our house there was lots of food and lots of love, but the two never met. Food wasn't love. Food was work. Our weekly menu wasn't an opportunity for my mother to express the joy of cooking, it was an assembly line for sustenance. Whatever her motives, it boils down to this: When I go out to eat, and it's Tuesday, and there's a breaded veal cutlet on the menu, that is what I always order. And it is always delicious.

THE 5 MOST EXPENSIVE FOODS IN THE WORLD

saffron ★ beluga caviar ★ fugu (blowfish) ★ foie gras ★ truffles

****

12 Great Web Sites for Gourmets

spoon.com (from American Spoon Foods)

epicurean.com

worldpantry.com (Greek foods)

idealcheese.com (fantastic selection)

Kalustyans.com

lamaisonduchocolat.com (high-end chocolates)

nbsmokehouse.com (smoked meats of all sorts)

SplendidPalate.com

outdoorcookingstore.com (everything for grilling and outdoor cooking)

winespectator.com

gourmetsleuth.com

iGourmet.com

****

12 CLASSIC SAUCES

espagnole	mornay	vinaigrette
velouté	béarnaise	mousseline
béchamel	beurre blanc	bordelaise
hollandaise	rémoulade	bigarade

4 Famous Chefs Who Couldn't Take the Heat

★ Bernard Loiseau: shot himself to death in 2003 because (among other reasons) his Côte d'Or restaurant dropped from nineteen to seventeen in the twenty-point Gault-Millau restaurant rating system

★ Gérard Besson: had a heart attack when he learned that his restaurant had lost one Michelin star

★ Alain Zick: shot himself to death when he found out that his Paris restaurant, Relais des Porquerolles, had lost a Michelin star

★ Francois Vatel: in 1671 killed himself with a sword, to avoid disgrace after a delivery of fish apparently failed to arrive when his employer was hosting King Louis XIV. The fish did, in fact, arrive soon after Vatel had been misinformed—but it was too late for Vatel.

And Speaking of Food . . .

Ludwig Bemelmans, La Bonne Table, 1964

The popular concept of the gourmet is that of a seallike, happy creature of Gargantuan appetite, who sticks a napkin inside his collar, dunks bread into the sauces and throws on the floor plates that are not properly heated. His nourishment is cataloged as caviar, pâté de foie gras, truffles, pheasant and crêpes Suzette. . . . He is thought of as a middle-aged man (never a woman), portly and jolly, given to reciting toasts that are spiked with French terms. His extravagant dinners take on the aspect of an eating contest rather than a good meal. Actually, the true gourmet, like the true artist, is one of the unhappiest creatures existent. His trouble comes from so seldom finding what he constantly seeks: perfection.

7 Other Sizes of Champagne Bottles

An ordinary bottle of champagne equals 750 milliliters.

★ split = ¼ bottle

★ magnum = 2 bottles

★ jeroboam = 4 bottles

★ rehoboam = 6 bottles

★ Methuselah = 8 bottles

★ Salmanazar = 12 bottles

★ Balthazar = 16 bottles

10 Stuffed Treats

mushrooms stuffed with seasoned breadcrumbs

classic stuffed grape leaves

stuffed cabbage

pita sandwiches

deviled eggs

dried figs stuffed with goat cheese

celery stuffed with peanut butter

baked apples stuffed with raisins, nuts, and brown sugar

halved winter squash stuffed with savory vegetables

baked potatoes stuffed with almost anything
from tuna to broccoli

What to Serve at a Luau

At a luau, food is eaten with fingers only.

★ one-, two-, and three-finger poi (the number of fingers depending on the thickness of the poi)

★ kulolo (taro pudding)

★ sweet potatoes

★ kalua (roast pig)

★ laulau (meat or fish steamed in ti leaf packets)

★ chicken long rice

★ fresh fish

★ salt fish

★ lomi salmon (cooked with tomatoes and onions)

★ coconuts

★ haupia (coconut pudding)

★ fresh pineapple, papaya, bananas

WHAT ON EARTH IS...

POI?

To understand poi you have to be familiar with taro, a staple food of Polynesia. Taro is an underground tuber (like a potato) with leaves growing aboveground. The leaves can be cooked and eaten or they can be used for wrapping other foods that are going to be cooked. The underground part of the taro—the corm—can be baked and eaten, or it can be cooked and pounded to make poi. That's what poi is: cooked taro that's been pounded to a paste with either no water, some water (thick poi), or more water (thin poi). Poi can be eaten as soon as it's pasty (sweet poi) or it can be allowed to ferment for several days (sour poi). As Sharon Tyler Herbst writes in *Food Lover's Companion*, "This native Hawaiian dish is definitely an acquired taste."

POI FACT: Poi is eaten with the fingers, so thick poi is called one-finger poi, thinner poi is two-finger, and thin poi is three-finger.

POP QUIZ!

1. Which of these is not made with ground corn?
   A. grits
   B. spaetzle
   C. posole
   D. polenta
   E. tamales

2. *True or false:* Port wine was originally made in Portofino, Italy.

3. A ptarmigan is
   A. a game bird
   B. an edible lizard
   C. a steak-and-kidney pie
   D. a utensil for crushing herbs
   E. a food-borne bacterium

4. To temper chocolate is to
   A. sweeten it
   B. flavor it
   C. combine it with other ingredients
   D. stabilize it
   E. enrich it

5. What is rumaki?
   A. a cocktail invented at a posh hotel in Barbados
   B. a Southeast Asian relish flavored with lemon grass, ginger, and garlic

C. an hors d'oeuvre of bacon, water chestnut, and chicken liver
D. a Russian stew of beef, onions, carrots, sour cream, and a dash of vodka
E. a strudel-like pastry spiced with cinnamon and nutmeg

6. If you were making mee krob, you would start out by
   A. braising
   B. grilling
   C. deep-frying
   D. poaching
   E. sautéing

7. If you were using a metate, you would be
   A. whipping
   B. chopping
   C. stirring
   D. grinding
   E. mashing

8. *Name that cuisine:* What country does nuoc mam come from?

Answers: 1. b; 2. false (it was made in Oporto, Portugal); 3. a; 4. d; 5. c; 6. c; 7. d; 8. Vietnam (it's a fermented fish sauce)

199

CHOWDER FOR ALL

In Boston there is a very famous restaurant called Durgin-Park, which has—for quite a lot longer than a century—specialized in Yankee food: oysters, clams, pot roast, corned beef, scrod, corn bread, apple pan dowdy, Boston cream pie, Indian pudding, and, of course, clam chowder. The restaurant has a very pleasant and homey Web site that offers, in addition to history and other odds and ends, recipes. To the experienced recipe reader's eye (mine), all the recipes seem to make sense, except one—the clam chowder. This New England–style chowder recipe requires four pounds of clams, forty-six ounces of clam juice, four to six potatoes, a pound of butter, a pound of flour, and a quart of half-and-half.

No problem, except that the yield is listed as four to six servings. Which means that each of those four servings will contain a pound of clams, around ten ounces of clam juice, a whole potato, a quarter pound each of butter and flour, and a cup of half-and-half. The mind boggles. I am a small-sized person, so perhaps I'm overreacting; Queequeg might find one serving of this stunningly rich chowder barely enough for a snack. When I queried the kind, friendly, utterly accessible Durgin-Park chef about this, he conceded, after giving it some thought, that his recipe would serve . . . six to eight.

Chowder is by definition a hearty dish. Its most famous American versions are New England clam chowder, Manhattan clam chowder, fish chowder, and corn chowder; some soup lovers might add chicken chowder, conch chowder, and vegetable chowder to the list. The broth can be thick or thin, but it's generally chock-full of chunky ingredients, well seasoned, and very satisfying. Chowder slots into the centuries-old fishermen's tradition of communal meals, and likely started as more of a stew than a soup—a big pot into which some combination of clams, bits of fish, salt pork, onions, potatoes, crackers, butter, savory herbs, salt, and pepper were layered and simmered. Ingredients varied according to what was available and what was customary, and they evolved over time: cream went in, potatoes came out, lobster went in, potatoes reappeared, and so on.

And then there was the Great Tomato Schism: some heretic—generally thought to have been living in Rhode Island in the early 1800s—added tomatoes to clam chowder. New England clam chowder devotees heaped scorn on the tomato-y interloper, blamed it all on New York City (for a change), and christened it Manhattan clam chowder. In 1939 the legislature of the state of Maine got into the act, famously: Assemblyman Seeder introduced a bill to make it illegal to put tomatoes in clam chowder.

DEFINITION OF CHOWDERHEAD: an unintelligent or irrational person.

8 Ways to Improve Basic Scrambled Eggs

★ Scramble with a handful of shredded Cheddar
and some chopped fresh herbs.

★ When eggs are almost cooked, gently fold in
some salmon caviar; dab with sour cream.

★ Sauté lots of chopped onion until caramelized;
add eggs and scramble.

★ Scramble with chopped scallion, tomato,
and pickled jalapeño.

★ Spread crisp tortillas with salsa verde;
top with scrambled eggs and crumbled queso fresco.

★ Scramble with sautéed fresh mushrooms;
top with crumbled goat cheese.

★ Add a deli favorite—minced salami or lox;
top with red onion rings.

★ Sauté minced bell peppers, onions, and
small pieces of bacon; add eggs and scramble.

HORN AND HARDART AUTOMATS

Sad but true: if you were born too late or in the wrong city, you missed one of the most astonishing phenomena in the history of American food service. Mr. Horn and Mr. Hardart opened their first glorious Automat in Philadelphia in 1912; the last extremely unglorious one closed in New York City in 1991. The heyday of Automats was in the 1930s, '40s, and '50s, and any child who was ever taken to an Automat has never forgotten it. It looked like no other eating venue, and you bought and ate your food in a way that was utterly different from any other restaurant.

Horn and Hardart Automats were impressive places. Because they were a chain of restaurants (180 of them at peak), the sleek, modern design elements were consistent (though not identical) from Automat to Automat; even the typeface used for the outside and inside signage was distinctive and uniform. There were steam tables serving hot food, but the thing that every former patron still sighs over with nostalgia

---

12 GOOD REASONS TO OWN A MICROWAVE OVEN

1. reheating cold coffee
2. reheating cold tea
3. ditto cold cocoa
4. heating a mug of soup
5. reheating many (but not all) leftovers
6. warming up take-out food that is cold by the time you get it home
7. melting butter
8. melting chocolate
9. steaming asparagus (with tips pointed toward the center of the oven)
10. defrosting frozen food
11. quickly reheating food prepared the old-fashioned way, just before dinner
12. making microwave popcorn for a couch-potato evening

---

was the wall of food—yards and yards of shiny white enamel-and-glass vending machines. Gigantic vending machines. A wall-sized grid of dozens and dozens of little metal food chambers with glass doors, behind each of which sat a thick china plate or dish of famous H & H mac and cheese or baked beans, a wedge of pie, freshly made sandwich, scoop of ice cream, slice of cake.

These were simple, reliable, tasty foods, and they cost only nickels. Literally. You took yourself and your quarter or dollar to a rubber-fingertipped lady who sat in a marble-and-steel cage, handed her your money, and watched her shoot a stack of five or twenty nickels into a marble trough. You scooped them out and headed for the vending machines. Clink, clink, clink, you dropped your nickels into a slot next to the window displaying the food of your choice. Then you twisted a little chrome-and-porcelain knob, and snick, the window popped open. You stuck your hand in and lifted out your pumpkin pie or ham sandwich. Magic.

Automats had the illusion of being automated, but of course they were not. Behind the scenes they were heavily staffed by very clean workers who restocked empty food chambers lickety-split. If you happened to be peering intently through the glass-door front of the chamber after you scored your baked beans, you might catch a fleeting glimpse of a finger or hand, just enough to disappoint you (too bad it wasn't real magic) and delight you (gotcha!) at the same time. The system was meant to be a sort of adaptation of an assembly line, and it was—sort of. The food kept coming in an orderly way, just as on an assembly line; the presentation, however, was as thrilling as a theatrical performance. When you spent your nickel on a cup of coffee, for instance, the liquid gushed from a polished chrome dolphin's mouth, hot and fragrant and for exactly the same number of seconds every time you did it. It was drama plus standardization, and it was compelling.

After you got your food, where you sat was entirely your own business. The Automats were democratic. There were lots of tables, but no table service. You bought your food—which might be only that five-cent cup of coffee—and found a seat, whether you were a film star or a garment worker or a professor. You could hang out for hours if you wanted to, reading your paper, sipping and munching, or just observing the food life of the city.

MEET...

CRAIG CLAIBORNE

There's a wonderful photo of Craig Claiborne taken in his own apparently small apartment kitchen in 1990, ten years before his death. He looks like a genial gnome, surrounded by copper pots and jars of herbs and spices, all perfectly orderly—and he's wearing his signature striped apron, tied at the waist, over a white shirt and dark tie. When was the last time you wore a tie (or a tie-analog, like high heels) in the kitchen?

Southern gentility and a soft charm hover around the man in the picture, but the facts of his life reveal a steelier story. He was born in Sunflower, Michigan, in 1920, into no financial comfort whatsoever. He studied journalism at the University of Missouri, joined the wartime navy as a communications specialist, and became an officer on a submarine. After the war he worked in public relations in New York City, studied food and hospitality in France, and enlisted again when the Korean War began. He went back to Europe, postwar, to study more food and hospitality in Switzerland, then took a lowly job at *Gourmet* magazine and worked his way up to food writer and editor. That's when his true dream began to seem possible.

In 1957 Claiborne applied for and got the job of food editor at the *New York Times*, a position customarily held by a woman. He rigorously reviewed and rated restaurants and also wrote about food, making his readers aware of international cooking in a way that was new (and welcome) to them. His first book, *The New York Times Cookbook*, published in 1961, became a classic—the cookbook every aspiring home cook had to have. It included recipes from all over the world, and though the original does have a dated quality now, it was revolutionary and ambitious at the time. Claiborne took his place as, arguably, the best-known food writer in America.

Craig Claiborne stayed at the *Times* until he retired in the late 1980s (with only one brief hiatus in the early 1970s), writing, critiquing, observing, and commenting on the food trends of a nation, and generally encouraging Americans to broaden their food horizons. He published more cookbooks, too, and his culinary partnership with chef Pierre Franey (more cookbooks . . .) was legendary. He died in January

2000, respected, remembered, but somehow out of sync with a food world he'd been instrumental in creating. When Claiborne started his career, he was a big fish in a small pond; when he died, the pool of food writers had grown to such enormous proportions that he was only one of many—unique, to be sure, but not the giant he had once been.

SOME CRAIG CLAIBORNE COOKBOOKS: The New York Times Cookbook; Craig Claiborne's Kitchen Primer; Cooking with Herbs and Spices; The New York Times International Cookbook; Memorable Meals: Menus, Memories, and Recipes from Over Twenty Years of Entertaining; Craig Claiborne's Gourmet Diet; The New York Times Menu Cookbook; The Best of Craig Claiborne.

AMAZING FOOD EVENT: 1796

First American Cookbook

In 1796 Amelia Simmons wrote and published the first wholly American cookbook, *American Cookery*. Until that time American women had been using British cookbooks that didn't include American ingredients or American recipes. Simmons included both. Turkey, corn, squash, cranberries, pumpkin, potatoes—very American and very present in *American Cookery*.

Subtitles, as all writers know, are important. Here's Amelia Simmons's: *The art of dressing viands, fish, poultry and vegetables, and the best modes of making pastes, puffs, pies, tarts, puddings, custards and preserves, and all kinds of cakes, from the imperial plum to plain cake. Adapted to this country, and all grades of life.* Amen to that.

WE GATHER TOGETHER

The first Thanksgiving was a three-day harvest celebration at Plymouth in 1621, attended by the fifty or so Pilgrim settlers and about one hundred Wampanoag Indians. They had a feast of some kind of wild fowl (not necessarily turkeys; could have been ducks, geese, swans, or eagles, for all we know), venison, clams, mussels, lobster, fish, boiled pumpkin, beans, peas, carrots, squash, leeks, onions, plums, raspberries, grapes, nuts, and more. A good time was had by all, but there was no second Thanksgiving a year later. In 1623 the colonists gathered together again to pray for rain, and then when—miraculously —it actually did rain, they gave more thanks. But that was the end of group thanksgivings for more than fifty years.

FOOD-OF-THE-MONTH
12 Great Gifts for Your True Love

JANUARY: caviar and champagne

FEBRUARY: sensational Valentine's Day chocolates

MARCH: homemade soup and bread

APRIL: wild strawberries

MAY: slender stalks of fresh asparagus

JUNE: plump cherries

JULY: blueberry pie

AUGUST: a bushel of sweet corn and a juicy watermelon

SEPTEMBER: pears, plums, persimmons, and pomegranates

OCTOBER: apples, doughnuts, and freshly pressed cider

NOVEMBER: cranberry chutney and cranberry muffins

DECEMBER: gingerbread boys and girls

In 1676 a new Thanksgiving Day was designated for June 29 of every year, but November didn't come into play until 1789, when President George Washington declared a one-time official national day of thanksgiving on November 26. (Thomas Jefferson thought it was silly.) In 1827 Mrs. Sarah Josepha Hale, editor of her own women's magazine and later the highly influential editor of *Godey's Lady's Book*, began her campaign for an annual national Thanksgiving holiday; she was frustrated until 1863, when President Abraham Lincoln proclaimed the last Thursday of each November to be a national Thanksgiving Day. President Franklin D. Roosevelt tried to change the date to the third Thursday of November, to allow for more days of Christmas shopping, but that attempt was a total flop. In December 1941 a joint resolution of Congress established the date we all know: the fourth Thursday of every November is Thanksgiving Day.

18 TRADITIONALLY WESTERN AND SOUTHWESTERN FOODS

Dungeness crab	California onion dip	barbecue
geoduck	Cobb salad	buffalo stew
smoked salmon	Caesar salad	Anasazi beans
cioppino	posole	sopaipillas
crab Louis	chile con queso	biscochitos
sourdough bread	chili (or chile) con carne	fry bread

HOW TO ROAST
A THANKSGIVING TURKEY

Face facts: there's no perfect solution to the November Turkey-roasting Dilemma. Big Thanksgiving turkeys take a long time to cook, so the breast will always dry out by the time the thighs are cooked thoroughly. Fine for guests who love dark meat, not so good for the ones who like a moist slice of the white. So here are your choices: roast two smaller birds instead of one huge one (like two eight-pounders instead of one sixteen-pounder), or settle for the best you can do with the big boy and make plenty of gravy.

Unless you're cooking a fresh bird, defrosting a frozen bird (or two) is your first assignment. The experts tell you to defrost a sixteen-to twenty-pound bird in cold water for about eighteen hours. Query: Who has a bowl big enough to hold a giant bird plus enough water to cover? You're supposed to change the water occasionally—are you strong enough to lift the bowl to tip out the old water and add new? Splish-splash, what a mess. And if you defrost the bird in a kitchen sinkful of cold water for eighteen hours, what do you do for a kitchen sink in the meantime?

So you decide to defrost the bird(s) in the fridge—whoa! That takes up a pretty big part of the fridge for about two whole days at exactly the time when the fridge is overflowing with ingredients for seventeen kinds of vegetables and eight different condiments for the feast. Experts don't think about stuff like this, but you have to.

One way or another, you defrost your birds and you're ready to roast—assuming your oven is big enough to hold the giant bird or the two smaller birds. Preheat to 350°F and figure fifteen minutes of roasting per pound of bird. If you opted for smaller birds, start them breast side down in the roasting pans, cook for an hour, and then flip onto their backs for the remainder of the roasting time; that gives you a fighting chance for a moister, thoroughly cooked turkey. If you've chosen Big Bird, put him into the oven breast side up and allow to roast until an instant-read thermometer inserted in the thigh shows 165°F, about four hours for a sixteen-pounder. Baste along the way, of course, and if the bird(s) isn't brown enough, raise the heat to 400°F for the last fifteen minutes.

The table is set, the guests are starving (since it's three hours past the appointed dinner time), you're totally exhausted, and you still have to make the gravy. Take a breath. Give thanks that doing the bird has exempted you from doing the dishes. Make the gravy.

What's the Difference between . . .

BROILER-FRYER, ROASTER, STEWING CHICKEN, CAPON, ROCK CORNISH GAME HEN, AND SQUAB CHICKEN?

There's no official definition of each kind of chicken, and the unofficial definitions vary from butcher to butcher, market to market, and cookbook to cookbook. Here are mine:

A broiler-fryer is your basic unit of chicken, a young bird weighing between two and four pounds. You can do almost anything with it—roast it whole or use the parts for broiling, grilling, frying, braising, poaching. A roaster is a little older, fattier, and bigger, anywhere from four to seven pounds, and roasting is what you usually do with it, although poaching and braising are definite possibilities. A stewing chicken is a mature bird weighing between four and seven pounds, flavorful but tough, so it's good for long, slow cooking—soups, stews, braises.

I wish there were another way to say this, but a capon is a rooster that was castrated before it was a couple of months old and then allowed to get fat (between five and ten pounds) for six or eight more months. Roast a capon, because it's tender, tasty, and juicy.

Most Rock Cornish game hens are one to two pounds—pretty small. Roast them whole or split them for the grill or broiler, one hen per person. Squab chickens (*poussin* in French) are very young birds that weigh around a pound, give or take a few ounces. (Don't confuse them with actual squabs, which are pigeons.) Broil, grill, or roast them.

10 Classic Cookbooks

Times change, styles of eating and cooking change. These cookbooks are legendary, and they belong in any serious cook's library—but they aren't necessarily the cookbooks to which you'd automatically gravitate today. Give them a look and decide for yourself.

The Fannie Farmer Cookbook, Marion Cunningham

The Joy of Cooking, Irma S. Rombauer and Marion Rombauer Becker

The James Beard Cookbook, James Beard

The New York Times Cookbook, Craig Claiborne

The Michael Field Cookbook, Michael Field

Simple French Food, Richard Olney

Mastering the Art of French Cooking, Volumes 1 and 2, Julia Child et al.

Classic Italian Cooking, Marcella Hazan

A Taste of India, Madhur Jaffrey

The Cuisines of Mexico, Diana Kennedy

And Speaking of Food . . .

Alice B. Toklas, *The Alice B. Toklas Cookbook*, 1954

There is for the French no way of understanding the American habit of having such attractively furnished and arranged kitchens as not only to make it possible but pleasant to eat one's meals in them. To them a kitchen is a room in which a great deal of preparation for cooking, as well as the cooking, takes place. The walls of the kitchen are therefore covered with suspended pots and pans and kitchen utensils, and the tables have at least two mortars and pestles and endless bowls, graters and sieves in evidence. And all this without any disorder but lacking the taste that prevails in the other rooms of the home. Taste there undoubtedly is—the cooking-culinary-gastronomic taste. It is a puzzlement to Americans.

HOW TO START A SUPPER CLUB

Consider the supper club. It's like a book club, but instead of devouring words, supper club (or dinner club or gourmet club) members gobble up good food that they and their friends prepare and present.

Here's what mystery writer Hallie Ephron Touger (whose nom de plume is G. H. Ephron) says about her club: "We get together once every two months or so, rotate houses, and cook a meal extravaganza that none of us could do alone. Each dish is labor-intensive, but since all you have to make is one thing, it's doable."

There are no hard and fast rules for organizing a supper club; different groups do it different ways. You'll want to form your club with congenial people (friends or acquaintances) and agree on your objectives: Are you out for the gourmet cooking experience? Are you just out for a good time? Are you interested in expanding your knowledge of food? Any goal is a good one, if you all agree on it.

Next decide how often and when you'll have your dinners—and your planning meetings. Some groups do all their menu planning and assignments by e-mail or telephone, but other groups think half the fun is getting together to hash out the menu. The actual dinner venue generally rotates from club member to club member; everyone should have a turn to host, though if the club is large you may have to split up and dine at two or more homes at each dinner.

Menu planning is the heart of the matter. Most groups pick a theme of some sort: a particular cuisine, such as Mexican, Greek, Indian, or Thai; a special food, such as soft shell crabs, apples, or fresh pasta; seasonal food, such as lamb, asparagus, and strawberries in spring. But menus can zero in on almost anything, so here are some other possible themes: special place (beach, Provence, Shanghai); method or technique (barbecue, roasting, stir-frying); holiday (Valentine's Day, birthday, July Fourth); cookbook (classic, vintage, dessert); family recipes (Grandma's best, holiday traditions, childhood favorites).

Budget may or may not be an issue—how much will you spend and how will you divvy up the costs? It's essential to figure this one out from the get-go, or you're going to end up with inequities and resentment. Don't forget to include the cost of wine in your calculations, if you serve wine. You might want members to supply the appropriate wine for whatever course they're preparing, or you might assign the choice and purchase of wines to one or two different members each time. Remember that this is a communal activity, so everyone's preferences should be addressed.

Dividing up the assignments should take into account the skill levels of the cooks; less skilled cooks may have to do the easier dishes, or they may want to try dishes that challenge. Take turns with different parts of the meal, too: no one should always do the appetizer or the dessert unless that's the way you decide to structure the club.

Not every dish will work every time, not every meal will be four-star, but that's part of the supper club experience—making friendships and history along with food.

15 SELF-DECLARED FOOD CAPITALS OF THE WORLD

AVOCADO CAPITAL OF THE WORLD: Fallbrook, California

BRATWURST CAPITAL OF THE WORLD: Sheboygan, Wisconsin

CHOCOLATE CAPITAL OF THE WORLD: Hershey, Pennsylvania

CRAWFISH CAPITAL OF THE WORLD: Breaux Bridge, Louisiana

GINSENG CAPITAL OF THE WORLD: Wausau, Wisconsin

GREEN CHILE CAPITAL OF THE WORLD: Hatch, New Mexico

MELON CAPITAL OF THE WORLD: Rocky Ford, Colorado

MUSHROOM CAPITAL OF THE WORLD: Kennett Square, Pennsylvania

PINTO BEAN CAPITAL OF THE WORLD: Dove Creek, Colorado

RAISIN CAPITAL OF THE WORLD: Fresno, California

SPINACH CAPITAL OF THE WORLD: Alma, Arkansas

WINTER STRAWBERRY CAPITAL OF THE WORLD: Plant City, Florida

SWEET POTATO CAPITAL OF THE WORLD: Vardaman, Mississippi

SWISS CHEESE CAPITAL OF THE WORLD: Monroe, Wisconsin

WHEAT CAPITAL OF THE WORLD: Sumner County, Kansas

HENRI SOULÉ

The 1964 edition of *Hart's Guide to New York City* says this: "Henri Soulé has enjoyed a reputation as one of the great restaurateurs of our time. His fame has spread to the ends of the earth. You will be served superb viands at Le Pavillon, but you will pay heavily for the privilege. . . . What you buy here is not only top-quality food . . . but entrée into the vortex of the dazzling society which frequents this sanctum sanctorum. Le Pavillon's well-deserved reputation for gourmetry is undoubtedly perpetuated by its exclusivity."

Henri Soulé was legendary, one of those French restaurateurs who by their very existence made even wealthy Americans of the post–World War II period feel like rubes. To eat in Soulé's restaurant, Le Pavillon, was to be anointed with Continental sophistication, to be approved by the Old World, to be reassured that Americans were not the culinary *parvenus* we truly were back then.

Soulé's American journey began at the 1939 World's Fair in New York City, at the French Pavilion. At the time he was hired away to be general manager of Le Restaurant du Pavillon de France, he was the manager of the Café du Paris, a position he'd worked his way up to. He had been waiter, captain, and maître d'hôtel at restaurants in Paris and other parts of France, and he knew the food business inside and out. His American debut, the French Restaurant, as it came to be called, was a fantastic success. At the French Restaurant, summer fair-goers experienced the full majesty of French haute cuisine, the fabulous food and the elegant service.

A detour came next for Soulé —a trip home to France to join the army, and a return to New York to reopen the French Restaurant in 1940. It was not a good year; there was a war on, and the French Restaurant did not do well. Undiscouraged, Soulé and his staff finagled status as war refugees, and on October 15, 1941, Soulé opened the restaurant that was to be his life's work, Le Pavillon on East Fifty-fifth Street in Manhattan. From the very first night he attracted—commanded—the most socially prominent and glamorous clientele, to whom he fed the most sublime food.

Petty politics and temper tantrums are an integral part of the restaurant game. Soulé and his landlord (Harry Cohn, notoriously mean head of Columbia Pictures) fell out, and in 1957 Soulé moved Le Pavillon to East Fifty-seventh Street. When Cohn died, Soulé pounced on the old Le Pavillon space and in it he opened his second, equally famous eatery, La Côte Basque. Soulé, who had become an American citizen in 1946, died in 1966. Le Pavillon outlived him by only five years.

And Speaking of Food . . .

John Steinbeck, *The Grapes of Wrath*, 1939

It was crowded now. The strange children stood close to the stew pot, so close that Ma brushed them with her elbows as she worked. Tom and Uncle John stood beside her.

Ma said helplessly, "I dunno what to do. I got to feed the fambly. What'm I gonna do with these here?" The children stood stiffly and looked at her. Their faces were blank, rigid, and their eyes went mechanically from the pot to the tin plate she held. Their eyes followed the spoon from pot to plate, and when she passed the steaming plate up to Uncle John, their eyes followed it up. Uncle John dug his spoon into the stew, and the banked eyes rose up with the spoon. A piece of potato went into John's mouth and the banked eyes were on his face, watching to see how he would react. Would it be good? Would he like it?

And then Uncle John seemed to see them for the first time. He chewed slowly. "You take this here," he said to Tom. "I ain't hungry."

6 Great Paintings Depicting Delectable Food

Pies, Pies, Pies, Wayne Thiebaud (1961)

The Breakfast Room, Pierre Bonnard (ca. 1930–31)

Nature Morte (Ananas, Compotier, Fruits, Vase d'Anémones),
Henri Matisse (1925)

Still Life with Apples and a Pot of Primroses,
Paul Cézanne (ca. 1890)

Still Life, Marsden Hartley (1912)

The Picnic, Claude Monet (1865–66)

TIDBIT: French Impressionist painter Claude Monet had a reputation for the style and content of the meals served at his home in Giverny. Monet and his wife were devoted to good food and they planned meals carefully, using the freshest ingredients from their own garden and farmyard, and from local suppliers, too. Their dining room was golden yellow, and Monet designed dishes to match—yellow with a blue band. When the couple entertained, guests were invited for an 11:30 lunch; lateness was unacceptable, and shilly-shallying over the meal was discouraged too. Monet's painting schedule was rigid, and when lunch was over, he went right back to his work.

RATING THE LEGENDARY
MOBIL TRAVEL GUIDES

If you are a woman, one of the ways you judge an eating place is by the quality and cleanliness of the ladies' room. You may *forgive* a bad bathroom if the dining room is serving up fantastic food, but you'll never *forget* it. And your enthusiasm for the ribs at Bob's Boffo Barbecue will always be dampened by the prospect of a future visit to the horrible loo.

The Mobil Travel Guides do not give out one, two, three, four, or five restaurant stars lightly, if their long lists of per-star criteria can be believed, and bathrooms are definitely on all five lists. Hundreds of criteria are on the lists, and as a restaurant gains stars it must pass muster for all the previous levels as well: a four-star restaurant has to meet the inspection criteria for four stars, three stars, two stars, and one star.

When you use a Mobil guide to choose a restaurant, you put yourself in the hands, eyes, and mouths of the people who have made these reputedly elaborate inspections, because the guides themselves offer you few details in their explanations of the quality ratings or in their actual descriptions of the restaurants. For instance, "[three-star] restaurants are of national caliber, with professional and attentive service and a skilled chef in the kitchen." That's all the MTG for New York/New Jersey has to say about a three-star rating. And here's the descriptive part of the entry for Union Square Cafe, arguably one of the most beloved upscale restaurants in Manhattan, awarded three Mobil stars: "Italian, American menu . . . Contemporary Amer [sic] bistro." That's minimal to the point of withholding.

If you log onto the Web site (mobiltravelguide.com) to find out more about the "Restaurant Star Criteria & Expectations," you might think the collective mind behind the MTG is curiously bloodless and devoid of personality in its quest for true objectivity, but you'll also find it fascinating and rather endearing in its finickiness. These points are from the list of two-star criteria: "Cubed ice, not crushed, is served. . . . Staff uniforms are matching/coordinated. . . . Music system, if in use, consists of CD or equivalent and is interruption-free, not commercial radio. . . . Service is pleasant, competent and able to assist guest with beverage and menu selection." Nice.

This evaluation system works best, of course, if you try some of the MTG's recommendations and discover that you trust the assessments. It's like finding a movie critic you agree with: if she liked the film and you liked the film, she's reliable for you. Stick with her.

A Few American Food Moments from the 1980S and 1990S

1980: 3 billionth can of Spam sold

1981: USDA declares ketchup a vegetable; NutraSweet goes on the market

1985: Coca-Cola tries to replace the old formula with a sweeter one

1986: 4 billionth can of Spam sold

1987: Nabisco introduces Ritz Bits

1990: Kraft introduces Fat Free Singles; Hershey's introduces Kisses with Almonds

1991: Salsa outstrips ketchup as the nation's number-one condiment

1992: We welcome Spam Lite; Nutri-Grain bars introduced

1993: Hershey's Hugs debut; the Food Network starts up

1996: Olestra approved by the FDA for use in "savory snacks"

DUNCAN HINES

So Rich. So Moist. So Very Duncan Hines. That's the pitch for the Duncan Hines baking products, and it seems to suggest that the man has morphed into the product. It's doubtful that the real Duncan Hines was rich and moist, but he was Very Duncan Hines: uncompromising, exacting, and totally reliable. His chosen career was traveling the country, usually with his wife Florence, testing the food in restaurants and assessing the quality of hotels. He was the Mobil guide, Michelin guide, and Zagat's rolled into one, and he did it in the 1930s and 1940s, when this sort of thing just hadn't yet been done.

He and Florence kept detailed notebooks cataloguing all the places they dined in and slept in, critiquing the cleanliness (which was of primary importance to Hines), safety, and atmosphere, the excellence (or not) of the food, the service, and the value. He took no payment from any of the places he recommended, and because he was so squeaky-clean his credibility was unassailable. When he turned this pure, uncompromising research into newspaper columns and travel guides, he became *the* trusted name in the hospitality business. A recommen-

---

10 EASY CAKE DECORATIONS

fresh flowers

whole or sliced berries (strawberries, raspberries, blueberries)

glacé chestnuts

chopped or whole nuts (walnuts, pecans, pistachios, almonds, hazelnuts)

glacé cherries, apricots, oranges, pineapple

dollops of whipped cream topped with chocolate sprinkles

chocolate truffles or filled chocolates

marzipan fruits or animals

Jordan almonds

miniature nonpareils

---

dation by Duncan Hines was the most important selling point an establishment could have back then. It is not an overstatement to say that Duncan Hines changed America's hotel and restaurant expectations.

But a twist was coming: In 1949, public relations man Roy Park convinced the sixty-nine-year-old Hines that they should start a company to market a "Duncan Hines" line of food products. Within a short time stores were stocking over two hundred food products and fifty kitchen items bearing the Duncan Hines brand label. Today we're most familiar with the mixes for cakes, cookies, brownies, and muffins, but back in the 1950s there was Duncan Hines ice cream, sherbet, sauce, pickles, jelly, bread, and more. The travel expert had been eclipsed by the food purveyor. Eventually the brand was sold to Procter and Gamble; Aurora Foods is the newest owner, and they still get a lot of mileage out of the Duncan Hines reputation.

FOLLOWING THE RULES: FOOD AND RELIGION

There's no separating food from religion, any more than you can separate food from life. Religions, especially in their orthodox forms, have a lot to say about what may and may not (or should and shouldn't) be eaten by their adherents. Not only that, fasting is an integral part of many religions, yet another demonstration that food (or the renunciation of it) can play a major role in religion. Rules about food are complicated in any religion that *has* rules, and they can vary from sect to sect or even from country to country. Not every member of a religion will follow the rules, or a member may follow some and ignore others. There are so many religions and so many rules that it would be impossible to describe them all here.

Christians, in general, have fewer food rules than other major religions. Protestants generally have no rules dictating what they eat. Catholics may give up certain foods at Lent or fast on certain days or at certain times (before taking communion, for example). Mormons don't drink alcohol or caffeinated beverages. Many Seventh Day Adventists eat no meat or dairy products, while other Adventists follow a sort of lacto-ovo-vegetarian diet. And there are smaller Christian sects with their own sets of rules.

Jews who "keep kosher" follow the kosher laws, and there are a lot of them. The milk and meat of some animals (cows, sheep, and others that have split hooves and chew their cud) can be eaten; the meat of pigs, rabbits, squirrels, and certain others can't. Domestic chickens, ducks, turkeys, and some other fowl are kosher, while predatory and scavenger birds are not. (And mammals and birds must be slaughtered and prepared for cooking according to very strict rules.) Meat and dairy are never eaten at the same meal; in fact, separate sets of utensils and dishes are used for each, and a certain amount of time must pass between meat and dairy meals. Water creatures with fins and scales are kosher; no others (such as shellfish, swordfish, and catfish) are acceptable. All fruits, vegetables, and grains are kosher.

Devout Muslims eat only foods that are *halal*, or lawful. Fresh vegetables, legumes, grains, fish, honey, milk (from cows, sheep, camels, and goats), fresh and dried fruits, and certain other foods are halal. Some animals are halal (cows, sheep, chickens, and ducks, to name a few), but only if they're slaughtered according to Islamic rites. Unlawful, or *haram*, foods, such as pigs, carnivorous animals, and most reptiles and insects, are strictly forbidden.

Hindus are governed less by rules about food than by a concern with karma, the actions in life that bring good or bad results in this or the next life. Though Hindus don't eat beef (cows are sacred animals), what they do eat is more a matter of individual choice or tradition. Vegetarianism is advocated but not required. Anything—alcohol, for instance—that gets in the way of spiritual enlightenment is usually avoided too.

And Speaking of Food . . .

Rumer Godden, In This House of Brede, 1969

[On Maundy Thursday] the Abbess, following her Master's example, became the servant of the whole community, serving them at midday dinner. The sight of the refectory was inviting: each place was laid with a snow-white napkin, a glass of wine, a bunch of grapes, a small wheaten loaf, and a brown earthenware bowl of vegetable soup. Apricot puffs and cheese were laid along the side tables. When the nuns were seated, the Abbess came in, wearing a white apron and white sleeves, and with her came the kitchener, Sister Priscilla, bearing a great silver salver of fish. The Abbess went to every nun, serving her and laying beside her plate a nosegay of small flowers: violets, wood anemones, primulas, grape hyacinths, tiny ferns, pink heaths.

What to Eat for Easter Dinner

Easter dinner breaks the Lenten fast and, traditionally, celebrates spring.

leg or rack of lamb

stuffed breast of veal

baked ham

asparagus

new peas

green beans

new potatoes

baby spinach and mushroom salad

Parker House rolls

strawberry-rhubarb pie or crumble

chocolate-dipped strawberries

lemon meringue pie

cheesecake

coconut cake

carrot cake

What to Eat during Ramadan

During Ramadan Muslims fast during the daylight hours, so meals are very early in the morning and at night. At the end of Ramadan there's a three-day celebration and *lots* of food, but here are some choices for the evening meals during the time of fasting.

lentil soup

lamb and lentil soup

chicken

pasta with yogurt sauce

spiced vegetables

pickled vegetables

meat-stuffed tomatoes

baba ghanoush

tabbouleh

pita bread

HANUKKAH FEASTS

Hanukkah is the eight-day Jewish "Festival of Lights," which generally starts in December. It's a sort of David and Goliath story: the Greek-Syrian ruler Antiochus IV sought, with the backing of his mighty army, to force Greek culture upon the Jews of Judea, and to prevent them from carrying out their religious practices or studying their Torah. This small band of Jews (called the Maccabees after their leader, Judah Maccabee) defended their community, their religion, and their temple. After three years of fighting, the Maccabees triumphantly reclaimed the temple, but when they went to rededicate it, there was only enough holy oil to kindle the temple light for one day. Nonetheless, the miraculous light burned for eight. The Hanukkah menorah, or candelabrum, holds eight candles to symbolize those eight days of light, plus one extra for transferring the light from one candle to the next.

Hanukkah foods reflect the traditional story. Latkes, the beloved potato pancakes, are made with oil to symbolize the temple oil. A kind of jelly doughnut (called sufganiyot) cooked in oil is a Hanukkah specialty too. Dairy foods are customary at Hanukkah, particularly those made with cheese, and there's a grisly tale to explain the presence of the cheese: A Jewish girl named Judith determined to save her village from the Syrian attackers. She fed salty cheese to the Syrian general Holofernes, which made him so thirsty that he had to lubricate his dry throat with a lot of wine. When he fell over drunk, Judith grabbed his sword, cut off his head, and took it home to her village in a basket. Next day Holofernes' troops found his decapitated body—and fled in panic.

THE PASSOVER SEDER FOODS
And What They Mean

★ three whole matzohs: the unleavened "bread" is a reminder of the hasty departure of the Israelites from Egypt, when there was no time to wait for leavened bread to rise

★ bitter herbs (maror): horseradish is usually chosen to represent the bitter herbs, symbol of the bitterness of slavery

★ roasted lamb shankbone (zeroah): symbolic of the paschal lamb sacrificed at the temple in ancient times

★ green vegetable (karpas) and salt water: parsley is the usual choice, to represent spring, new life, and hope; salt water symbolizes the tears shed during slavery

★ mixture of apples, walnuts, wine, and cinnamon (charoset): represents the mortar used by the Jewish slaves when building for the Egyptians

★ roasted or boiled egg (beitzah): the traditional food of mourners, and also the symbol of life and the continuity of existence

★ four glasses of wine: represents God's fourfold promise of freedom and redemption

A CRÊPE IS A BLINTZ IS A PANCAKE

There's hardly a culture in the world that doesn't eat pancakes in some form. Thin or thick, plain or fancy, light or hearty, for breakfast, lunch, dinner, or dessert—everyone's got a version or two or three. Basically, a pancake is made by mixing up a batter, pouring it onto a hot griddle or skillet, and cooking it quickly on one or both sides. Most are then either topped with something, rolled up around a filling, or folded over a filling.

Americans love pancakes for breakfast, and we make them every which way. The basic batter can be made with plain flour, buckwheat flour, or cornmeal, with sweet milk, sour milk, buttermilk, sour cream, or yogurt. We stir all kinds of things into the batter for sweet pancakes—blueberries, strawberries, apples, banana slices, chocolate chips, chopped nuts. We make savory pancakes with corn kernels or rice, scallions, cheese, bacon bits, hot peppers. We make them round, heart-shaped, free-form, and silver-dollar-sized. We top them with syrup, honey, molasses, jam, jelly, fresh fruit.

But we eat a lot more kinds of pancakes than just the good old "American" pancake that dates back to colonial times, because we're a nation of immigrants and we've learned to love pancakes of all nations. We eat French crêpes (there are crêperies all over the country), Russian blinis (with sour cream and caviar), blintzes, latkes (potato pancakes), Austrian *palatschinken* and Hungarian *palacsinta*, puffy German pancakes, Swedish pancakes with lingonberries, crespelle from Italy, Chinese pancakes for moo shu pork, rice pancakes wrapped around spring roll fillings. There's just no stopping us where pancakes are concerned.

PANCAKE FACT: The first International House of Pancakes opened in California in 1958. There are now more than eleven hundred IHOPs across the United States and Canada.

KNOW YOUR OILS

Oils are liquid fats (a somewhat icky thought if you happen to be dieting, though not as icky as picturing pounds of solid fat like butter, lard, or Crisco). We can break them down, for practical cooking purposes, into four sorts: olive oil, neutral oils (canola, corn, safflower, sunflower, grapeseed, and a few others), flavorful oils (dark sesame, walnut, hazelnut), and peanut oil.

Olive oil is virtually all-purpose for cooking and absolutely essential for salad dressing. See page 167 for more info on the various kinds of olive oil. The fruitiest olive oils add pizzazz to most foods, and the lightest ones (in color and fragrance) are unobtrusive and can be used at high cooking temperatures.

Neutral oils are just that—neutral in flavor and perfectly good for high-temp cooking. They don't add any interest to food, but they don't detract, either.

The flavorful oils are best reserved for noncooking purposes: add them to salad dressings or, in the case of dark sesame oil, when you've turned off the heat (sesame oil has a low burning point) and want to contribute a rich sesame taste to your food. These oils are fragile and should be refrigerated after opening.

Peanut oil has a foot in each camp: it's fairly neutral, but it does impart a slight flavor that suits Asian cooking very well. In a pinch you can use it for most kinds of cooking, and it's great for Asian-inspired salad dressings.

KNOW YOUR VINEGARS

Commercial vinegar happens when yeast converts sugar to alcohol, and then bacteria converts the alcohol to acid, all under carefully controlled conditions. Vinegar is hardy stuff: it preserves itself unrefrigerated and lasts almost indefinitely. You may notice slight changes in color or some sediment or cloudiness in the bottle, but these are cosmetic issues—the vinegar is still good.

Most ambitious cooks have quite a variety of vinegars tucked away in the pantry: balsamic, white wine, red wine, sherry, rice, cider, and maybe a fruit or herb vinegar as well. Each tastes different from the others, according to whatever the starting material was (fruit, wine, grain, and so on) or whatever flavoring was added later (basil, garlic, tarragon, or raspberry, for instance). They have varying degrees of acidity, too, which yield a milder or sharper bite.

Balsamic vinegar, made from grapes, is either wildly expensive (if it's the real, aged, regulated item) or completely affordable. Taste different brands until you find a warm, rich, slightly sweet, slightly oaky flavor in a price range you can handle.

Wine vinegars (red, white, sherry, Champagne) should contain exactly that: wine, and nothing else. And a wine vinegar should put you at least vaguely in mind of the wine from which it was made.

Japanese and Chinese rice vinegars, essential for making Asian dishes, come in a variety of shades (pale gold, clear, black, and red) and flavors from mild to rich to sweetish to spicy. If you're adventurous, you may find yourself using these vinegars more and more often in non-Asian dishes.

Cider vinegar, fermented from apple cider, has a caramel color and a somewhat fruity taste. It's used most often for pickling and preserving.

KNOW YOUR SALAD GREENS

Let's get acquainted with, or at least reminded of, the possibilities: arugula; baby dandelion, turnip, or beet greens; Belgian endive; Bibb lettuce; Boston lettuce (butter, butterhead); cabbage (red, green, Savoy); chicory (curly endive); Chinese cabbage (celery cabbage, Napa); escarole; frisée; iceberg lettuce; leaf lettuce (or looseleaf lettuce, including red leaf, oak leaf, and green leaf); mâche (field lettuce, corn salad, lamb's lettuce); mizuna; radicchio; romaine lettuce (cos); spinach; watercress.

When you're choosing tight-leafed greens (Bibb, Boston, Belgian endive, cabbage, radicchio, and the like), look for firm, compact heads that seem heavy for their size. Loose-leafed greens (arugula, leaf lettuce, spinach, watercress, and so on) should be crisp and lively, never limp

FROM ARTICHOKE TO ZUCCHINI:
15 Specialty Food Festivals

Artichoke Festival, Castroville, California
World Catfish Festival, Belzoni, Mississippi
National Cherry Festival, Traverse City, Michigan
Hatch Chile Festival, Hatch, New Mexico
Sweet Corn Festival, Sun Prairie, Wisconsin
National Cornbread Festival, South Pittsburg, Tennessee
National Date Festival, Indio, California
Frog Leg Festival, Fellsmere, Florida
Gilroy Garlic Festival, Gilroy, California
Maine Lobster Festival, Rockland, Maine
Pecan Festival, Okmulgee, Oklahoma
Crystal Springs Tomato Festival, Crystal Springs, Mississippi
Vidalia Onion Festival, Vidalia, Georgia
Black Walnut Festival, Spencer, West Virginia
Zucchini Festival, Ludlow, Vermont

and droopy. Both types of greens should be free of wilted, bruised, or discolored leaves, and free of mushy brown spots or sliminess (including on the stem end).

The hot issue is how to store salad greens: Wash immediately or when you need them? Put them in an open or closed plastic bag? Tuck a paper towel in the bag or not? Every cookbook used to have a theory, and they differed like cats and dogs. Here's mine: Don't buy more than you need for the next four or five days. Wash greens when you need them—who wants to come home from the market and start washing lettuce? Use the fragile types (arugula, baby greens, dandelion or beet greens, spinach) first. Wrap each head in a couple of paper towels (to absorb moisture), stash in a plastic bag, close the bag, stuff into the already-overstuffed vegetable bin in your fridge. You will lose a few leaves, but that's just the nature of greens.

****

13 *Web Sites with General Information about Food*

food.oregonstate.edu

gourmetspot.com

epicurious.com (*go to the dictionary*)

switcheroo.com/FGDairy.html (*Cook's Thesaurus*)

www.food-info.net (*European, but interesting*)

Kashrut.com (*Kosher info*)

http://www.consumer.gov/food (*health, safety, nutrition*)

Pillsbury.com (*lots more than just flour and baking*)

foodreference.com (*terrific site*)

wholefoods.com (*excellent info*)

whatscookingamerica.net (*great site*)

www.hungrymonster.com (*then click on "food facts"*)

homecooking.about.com

****

HOW TO DRESS UP A SALAD

Start with a nice big bowl of bite-size greens, simple and basic, like a little black dress. Accessorize. Add the finishing touch. Toss well. *Voilà!* Something special.

★ L.A. salad: red leaf lettuce; cubed avocado, chopped hard-cooked egg, alfalfa sprouts, crumbled blue cheese; creamy vinaigrette

★ summer salad: leaves of baby lettuce; thin slices of ripe peach or nectarine, snipped chives; raspberry vinaigrette or creamy ginger dressing

★ Greek salad: romaine lettuce; diced cucumber, diced tomato, diced green pepper, sliced sweet onion, pitted black olives, crumbled feta cheese; oil, vinegar, salt, fresh pepper

★ spring salad: new lettuce (any kind); small whole sugar snap peas, fresh petite peas (raw or cooked); lemon-garlic dressing

★ another spring salad: baby Bibb lettuce; asparagus tips, artichoke hearts, sprinkling of toasted pine nuts; white wine vinaigrette

★ autumn salad: romaine, beet greens, finely shredded red cabbage; thin slices of apple, matchsticks of jícama; creamy herb dressing

★ winter salad: romaine, radicchio, frisée; chopped toasted walnuts, red onion rings, crisp bacon or cubes of pancetta; mustard vinaigrette

★ Italian salad: arugula, radicchio, tender inner leaves of escarole; cracked Sicilian olives, slivers of roasted red pepper, shavings of Parmesan; balsamic vinaigrette

★ Asian salad: watercress, baby spinach leaves; diced tofu, sautéed enoki or shiitake mushrooms; soy-ginger dressing

★ New York salad: Bibb lettuce; thin slices of almost-ripe pear, chopped toasted hazelnuts, crumbled Roquefort cheese; red wine vinaigrette

★ Tex-Mex salad: red leaf and green leaf lettuce; diced tomatoes, sliced pickled jalapeños, chopped fresh coriander; cumin vinaigrette or olive oil, fresh lime juice, and salt

★ San Fran salad: mesclun; sourdough croutons, shredded Monterey Jack cheese; garlic vinaigrette

HARDTACK, GROG, AND OTHER INEDIBLE SEAFARING FARE

Grog as we know it now is anything but inedible—or undrinkable, to be more accurate. It's a warming drink of rum, sugar or honey, boiling water, a slice of lemon or lime, and a few whole cloves or a cinnamon stick. In other words, a delicious hot toddy. But grog wasn't always so yummy. When Admiral Sir Edward Vernon, whose nickname was "Old Grog," saw in 1740 that sailors were getting too drunk on their small but unadulterated rum rations, he had the rum watered down: three parts water to one part rum. Efficiency aboard ship improved, and the drink was dubbed "grog" in his honor. Until that time, plain slimy water and sour beer had been the main quaffs, so even weakened rum was a major improvement. Later, sugar was added for taste and, after Dr. James Lind discovered the connection between scurvy and vitamin C deficiency, lime was added too. That made grog even tastier.

From the early 1800s, hardtack (also called ship biscuit, sea bread, sea biscuit, or pilot bread) was a staple food of sailors. It was a hard—very hard—square or rectangular cracker made of flour and water, and occasionally salt, but no shortening or yeast. In the hardtack factory, the crackers were baked first, then allowed to dry out even more to increase

WHAT TO SERVE AT A NEW ENGLAND CLAMBAKE

The important food at a real beach clambake is steamed in sand pits that are lined with hot rocks and topped with seaweed.

steamed lobster

steamed clams (soft-shell, cherrystone, littleneck)

steamed sweet potatoes

steamed sweet corn

drawn butter

potato salad

watermelon

And Speaking of Food . . .

Herman Melville, *Moby-Dick; or, The Whale*, 1851

It is upon record, that three centuries ago the tongue of the Right Whale was esteemed a great delicacy in France, and commanded large prices there. Also, that in Henry VIIIth's time, a certain cook of the court obtained a handsome reward for inventing an admirable sauce to be eaten with barbecued porpoises, which, you remember, are a species of whale. Porpoises, indeed, are to this day considered fine eating. The meat is made into balls about the size of billiard balls, and being well seasoned and spiced might be taken for turtle-balls or veal balls . . .

The fact is, that among his hunters at least, the whale would by all hands be considered a noble dish, were there not so much of him; but when you come to sit down before a meat-pie nearly one hundred feet long, it takes away your appetite.

---

their longevity on extended sea voyages. They were tasteless, tough enough to break teeth, and sailors had to eat a lot of them. Weevils shared the hardtack with the seamen too. Clearly, eating the crackers plain was the least desirable menu option, so they were often soaked in water or coffee, or crumbled (smashed, more likely) and fried with salt pork or bacon grease.

Sailors of the 1800s ate other things as well: bread, beef, pork, salt fish, fresh fish, peas and beans, cheese, potatoes, turnips, molasses, and oil. Rations weren't huge, and no one expected fine dining. There were, for example, some rather peculiar stews called lobscouse and daddyfunk. Lobscouse was a hash of meat, vegetables, and hardtack; daddyfunk was a mess of water-soaked hardtack baked with grease and molasses. You'll notice that fresh vegetables and fruits are nowhere to be found in the list of larder supplies. How could they be, with months at sea and no refrigeration? Getting ashore must have been a heady experience in every way.

HOW TO BUY FISH

Buying fish makes a lot of people very nervous. How do you know if it's fresh? What's it supposed to look and smell like? The first and most important rule is *buy from a reliable fish store or fish counter.* What's reliable? Cleanliness. No bad smells. Knowledgeable service. Rapid turnover—of the merchandise, not the help.

The second rule: If at all possible, buy fresh fish (no packaging) that you can see and smell and that's sitting neatly on a bed of ice. Whole fresh fish should have firm, resilient flesh: poke the flesh with your finger; it should spring back. The skin should be bright, the gills should be red or pink, and the eyes should be bright and clear. Really fresh fish does have a smell—a mild and pleasant one. Slime, gook, and brown spots are no-nos. When you get right down to it, the fish should look as if it's just been pulled from the water. Fresh fish fillets and steaks should look bright, clear, firm, and moist. Avoid pink, red, or brown spots that indicate bruising and spoilage. Again, sniff around for the right odor—a good one. Don't settle for inferior quality and do make a fuss if anyone tries to wave off your concern. Better yet, complain to the manager and don't buy your fish in that store again.

A wise shopper will make the fish market or counter the last stop before heading home, because fish (and other seafood) must be kept cold: once you've bought your fish, get it home and into the fridge ASAP. Cook and eat it that day.

FISH TIPS: Attractively prewrapped fish *may* be all right, but how will you know? Looks aren't everything, especially where fish are concerned. In general, try to avoid buying frozen fish, but definitely avoid frozen fish in damaged wrapping or frozen fish that smells bad or looks a little thawed.

Priscilla Goodmanners Tells It Like It Is:
WHAT TO DO IF YOU SPILL

Spilling food or drink in company is embarrassing. The moment your water glass goes flying, you forget that everyone, even Her Majesty the Queen, has spilled something sometime and usually at the worst possible moment.

Dealing with spills is simple: Make the least amount of fuss. Your impulse will be to moan, beat your breast, giggle, apologize profusely, burst into tears, or deliver a monologue on your habitual clumsiness. No. Wrong. That only embarrasses *everyone else*. Your job when you spill is to apologize *once* (okay, twice) in a quiet, heartfelt tone and—if you're visiting—get up and help the hosts mop up the mess. If, heaven forbid, you spill red wine, coffee, or anything equally dire on your host's pale green upholstery or white rug, you must immediately and firmly offer to pay for professional cleaning.

If you spill in a restaurant, make even less fuss, let the staff clean up, and thank them briefly. If your red wine has flowed across the table and dripped onto someone's lap, you must offer to pay for the dry cleaning and you must follow through. Friendships have foundered on less.

---

9 INTERESTING THINGS TO SERVE ON OR WITH GRILLED FISH

flavored butter	chutney	parsley or basil pesto
red or green salsa	horseradish sauce	tapenade
aioli	honey mustard	caper-anchovy sauce

HOW DO YOU EAT A LOBSTER?

With your bare hands and wearing a bib, of course, and with a stack of paper napkins nearby. Don't forget to grab your nutcracker and lobster pick. Now you're armed and ready.

Start with the claws: Twist them at the joint close to the body; they'll pop right off. Crack them here and there with the nutcracker, and then fork, suck, and pick out the meat.

Now work on the body: Twist the tail and body in opposite directions to separate them. Flip the tail over and cut through the soft side with a knife; split it open by hand and eat the meat. There are small bits of meat to be found in the body, so you might want to do a little scavenging there. Sucking the juice out of the skinny legs is fun too.

FOOD AT SEA:
What Does It Take to Stock the Queen Mary 2's Larder?

A lot. Each year the staff on the Queen Mary 2 will use up almost seven thousand boxes of strawberries, serve a million and a half drinks (excluding wine), and make enough tea to fill an Olympic-size swimming pool. On a six-night transatlantic crossing, the passengers on the QM2 will lay waste to the following, just to give a few impressive examples:

116 pounds of caviar
4,261 portions of marmalade
894 pounds of lobster
66,251 eggs
507 pounds of rack of lamb

Sear meat to seal in the juices.

Total myth. Just think about it: last time you carefully seared a piece of meat on both sides, got that nice crunchy brown crust, did it *really* keep the juices from seeping out? Of course not. Lots of beads of moisture formed on the seared brown surface; that was the juice escaping. The thin crust is delicious and aesthetically pleasing, but it doesn't seal a thing. Do it or not, as the spirit and your recipe move you.

8 KINDS OF WOOD FOR GRILLING

mesquite ★ hickory ★ apple ★ alder
cherry ★ pecan ★ oak ★ maple

16 MEATS AND FISHES FOR THE SUMMER GRILL

rib-eye steak	pork spare ribs	shrimp on skewers
flank steak	pork kebabs	scallops, ditto
butterflied leg of lamb	assorted sausages	whole fish (tricky— use fish basket)
loin lamb chops	chicken parts	fish steaks
lamb riblets	split Cornish hens	split lobsters
	soft-shell crabs	

BARTENDER'S CHECKLIST
(EXCLUDING ALCOHOL)

★ glassware

★ napkins

★ ice bucket and tongs

★ corkscrew

★ can and bottle openers

★ cocktail shaker

★ bar strainer

★ glass stirring rod or long spoon

★ muddler

★ shot glass (for measuring)

★ measuring spoons

★ club soda, tonic water

★ ginger ale, other sodas

★ fruit juices (cranberry, tomato, orange, grapefruit)

★ simple syrup

★ bitters

★ Worcestershire and Tabasco sauces

★ Rose's Lime Juice

★ lemons, limes

★ small green olives, cocktail onions

★ coarse salt, pepper

★ mint leaves

TYPICAL MENUS

The Edwardians

Though King Edward VII of Britain ascended the throne in 1901, his extravagant, self-indulgent lifestyle influenced English high society both before and after his mother, Queen Victoria, died. It's titillating to read a menu from a royal banquet or even a royal breakfast, and shocking to compare it to what ordinary working people ate. The gap between upper-class Brits and working-class Brits was huge in every respect, not least in the food they put on their tables.

Rich Edwardians ate meals of many courses (an ordinary dinner might consist of twelve!) and many dishes that were delicacies at the time: foie gras, asparagus, caviar, oysters, truffles, lobster, melon. And they put away huge amounts of more ordinary—but very British—fare: eggs, bacon, sausage, chicken, duck, lamb, mutton, beef, pork, rabbit, game birds (grouse, pheasant, woodcock, partridge, quail, and so on), haddock, turbot, salmon, sole, fresh vegetables and fruits from the kitchen gardens and home farms of their estates, luscious ice creams and ices, cakes, trifles, charlottes, puddings, tea cakes, and biscuits. And wine. And champagne. And chocolate. And more.

Listed on the next page are some of the dishes suggested for an autumn breakfast for twelve, from a book called *The Duchess of Duke Street*.

EARLY MEDIEVAL ANGLO-SAXON FOODS WE'D RECOGNIZE TODAY

beef, pork, mutton

chickens, geese, ducks

oysters, mussels, eels

salmon, herring, pike, perch

parsnips, peas, beans

onions, leeks

crab apples, plums, cherries

The book is based on the BBC television series of the same name, which was based on the life of Rosa Lewis, a famous cook and hotelier of the Edwardian era who was also, briefly, the king's mistress. The breakfast menu: partridges, roasted and glazed; Lyons sausage; pickled cockles; potted cold boiled beef; pheasant patties; marbled veal; canapés of sardines; oyster sausages; deviled turkey; ham toast; game puddings; polpettes of cold meat; bloaters; grouse; goose; terrine of hare; truffles; omelette of mushrooms; biscuits, marmalades, bonbons, and the usual accessories.

According to James Trager in *The Food Chronology*, by 1900 "[m]eat consumption among British working-class families has more than doubled since 1880, and consumption of butter and milk also shows a marked increase. The wages of Lancashire factory workers allow them a breakfast of coffee or tea, bread, bacon, and eggs (except when egg prices are too high), a dinner of potatoes and beef, an evening meal of tea, bread and butter, cheap vegetables and fish, and a light supper."

HIGH AND LOW NOTES: Trager also tells us that in 1897, for Queen Victoria's Diamond Jubilee, Auguste Escoffier, the most exalted chef in London, created a special dish: Cherries Jubilee. For the same occasion, Thomas Lipton, who had made a fortune in tea, contributed thousands of pounds to help feed hundreds of thousands of London's poor. This, one suspects, might have helped quell any rumblings of discontent during the lavish festivities.

11 FUSSY OLD EATING AND SERVING UTENSILS

pickle fork	cream soup spoon	bacon fork
strawberry fork	food pusher	lemon fork
ice cream fork	sugar sifter	olive spoon
five o'clock spoon		bon bon spoon

The Early Days of
DRIVE-IN RESTAURANTS

Legend has it that Mr. J. G. Kirby opened the first drive-in restaurant, a pork barbecue joint called the Pig Stand, in Dallas in 1921. Think about that: automobiles were rolling off the assembly lines, average Americans were newly in love with the driving experience—and they had to eat. Cars plus hunger equaled drive-in. Seems obvious, like many brilliant ideas.

Why drive-ins? Why not park your car outside and eat inside? There was the novelty of the drive-in concept, which can't be overestimated; Americans go for the new. Convenience, such as it was, must have been appealing too: you sat in your car, a girl or boy came and took your order (or you shouted it into a speaker), the food was delivered right to your car, and then you simply ate and drove home. It was an excursion for the family, and Mom didn't have to cook.

(Are you getting a glimmer of the imminent appearance of fast-food franchises? They were a twinkle in the eye of Ray Kroc in 1954, when he drove west to inspect a San Bernardino, California, hamburger stand owned by Dick and Mac McDonald.)

The design of drive-ins was unique: a central structure—usually, by the 1940s and '50s, with a large vertical neon sign sticking out of the roof and lots more neon in the windows and at roadside—surrounded or flanked by parking spaces. Cars nosed up to the main building and food was dispensed. Maybe Mr. Kirby, of the Pig Stand, was unconsciously influenced by the notion of a milk-swollen sow with her piglets nosing in for nourishment.

Teenagers were attracted to drive-ins like iron filings to magnets. They hung around for hours, often to the dismay of the managers or owners. Teens couldn't afford to eat or drink much, they were often rowdy (or just exuberant), and they sometimes scared away the families that made for more lucrative business. Moms and dads with little kids were uncomfortable with the atmosphere of a drive-in where teenagers were acting up or acting out. But teenagers loved lolling in, on, and around their jalopies, schmoozing and flirting, and they were hard to get rid of.

Drive-ins gradually morphed from exclusively "curb service" restaurants to restaurants that offered diners a choice of speedy indoor or in-the-car eating, a prediction of where the business was heading: the immense popularity of drive-ins was waning. By the late '50s, cars were just cars, and fast-food franchises were taking over where drive-ins left off.

TELL ME ABOUT...

HAMBURGERS

More than half the sandwiches Americans consume each week are hamburgers, a debt we owe to...whom? If anything in the food world is unclear, it's the true origin of the hamburger. Many have claimed, few have proved. There was the tenderized beefsteak served in the German city of Hamburg in the mid-1800s; the "hamburger" that appeared on Delmonico's restaurant menu ostensibly in 1834 but maybe in 1826; the hamburger offered by Ohioans Frank and Charles Menches at the Erie County Fair in Hamburg, New York, in the summer of 1885; the hamburger sold between two slices of bread by Seymour, Wisconsin (home of the Hamburger Hall of Fame), native Charlie Nagreen at the Outagamie County Fair in 1885; the hamburger recipe in *Mrs. Rorer's New Cook Book* in 1902; and the hamburger that showed up at the Louisiana Purchase Exposition in St. Louis, Missouri, in 1904.

Whose burger was the real "first burger"? My candidate is the hamburger made by Oscar Weber Bilby on July 4, 1891, on a farm west of Tulsa, Oklahoma. Grandpa Bilby's descendants claim he cooked his burgers on a coal-fired grill and served them up hot and juicy on Grandma Bilby's fresh yeast buns. Now, that's a burger to build a national obsession on.

PICNIC CHECKLIST
(EXCLUDING FOOD AND DRINK)

★ tablecloth or blanket

★ napkins

★ paper or plastic plates

★ paper or plastic cups, mugs

★ plastic or regular flatware

★ corkscrew

★ sharp knife

★ serving utensils

★ salt and pepper

★ sealable containers

★ resealable plastic bags

★ matches, fire starter

★ charcoal

★ grilling utensils, hot mitts

★ serving platters, bowls

★ garbage bags

★ paper towels

★ plastic wrap, aluminum foil

★ disposable wash-and-dry squares for sticky hands

★ cooler, freezer packs

10 Great Food Autobiographies

From My Mother's Kitchen: Recipes and Reminiscences, Mimi Sheraton

The Tummy Trilogy, Calvin Trillin

Kitchen Confidential: Adventures in the Culinary Underbelly, Anthony Bourdain

Tender at the Bone: Growing Up at the Table, Ruth Reichl

Waiting: The True Confessions of a Waitress, Debra Ginsberg

The Gastronomical Me, M. F. K. Fisher

French Lessons: Adventures with Knife, Fork, and Corkscrew, Peter Mayle

Pig Tails 'n Breadfruit: A Culinary Memoir, Austin Clarke

Delights and Prejudices, James Beard

Cooking for Mr. Latte: A Food Lover's Courtship, with Recipes, Amanda Hesser

---

15 RED FOODSTUFFS

strawberries	ketchup	corned beef
cherries	tomatoes	red potatoes
cranberries	radishes	chili
steak tartare	caviar	kidney beans
salsa	apples	red peppers

HOWARD JOHNSON

Howard Dearing Johnson (1896–1972), founder of the original Howard Johnson's restaurants and motor lodges, started in 1925 with a small drugstore and soda fountain in Wollaston, Massachusetts. He made great ice cream and he dreamed big. Johnson, like others, was convinced that cars and roads were the future of America. His goal was to put clean, reliable, standardized, family-friendly restaurants along the roadsides so that travelers would recognize them, feel comforted by their familiarity, know what to expect from them, and therefore flock to them.

He was right on target: in a 1930s and '40s world of unpredictability, sameness had value. If you're a little older than a baby boomer and you come from the East, you may remember the earliest HoJo restaurants with their bright orange roofs, on major highways. From Maine to Florida, at every HoJo's, you were going to get the same pretty good chicken pot pies, baked beans, turkey dinners. Sameness was safeness, and business boomed until World War II. Then, with gas and food rationing, it shrank almost to invisibility: only twelve restaurants remained in 1944.

After the war, conditions were once again perfect for a HoJo boom: Americans were buying new cars and suburban homes, having families, enjoying leisure, traveling again—and laying down a network of new highways along which HoJo's could build restaurants and motor lodges. If you're a genuine baby boomer, you'll remember the look-alike restaurants—colonial style, three dormer windows, cupola on the roof, Simple-Simon-Met-a-Pieman weather vane—and you'll surely remember the food: "frankforts" cooked in butter, fried clam strips, mac and cheese, tuna fish sandwiches, saltwater taffy, twenty-eight flavors of ice cream.

By 1954 there were over four hundred restaurants (both company-owned and franchised) in thirty-two states, and Mr. Johnson opened his first HoJo motor lodge. Families on vacation needed good accommodations, and so did the business travelers who were becoming an important part of the postwar economy. The HoJo motor lodges changed the hospitality industry by offering more standardization: clean rooms, modern bathrooms, air-conditioning, and even TVs. When the company went public in 1961 there were 605 restaurants and 88 motor lodges; by 1975 there were over 1,000 restaurants and over 500 motor lodges.

So have you noticed a HoJo's lately? Probably not. By the 1980s the ones that hadn't succumbed to the travel slowdown (remember the gasoline shortages of the 1970s?) had disappeared into the forest of all the other newer, faster, cheaper eating spots—such as Hot Shoppe, Denny's, Roy Rogers, McDonald's—that had proliferated along the expressways, in the malls, and in the commercial strips at highway interchanges. Along the Pennsylvania Turnpike, the HoJos became Burger Kings. But Big Business hasn't quite given up on Howard Johnson's; what's left of it has been sold from congomerate to conglomerate, a testament to the strength and endurance of the brand, which (if the past is any indication) may still have a future.

ICE CREAM NOTE: How many of HoJo's twenty-eight flavors of ice cream can you name? Here they are, in alphabetical order, just as they were listed on the wall menu back in the day: Banana, Black Raspberry, Burgundy Cherry, Butter Pecan, Buttercrunch, Butterscotch, Caramel Fudge, Chocolate, Chocolate Chip, Coconut, Coffee, Frozen Pudding, Fruit Salad, Fudge Ripple, Lemon Stick, Macaroon, Maple Walnut, Mocha Chip, Orange-Pineapple, Peach, Peanut Brittle, Pecan Brittle, Peppermint Stick, Pineapple, Pistachio, Strawberry, Strawberry Ripple, and Vanilla.

WHICH STATES HAVE THE MOST RESTAURANTS?

According to industry statistics of March 2004, the following ten states have the most eating and drinking spots.

California: 86,310	Florida: 39,027	New Jersey: 22,388
New York: 55,983	Pennsylvania: 31,628	Michigan: 22,188
Texas: 51,088	Illinois: 29,996	Georgia: 18,453
	Ohio: 27,112	

The Facts According to the Fast-food Franchisers

★ McDonald's has 30,000 restaurants in 119 countries, serving 47 million customers daily. And they add approximately 100 new franchises every year.

★ Burger King has a mere 11,220 restaurants in 61 countries.

★ Wendy's opened its 6,000th restaurant in October 2001, in Tijuana, Mexico.

★ Kentucky Fried Chicken has more than 11,000 restaurants in more than 80 countries and territories, serving nearly 8 million customers each day.

★ Krispy Kreme Doughnuts claims that it produces 7.5 million doughnuts daily and 2.7 billion annually. It has 390 stores in 45 states.

★ Domino's Pizza has more than 7,500 stores, 2,000 of them outside the United States. In the year 2000 their worldwide sales exceeded $3.5 billion, and in 2003 they delivered more than 400 million pizzas.

★ Hardee's has 2,400 restaurants in 32 states and 11 foreign countries. Wilber Hardee opened the first restaurant in Greenville, North Carolina, in 1960.

★ Subway has more than 21,000 restaurants in 75 countries and territories. As of the year 2003 their worldwide sales were $6.8 billion—$5.7 billion in the United States alone.

★ Taco Bell serves more than 35 million customers each week, in 6,500 restaurants in the United States. In 2003 they had sales of $5.4 billion.

★ Papa John's Pizza has nearly 3,000 restaurants in 49 states and 16 international markets. As of December 2003 they employed approximately 14,600 workers.

THE WHITMAN'S SAMPLER

For millions of lovers, Valentine's Day wouldn't be Valentine's Day without a Whitman's Sampler. That familiar red one-pound heart-shaped box full of chocolates is the very essence of romance. The rest of the year, the even more familiar rectangular yellow box with the printed cross-stitching and the tasting map in the lid speaks to us of love and devotion. Whitman's has been the mass-market chocolatier to America for over 160 years (the sampler box has been around for more than ninety), and it's still going strong. According to the folks at Russell Stover, current owner of Whitman's, someone buys a sampler box every 1.5 seconds.

It all started in Philadelphia in 1842, when a teenaged Stephen F. Whitman opened a candy shop near the waterfront. His chocolates were much admired for their flavor, freshness, and high-quality ingredients, but Whitman's real genius seems to have been his marketing skill: his packaging was especially attractive, and he spent plenty of money on advertising to let his customers know about his fine products.

Stephen's son Horace assumed leadership in 1888, and he was just as innovative as his father. The Whitmans were adamant about selling a product that offered (for that time) an out-of-the-ordinary combination of features: deliciousness, cleanliness, accessibility, and customer satisfaction. So Horace introduced the use of cellophane, a brand-new packaging material he had found in Europe, which gave a clean, crisp look to his chocolates. He and his new sales managers franchised their products only to better drugstores, and only to one per town. In 1911 the newest president of the company offered customers a money-back guarantee of satisfaction, a concept that was taken totally seriously by the company; they wanted to know what their customers liked, and they wanted to give it to them.

But the Big Moment came in 1912 with the introduction of the first Whitman's Sampler. The company labored long and hard to arrive at the right image for the top of that box: a subtle and beautifully designed play between the notions of a sampler of stitches and a sampler of chocolates, with all the appeal of the old-fashioned incorporated into the best of the then-modern. The proof came quickly: within three years the box had become Whitman's biggest seller and the nation's most popular box of chocolate.

The brilliance of the box design has been borne out. Over the years modifications have been made to it (a compartmented inner tray, a hinged lid, better liners, brighter colors, a fancy overhanging "French" edge, the elimination of the hinged lid, and so on), but the basic recognition factor remains—and remains beloved. People know and want a Whitman's Sampler when they see one.

The quality of Whitman's Sampler chocolates might not be up there with haute European brands, but it's not just the chocolate (or the box top) that wins and keeps customers. The Whitman's Sampler is a trigger for memories of the box you got or gave on Valentine's Day, the box you saw your dad give your mom, the box you bought yourself when you got the new job, the box your guests brought at Christmas, the box you sent to a soldier overseas, the boxes you saved and used for stashing buttons or crayons or picture postcards. The sampler box has continuity. It has tradition. It has history—its own and yours too. It's a constant in a world of change.

> **TIDBIT:** We can thank Mexico for both vanilla *and* chocolate. It's true: they're both native to our southern neighbor, were used extensively by the Aztecs, and were then introduced to the invading Europeans. The Aztecs also figured out that chocolate itself is greatly enhanced by the addition of vanilla, a culinary leap worthy of any great cuisine.

TRUE TALES OF THE DINNER TABLE:
LIMA BEANS

Peter Small, retired businessman

I was one of four siblings born in the 1920s and early 1930s. My father ruled the roost, and dinner didn't happen until he got home each evening. His arrival was anxiously anticipated by all of us. The family sat down together, with amazing aromas coming from behind the swinging door to the kitchen.

We had a lovely dining room, and a wonderful housekeeper-cook named Addie (her proper name was Angelina Butler Gaines), who wore a freshly starched white uniform to serve the meal. Our family wasn't big on religion, so "grace" was not part of the routine, but each of us got a chance to talk about our day, and the conversation was fast and without let-up for the hour or so we were at the table.

The meal usually started with soup and a lesson from our father on how to eat soup without slurping. You're not to suck the soup noisily off the spoon, he'd tell us, but tilt the spoon and silently pour it into

✳✳

10 Great Mail-order Food and Cooking Catalogs

chefscatalog.com

deandeluca.com

http://www.goldminenaturalfood.com/

http://www.shop.bakerscatalog.com/items/

ecookbooks.com (for the famous Jessica's Biscuit catalog)

kitchenkrafts.com (baking, candy, candy supplies)

penzeys.com (spices)

http://www.sweetc.com/

Zingermans.com

cookswares.com

✳✳

your mouth—something I never got the hang of and still don't believe can be done. Whenever I try this the soup pours all over my chin, so I guess I'll always be a slurper.

Addie would clear away the soup bowls (always from the right . . . the serving was always from the left) as my mother had trained her, and then bring in the main course, perhaps roast beef or leg of lamb or her special southern fried chicken. Addie was originally from Georgia, and she had nothing but contempt for what we called southern fried chicken. Hers was not dry and crispy, but moist, with a delicious creamy sauce. This, she said firmly, was the real southern fried chicken.

One evening the green vegetable of the night was lima beans, and they remained untouched on my plate. My father stopped Addie as she went to remove my plate.

"Please leave it until he finishes those lima beans," Dad told her.

"I can't eat them," I said, "I hate them!"

"You will eat them," said Dad, "and you won't leave the table until you do eat them."

So I sat staring at the damn lima beans for a couple of hours, and everyone else in the house went about their business silently, as if the lima bean impasse had stifled all sound. Eventually I was moved into the kitchen to sit staring at the lima beans some more, and when I thought no one could hear me, I dumped them into the garbage can. But good old Dad did hear me, and he ordered me to fish them out and eat them NOW. Which I did with much gagging and faked puking. Thank goodness most parents today are enlightened enough not to visit this kind of torture on their children.

TIDBIT: It's called a Hamdog, but the name doesn't do it justice. They serve this food phenom at a bar called Mulligan's, in Decatur, Georgia. Here it comes, the Hamdog: a hot dog wrapped in a beef patty that's deep-fried, blanketed with chili, cheese, and onions, topped with a fried egg and two handfuls of French fries, and served on a hoagie bun. Eat up, your ambulance awaits.

TYPICAL MENUS

Luncheon Then and Now

If you're meeting your friends for luncheon, you're probably a woman. Women have a long tradition of cozy, nonbusiness luncheons. You meet at a pleasant restaurant, eat lightly, have dessert even though you shouldn't, have a second glass of wine even though you shouldn't, and you discuss everyone's current issues for so long that you have to leave a very large tip for the waitperson. You kiss, kiss, kiss goodbye and stagger back to the office.

You may find this hard to believe, but women used to invite other women over to their homes for luncheon parties. It's true. They'd spend all morning preparing dainty (but not too dainty) dishes, set the table with the best china, arrange flowers, and entertain at luncheon. In the 1940s and '50s, everyone did it, even the president's wife.

James Beard, in the *Fireside Cook Book* (1949), suggests this menu for luncheon: avocado with fresh crabmeat and French dressing; eggs Florentine; popovers; watermelon. According to *Betty Crocker's Picture Cook Book* (1956), former first lady Bess Truman, wife of President Harry S. Truman, served this luncheon in her Independence, Missouri, home: chicken salad on tomato slices, garnished with watercress and olives; butter dips (a sort of biscuit); frozen lemon pie; coffee and tea. Mrs. Truman was a plain person; here's a fancier luncheon from the same period: individual cheese soufflés with crabmeat sauce; asparagus

---

BEYOND THE TOASTER:
12 SPECIAL-USE ELECTRIC KITCHEN APPLIANCES

ice cream maker	popcorn popper	food dehydrator
waffle iron	yogurt maker	iced tea maker
crêpe maker	quesadilla maker	pasta machine
meat grinder	electric cookie press	rice cooker

vinaigrette; melba toast; Mr. John's French Beret Pancake Dessert (mini-crêpes with jam); coffee. A much less chic luncheon: salmon au gratin, apple salad, and cake. Or Welsh rarebit, vegetable salad, fruit, and cookies.

And the 1975 edition of the *Joy of Cooking* offers no less than fifty-six luncheon menus—luncheons with meat, luncheons with fish, luncheons with eggs and cheese, and one-plate luncheons. Here's one menu: mushrooms stuffed with clams; puree of peas; Bibb lettuce salad with green goddess dressing; rolls; caramel custard with apricot-pineapple sauce. And another: jellied ham mousse; corn pudding; sliced fresh cucumbers and basil; brownies. A far cry from a grilled chicken Caesar and a diet soda.

12 POPULAR COOKBOOKS
of the 1940s and 1950s

1940: Hors D'Oeuvres and Canapes, James Beard

1940: 250 Classic Cake Recipes, Ruth Berolzheimer

1941: The American Woman's Cookbook

1941: Ann Batchelder's Own Cook Book

1947: Adventures in Good Cooking (Famous Recipes) and the Art of Carving in the Home, Duncan Hines

1947: Let's Cook It Right, Adelle Davis

1949: Antoinette Pope School Cookbook, Antoinette Pope and Francois Pope

1950: Betty Crocker's Picture Cookbook

1952: Ida Bailey Allen's Step by Step Picture Cookbook

1954: Alice B. Toklas Cookbook

1955: The Good Housekeeping Cookbook, Dorothy B. Marsh (editor)

1959: Farm Journal's Country Cookbook, Nell Nichols

LUNCH BOXES
THROUGH THE DECADES

Think about this if you're a baby boomer: Didn't you and every kid you knew have a rectangular metal lunch box with Hopalong Cassidy or Roy Rogers and Dale Evans smiling out from one side? No? Oh, then you had a lunch box with Superman or Howdy Doody or Davy Crockett or Mickey Mouse or a ponytailed bobby-soxer printed on it, right? Everyone had a lunch box, but the image you chose from the (then) limited possibilities was how you defined yourself.

The story of lunch boxes (or lunch kits, as they were called in the industry) after 1949 is a story of war—war between the companies that made them, war to come up with the pop culture images most

13 Very Popular Kids' Foods

raw cookie dough and cake batter

frosting left on the beaters and bowl

mac and cheese

Spaghetti-Os and canned ravioli

crunchy weird dry cereal with too much sugar and milk

chicken fingers

Sloppy Joes

noodle soup

Slurpees

ice cream cones and Popsicles

Jell-O with whipped topping

whatever their younger siblings are eating

whatever their older siblings are eating

likely to sell more and more lunch boxes. The 1950s choices were TV heroes, Disney cartoon characters, and the utterly uncool plaid pattern. In the '60s vinyl lunch boxes appeared alongside the metal ones, and the imagery included careers (space, law, athletics), TV cartoon characters (like the Flintstones and the Jetsons), TV stars (remember the Beverly Hillbillies? The crew of *Star Trek*?), girlie stuff (flowers, Barbie, Archie, and more ponytails), and the Beatles.

By the '70s there were so many pop icons in use that if your lunch box was your means of personal expression, you could get pretty specific. Or you could have a wardrobe of boxes: Peanuts characters, Muppets, rock groups, the Osmonds, athletic teams, TV shows and TV stars by the dozen, and loads more. Ditto for the '80s, with the addition of cutesy favorites like Care Bears and Cabbage Patch Kids. The list was long.

A strange note, but probably not a surprise to you nonboomers: There's an unvalidated story going around that metal lunch boxes were banned in Florida (and later in other states) in the early 1970s because children were whacking each other on the head with them. Whacking so hard that the Florida legislature supposedly called them "lethal weapons." And speaking of lethal weapons, the last metal lunch box that was produced (in 1985) carried a picture of Sly Stallone as—Rambo.

20 THINGS TO PUT IN A CARE PACKAGE FOR YOUR HARDWORKING, SNACK-STARVED COLLEGE KID

trail mix	crackers	instant hot cereal
mixed nuts	rice cakes	pop-top tuna and
dried fruit	cookies	pop-top pudding
energy bars	animal crackers	juice boxes
granola bars	microwave popcorn	chocolate mints
peanut butter cups	microwave soup	tea bags
peanut butter	microwave noodles	instant coffee

THE ORIGINAL IRON CHEF

Stumbling onto the original Japanese *Iron Chef* TV show on the Food Network was, for a lot of American viewers, both mystifying and fascinating. Japanese personality Takeshi Kaga came up with this Iron Chef idea and FujiTV put it on the air in Japan in 1993.

Described objectively: In every weekly show, one of four master chefs (dubbed Iron Chefs), each of whom specialized in a different cuisine (Japanese, Chinese, French, and Italian), engaged in a culinary contest with a non–Iron Chef challenger. The goal was to prepare a meal of several courses using that week's theme ingredient in each dish. A panel of judges tasted the food, commented, discussed, and awarded points. The chef whose dishes best expressed the theme ingredient—and tasted good too—got the most points and won the battle.

Described subjectively: In a large and confusing space (actually

A MOMENT OR TWO WITH...

SPAM

Spam is an incredibly popular food. Billions of cans have been sold since George A. Hormel and Company started making the stuff in 1937. Convenience and versatility were the selling points: you popped the chunk of gelatin-coated spiced ham out of the round-cornered can and used it for breakfast, lunch, or dinner. You could slice it, dice it, mince it, or cut it in a julienne; fry it, bake it, sauté it, or eat it without doing a thing to it. It required no refrigeration, so it made perfect rations for the GIs in World War II. In fact, Spam wasn't rationed during the war, so meat-starved Americans got very attached to it.

Today Spam Classic (yes, that's what they call it) is eaten all over the world, and it's been joined by low-salt Spam, hickory-smoked Spam, hot and spicy Spam, and a few more flavors, too. And if you're a true Spam fan, you can visit the 16,500-square-foot Spam Museum in Austin, Minnesota, to be, according to the Hormel Web site, "welcomed to the world of SPAM Family of Products [*sic*] with a variety of interactive and educational games, fun exhibits and remarkable video presentations." See you there.

chef's knife	measuring spoons	scissors
bread knife	rubber spatula	basting brush
paring knife	pancake turner	tongs
wooden spoons	wire whisk	oven thermometer
metal spoons	small strainer	timer
slotted spoon	lemon squeezer	easy-to-use
kitchen fork	vegetable peeler	can opener

called "Kitchen Stadium" by the producers) there were two elaborate kitchen setups. Each setup was occupied by a sweating, scowling, intensely focused chef and a pair of traumatized-looking assistants, all apparently attempting to cook something. Food flew around at breakneck speed, and it was almost impossible to figure out what was going on as the camera wove in and out within and between the setups. The job of the Liberace-costumed host, Chairman Kaga, and his subordinate commentators seemed to be to whip viewers into a frenzy of excitement about—what? Guys in whites cooking fancy food?

The theme ingredients (foie gras, shark fins, or truffles, for instance) were sometimes wildly extravagant, which added to the piquancy; the celebrity judges (rap star, businessman, politician, actor, baseball player) were sometimes wildly ignorant about food, which added to the strangeness. The finished dishes were often a stunning sight to see. The show could get very, very personal—there were tears, tantrums, terror, and triumph—and even if some of the acting out was real, it felt as fake as Monday-night wrestling. It was like watching a ten-ring circus crossed with a game show crossed with a class in advanced garnishing, in a foreign language.

The show ran in Japan for six years, with more than three hundred episodes. And then, in January 2005, Iron Chef America debuted on the Food Network, featuring Iron Chefs Bobby Flay and Mario Batali, among others. The Battle of the Ingredients began again, adrenaline running wild, egos on parade.

8 Specialized Utensils and What They Look Like

citrus juicer

pastry wheel

pastry blender

oyster/clam knife

zester

grapefruit knife

melon baller

meat tenderizer

KNOW YOUR POTS AND PANS

The first thing to know about pots and pans isn't about pots and pans. It's about who you are. What sort of pots and pans you buy (or request for your birthday or wedding) depends on who you are. If you set store by good looks, you'll want good-looking, high-end (expensive!) cookware. If you have weak wrists and arms, you'll want lighter-weight pots and pans (no cast iron for you). If you're always dieting, you'll want nonstick pans that cook well with very little (or no) oil. If you're saving your money for a trip to Tahiti, you'll want low-end (but serviceable) pots and pans. If you have no time for pot-scrubbing, you'll want easy-clean stainless steel.

Unless money and kitchen space are no objects, don't buy packaged sets of cookware out of which you'll use only one or two pieces. Don't be intimidated by salespeople who haven't a clue about what you

---

12 Pots and Pans Every Kitchen Should Have

small skillet (7 to 8 inches in diameter)

medium skillet (10 inches)

large skillet with lid (12 inches)

small saucepan with lid (2 to 3 cups)

medium saucepan with lid (1 to 1½ quarts)

large saucepan with lid (3 to 4 quarts)

pasta pot or stockpot with lid (8 quarts)

metal roaster pan

oven-safe glass or ceramic casserole

baking sheet (cookie sheet)

brownie pan (8 by 8 inches)

jelly-roll pan (10½ by 15½ inches, with 1-inch sides)

really need or who look down their noses at purchases of anything less than gourmet-quality cookware. Don't be seduced by cataloge photos of specialty pots and pans full of fabulous food that you're unlikely ever to cook.

New kinds of pot-and-pan materials are coming on the market all the time, but here are some guidelines for the classics:

★ Copper: expensive; great heat conductor; reactive with acid unless lined with stainless steel or tin; high maintenance; can be heavy

★ Clad: means stainless steel plus a base or core of copper or aluminum for excellent heat conductivity; can be expensive; nonreactive; low maintenance; a favorite of good cooks; can be heavy

★ Stainless steel: less expensive; poor heat conductor; nonreactive; low maintenance; lightweight

★ Cast iron: less expensive; excellent heat conductor; reactive; high maintenance; very heavy

★ Enameled cast iron: expensive; excellent heat conductor; nonreactive; low maintenance; very heavy

★ Stoneware: can be expensive; good heat conductor; nonreactive; low maintenance; heavy; limited uses (oven and microwave, but usually not stovetop)

★ Aluminum: less expensive to moderate; excellent heat conductor (look for higher gauges); reactive (unless anodized, which reduces reactivity); low maintenance; lightweight to heavy

★ Nonstick: less expensive to expensive; good heat conductor (anodized aluminum is often the base under the nonstick coating); nonreactive; low maintenance; lightweight to heavy

And Speaking of Food . . .

Robert Farrar Capon, *The Supper of the Lamb*, 1967

I despise recipes that promise results without work, or success without technique. I have eaten too many short-cut piecrusts to trust anyone who tells women that pastry made with oil is just as good as the "hard" kind. Mere facility, of course, is no more a guarantee of good taste in cooking than it is in music; but without it, nothing good is possible at all. Technique must be acquired, and, with technique, a love of the very processes of cooking. No artist can work simply for results; he must also *like* the work of getting them. . . . Interest in results never conquers boredom with process.

---

8 Hard-to-spell Foods and Beverages

How hard is it to spell *espresso* correctly? Pretty hard, evidently, since you see it spelled *expresso* at half the cafés in America. We can do better, can't we? Here's some help. Don't bother thanking me.

hors d'oeuvres

liqueur

cappuccino

pomegranate

zucchini

geoduck

broccoli

crème fraîche

261

POP QUIZ!

1. Egg creams, we all know, contain no eggs. What *do* they contain?
   A. chocolate syrup, milk, seltzer
   B. vanilla syrup, milk, seltzer
   C. chocolate syrup, cream, seltzer
   D. cocoa powder, milk, seltzer
   E. chocolate syrup, ice cream, seltzer

2. A potlatch is a
   A. lid for a pot, with flip-down fasteners to help retain heat
   B. lavish American Indian feast
   C. cast-iron trivet for hot foods
   D. kind of skillet bread popular in the Old West
   E. variation on Hungarian goulash

3. What is grappa?
   A. the topping on tortoni
   B. a kind of pasta shaped like a small bowtie
   C. a variety of Italian salami
   D. hazelnut-flavored Italian chocolate
   E. an Italian brandy

4. MSG stands for
   A. monosodium glycerin
   B. monosodium glyceride
   C. monosodium glucose
   D. monosodium glutamate
   E. monosodium glutinate

5. Adam's ale is a colloquial term for what?

6. What does the term *lamb's quarters* refer to?
   A. the haunch of a lamb, prepared for roasting
   B. a kind of wild greens
   C. a wildflower used in making a fragrant tea
   D. a New Zealand delicacy something like lamb stew
   E. none of the above

7. *True or false:* Bonzo bread was a Christmas specialty in the Reagan White House.

8. If you were consuming kolache, you would be
   A. having an appetizer
   B. using a soup spoon
   C. drinking from a tall glass
   D. snacking at coffee break
   E. detoxing your system

9. *Name that cuisine:* Where is chaurice used?

Answers: 1. a; 2. b; 3. e; 4. d; 5. water; 6. b; 7. false (it was monkey bread that Nancy Reagan served at Christmas); 8. d; 9. in the United States (it's a Cajun-Creole hot and spicy sausage).

262

A Few American Food Moments from the
1960s

1960: first Domino's Pizza opens, Detroit, Michigan

1961: Knopf publishes Julia Child's *Mastering the Art of French Cooking*; Charlie the Tuna is born; Coffee-mate nondairy creamer comes out

1962: Diet Rite Cola introduced nationwide

1963: *The French Chef* debuts on TV; Weight Watchers incorporates; Tab introduced

1964: Maxim, America's first freeze-dried coffee, goes on the market; so do Pop Tarts

1965: Diet Pepsi comes out

1966: Cool Whip, America's first nondairy topping, introduced; Doritos appear; Bac-Os do too

1968: Hershey's chocolate bar jumps from a nickel to a dime

1969: Tang goes to the moon on the Apollo mission

A Few American Food Moments from the
1970s

1970: Cocoa Pebbles appear

1971: first Starbucks opens in Seattle, Washington

1972: Snapple started by three New York guys selling all-natural juices; Stove Top stuffing mix introduced

1973: Cuisinart food processor goes on the market

1975: Miller Lite goes on the market

1976: Jelly Belly jelly beans born; Americans eat more than 50 billion hamburgers

BABY'S FIRST FOOD: ALL ABOUT BREAST MILK

Your government, in the shape of the Department of Health and Human Services, Office on Women's Health, recommends that for at least the first six months of life (preferably the first year) a baby should be fed on breast milk only. Here, straight from their Web site, are some of the benefits:

★ Breast milk has agents (called antibodies) in it to help protect infants from bacteria and viruses. Recent studies show that babies who are not exclusively breastfed for six months are more likely to develop a wide range of infectious diseases, including ear infections, diarrhea, and respiratory illnesses, and have more hospitalizations. Also, infants who are not breastfed have a 21 percent higher postneonatal infant mortality rate in the United States.

★ Some studies suggest that infants who are not breastfed have higher rates of sudden infant death syndrome (SIDS) in the first year of life, and higher rates of type 1 and type 2 diabetes, lymphoma, leukemia, Hodgkin's disease, being overweight and obese, high cholesterol, and asthma. More research in these areas is needed (American Academy of Pediatrics, 2005).

★ Babies who are not breastfed are sick more often and have more doctor's visits.

★ When you breastfeed, there are no bottles and nipples to sterilize. Unlike human milk straight from the breast, infant formula has a chance of being contaminated.

---

7 FOOD-RELATED ILLNESSES AND CONDITIONS

anorexia nervosa	night-eating syndrome	food allergies (most commonly to milk, eggs, peanuts, tree nuts, fish, shellfish, soy, wheat)
bulimia nervosa		
binge-eating disorder	gluten intolerance (celiac disease)	
lactose intolerance		

★ Breast milk is the most complete form of nutrition for infants. A mother's milk has just the right amount of fat, sugar, water, and protein needed for a baby's growth and development. Most babies find it easier to digest breast milk than they do formula.

★ As a result, breastfed infants grow exactly the way they should. They tend to gain less unnecessary weight and to be leaner. This may result in being less overweight later in life.

★ Premature babies do better when breastfed compared to premature babies who are fed formula.

★ Breastfed babies score slightly higher on IQ tests, especially babies who were born prematurely.

★ Nursing uses up extra calories, making it easier to lose the pounds of pregnancy.

★ Breastfeeding makes your life easier. It saves time and money. You do not have to purchase, measure, and mix formula. There are no bottles to warm in the middle of the night!

★ A mother can give her baby immediate satisfaction by providing her breast milk when her baby is hungry.

★ Breastfeeding requires a mother to take some quiet relaxed time for herself and her baby.

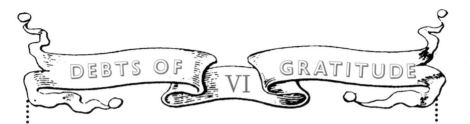

CARL SONTHEIMER (1914–1998), an American engineer, designed the Cuisinart food processor and got it onto the market in 1973. He adapted it from an industrial-grade blender, and it revolutionized home cooking. With a Cuisinart even a novice could chop, slice, grind, blend, grate, knead, cream, and do other previously difficult, time-consuming cooking chores like a pro.

In 1927 Nebraskan **EDWIN E. PERKINS** invented Kool-Aid. It's Nebraska's official soft drink, and more than 563 million gallons are slugged down worldwide each year.

SYLVAN GOLDMAN (1898–1984) invented the supermarket shopping cart in 1936. Up to then the (mostly female) customers at his chain of markets lugged heavy shopping baskets around the stores. The newfangled carts were a hard sell, though, and to accustom his wary customers to progress, Goldman hired ringers to shop the aisles, demonstrating by example the proper use and amazing ease of the shopping cart.

TOM CARVEL (1908–1990) invented the recipe (in 1936) and then the machine (in 1939) for making the first soft-serve ice cream. He turned his inventions and his business acumen into a chain of Carvel ice cream store franchises and went right on inventing products (the Flying Saucer, Lo-Yo frozen yogurt, Thinny-Thin diet dessert) and expanding his empire. He trained his new franchisees at the Carvel College of Ice Cream Knowledge; the franchisees called it Sundae School.

TRUE TALES OF THE DINNER TABLE:
MY ISSEI MOTHER

Grace Shibata, wife and mother

Mother loved the outdoors and the sea and made the most of it whenever she could spare time from the farm. She watched the tide by the position of the moon. Whenever it was close to full moon, the tide low, she would urge Father to drive us out to Pismo Beach for clams, or, more often, to Pecho for abalone hunting. Mother took four or five sacks and tire wrenches to pry the mollusks from the rocks. With our trousers rolled up, we scrambled down the craggy hillside to the rocky beach below. Carefully stepping from one slippery, seaweed-covered rock to another, we'd peer under a large boulder to find abalone, always with one eye to the oncoming wave. Mother was always quickest to find her limit of five abalone. Then she would come to help us find ours, we meanwhile having been more interested in playing than looking for abalone. We also found among the tide pools crabs, mussels, small black sea snails, and sea urchins. Mother would boil these in a huge pot as soon as we returned home. Eating these delicious morsels capped our day.

Masaji, our brother, used to hunt for rabbit, duck, and quail at the farm, which contained a five-acre lake surrounded by lush pampas grass. Some of the best lunches Mother packed for us included roast quail with *onagiri* (rice balls). When Masaji had luck hunting, he brought down mallard ducks or sea brant geese and, occasionally, a Canadian goose. While dressing the wild game or fish, my mother

---

10 GREAT FILMS ABOUT FOOD

Babette's Feast	Eat, Drink, Man, Woman	Chocolat
Big Night	Tampopo	What's Cooking?
Like Water for Chocolate	Mostly Martha	Tortilla Soup
	Life Is Sweet	

9 FOOD WORDS THAT ALSO MEAN "MONEY"

dough	bread	beans
cabbage	kale	peanuts
lettuce	sugar	gravy

would explain the anatomy of the carcass to us.

Mother loved to go mushroom hunting. She found small mushrooms, firm and white, in the willow forest, or *kashi naba* (oak tree mushrooms) under large oak trees surrounded by peat moss about a foot deep. She also picked mushrooms from pastures, miraculously never poisonous ones. How she knew the difference remains a mystery to me. I used to watch her put a dime into whatever pot the mushroom was cooking in, to see if it would turn black, but in later years I learned that this was not an accurate test of toxicity.

Once a week we went shopping, usually on Saturdays when Father was available to drive. This was a big day, going into "town," and we all had something on the list. Grocery shopping came last so the food would not spoil in the car. The best part was at the end, when Father would say, "*Orai,* [all right], everybody finish?" And Mother would say, "*Hai,* Papa. Ice cream *wa doh?*" That was music to my ears, for I knew Father would say with a grin, "*Orai, orai.*" Our heads poking out the window, we eagerly watched Father come out of the ice cream parlor with six vanilla cones stuck firmly in a cardboard container. They dripped a little on the side, softening the white paper napkins wrapped around them. Mother beamed as she looked at our happy faces.

THE JAPANESE TEA CEREMONY

The Japanese tea ceremony is a solemn rite of preparing, serving, and drinking green tea. It is called either chanoyu, sado, or chado. Its formal practice is attributed to a sixteenth-century Zen master named Sen No Rikkyu, who shaped it into a ritual of simplicity, humility, and self-cultivation. The tea ceremony takes place in a special venue, either a teahouse built specially for the purpose or a room specifically designated and arranged for the purpose. The space is furnished simply, with tatamis on the floor, a flower arrangement in the Japanese style, a calligraphy scroll on the wall. No more than five guests participate with the host. The ceremony is a performance of ritualized steps offered in a calm, unhurried, graceful manner.

The procedure for the actual making and drinking of the green tea is roughly this: The guests are escorted to the teahouse or tearoom. The guests remove their shoes, enter, and kneel on the tatami, facing the kettle on the hearth. The host enters, arranges the tea utensils, cleans them ritually, and silently begins to prepare the green tea. A bamboo whisk is used to mix green tea powder with water in a special tea bowl. The bowl is passed to the first guest, who sips, wipes the edge of the bowl where his mouth has touched, and passes the bowl to the next guest. When all the guests have tasted the tea, the bowl is returned to the host, who rinses it and the other utensils. The guests then examine and admire the utensils reverently. The host collects the utensils, the guests leave, and the ceremony is over.

To an outsider the tea ceremony might seem rigid and stiff, though

12 KINDS OF TEA FROM TEA SHRUBS

Assam	Keemun	Yunnan
Darjeeling	Sencha	Nilgiri
Ceylon	Formosa oolong	gunpowder
Earl Grey	Lapsang souchong	bancha

chamomile	spearmint	hibiscus
peppermint	alfalfa	birch
rosehip	persimmon	linden flower
sassafras	licorice	yerba mate

it would be more accurately described as having carefully defined structure and prescribed goals. The goals themselves—harmony, respect, purity, and peace of mind or serenity—have immense scope, but the path to the goals, the path of the tea ceremony, is focused, systematic, and formal. The purpose of the tea ceremony—to be in the moment, to appreciate both the anticipated and the unanticipated, to find tranquility—is large; its method for achieving that purpose has been honed down to the most basic actions.

Though the ceremony is so defined, there is room for individuality in the choice of the particular scroll, the choice of the water jar, tea caddy, and other tea utensils. The host chooses these objects with great care, and the good guest will compliment the host's choices with sincerity. The good guest will always behave according to proper tea ceremony etiquette, speaking or keeping silent at the appropriate times, drinking and eating what is offered. The good guest will give himself over to the experience that has been so carefully planned and prepared for him, and after several days will call or write to the host to thank him for the experience.

ALL ABOUT CHUTNEY

We are told, in a cookbook called *Cooking the Indian Way*, published in India in 1962, "Chutneys . . . form an accompaniment to the main courses of a meal, but, unlike raitas and salads, are eaten in a small quantity, to add just a slight touch of piquancy. The most popular chutneys in India are freshly made of onion or coriander leaves or fresh mint."

This charming little book then offers recipes for about twenty traditional chutneys, including apple, tomato, coconut, mango, sultana (raisin), date, plum, mint, onion, and coriander. Most contain green chiles (spelled an Indian way, *chillies*) or chile powder, garlic, ginger, vinegar, salt, and spices in combinations that appear simple but yield a complex whole much greater than the sum of the parts. Some chutneys are chunky, others are smooth; some are cooked, others are not. All are meant to be prepared fresh, in small amounts, to eat immediately with the meal for which they are designed. This is still the general approach to chutney in India: make it fresh, using local fruits or vegetables and the best spices and vinegar.

Chutney can be sweet, hot, or sweet-hot, but in America we usually opt for a sweet-hot, spicy, thick, jamlike mixture. We like cranberry, rhubarb, beet, peach, pear, and fig chutneys in addition to the traditional kinds, and we slather our chutney on turkey sandwiches or spoon it onto cheese and crackers. But we aren't too eager to make chutney. It's a proven fact that inside every fridge door in the United States there is, among the jars of mustard and cocktail onions, at least one half-eaten jar of store-bought mango chutney.

15 THAI FOOD INGREDIENTS

nam pla (fish sauce)	coconut, coconut milk	mint
ginger	kaffir limes	coriander
lemon grass	shrimp paste	turmeric
palm sugar	chile paste	bird's eye chiles
tamarind	Thai basil	rice flour

INDIAN BREADS

Though there are many varieties of Indian breads, they do fall into five main categories: chapati, roti, paratha, poori (or puri), and naan. These are the names you'll usually see on the menu in an Indian restaurant, and they can get a little confusing. Interestingly, these are all flatbreads, and they're mostly cooked on a hot griddle or baked in a clay oven called a tandoor.

Chapatis are rather like flour tortillas—unleavened rounds made of whole-wheat flour and water kneaded into dough. Some variations have butter or ghee (a kind of clarified butter) worked into the dough too. Egg- or golf ball–sized pieces of the dough are patted or rolled out very thin and then cooked on both sides on a very hot griddle just until brown spots appear.

Rotis are basically chapatis, but some cooks (or restaurants) make them a bit thicker and coarser than chapatis. Each roti is held over an open flame for a few seconds, and whoosh! it puffs up like an air-filled pillow.

Parathas are unleavened, round, thin, made of whole-wheat flour dough, and cooked on a griddle—but here's what makes them different: they're tender and flaky. A ball of dough is rolled out, brushed with ghee or oil, then folded in half (like a half moon), brushed with more ghee or oil, and folded over into a quarter circle. It's rolled out once again to make a wedge-shaped piece of layered dough (similar to puff pastry) and then cooked on a hot griddle.

Pooris are also unleavened, round, and thin, but they're made of dough a little drier than chapati dough. They are smaller than chapatis, and they're deep-fried one at a time until they puff up and turn golden.

Naan, unlike the other breads, is leavened with a small amount of yeast. The dough is often made with white flour instead of whole-wheat flour, and it usually has some yogurt, too. The balls of naan dough are patted into teardrop or oval shapes and baked in a tandoor until puffed and brown.

SOUL FOOD

In the early 1960s, when the American civil rights movement was in the ascendancy, African Americans began to use the word soul: soul man, soul sister, soul brother, soul music—and soul food. The term soul food caught on in the mainstream culture and came to mean the dishes traditionally eaten by black Americans in the South: a passionately expressive new name for a very well established style of cooking. Soul food conjured up a vision of home and community, culture and history, creativity and invention—tasty, rich, satisfying food that nourished not just the body but the soul.

This culinary style evolved during the years of slavery, when black plantation workers cooked for their white masters. African cuisine met southern ingredients and palates and produced (or improved on) many of the dishes we think of as southern food: fried chicken, sweet potato pie, corn bread, biscuits, pecan pie, country ham, candied yams, fried okra, black-eyed peas, and dozens more. But slaves did not eat the foods their owners ate. For their own meals they were reduced to using the meat scraps and leftover fish from the master's  kitchen, the vegetable discards such as turnip or beet tops, wild game, wild greens (such as pokeweed, cress, and mustard), nuts and beans, lard and skin from slaughtered hogs, as well as the rations of molasses and cornmeal they were allotted weekly. Everything that could be used was used, from "pot likker" (the liquid in which vegetables had been boiled) to stale bread to the parts of the pig that the masters rejected.

After Emancipation, parallel cuisines continued to exist: one for the rich and another for the poor. Former slaves could only afford to buy the cheapest meat and bones, eat the chickens they raised, use garden stuff that grew easily and without too much time-consuming care, catch catfish and porgies and other fish and shellfish, forage for wild plants and fruits. Rice, beans, white and sweet potatoes, grits, and cornmeal were their starchy staples. As decades went by, more overlap developed between the two cuisines. Blacks were hired to cook in white homes and restaurants and introduced certain dishes into the white cuisine; blacks took recipes away from their white employers and added them to their own repertoires. The lines between African American cooking and white southern cooking sometimes blurred, and for a very long time the term *southern food* encompassed both cuisines—until the term *soul food* made food historians pay attention to (and take seriously) the political events and sociological conditions that had produced the differences between the two.

Here's a mouthwatering list of some dishes commonly claimed as soul food, though some of them are still thought of equally as southern food and some of them are so much a part of American cooking that no labels really apply: buttermilk biscuits; crackling corn bread; barbecued pork; barbecued short ribs; smothered chicken; fried chicken; chicken livers and onions; pickled pigs' feet; hog head cheese; crab cakes; fried catfish and other fish (dredged in seasoned cornmeal or corn bread crumbs); chitterlings (or chitlins); chicken-fried steak; fried breaded pork chops; hush puppies; black-eyed peas; red rice; lima beans and butter; fried okra; stewed okra and tomatoes; fried cabbage; cole slaw; collard, kale, mustard, turnip, and other greens; boiled string beans with ham; potato salad; candied yams (actually sweet potatoes); sweet potato pie; peach cobbler.

TIDBIT: Southerners may claim hominy grits for their own, but grits didn't originate below the Mason-Dixon Line. Northeastern American Indians introduced the first European colonists to the dried, hulled corn kernels we call hominy, which was ground into what we call hominy grits, little bitty bits of corn. Grits come in coarse, medium, and fine grinds—but take care: grind a little too fine and you have cornmeal. Northerners never really took to grits; grits had to migrate south to be incorporated into soul and southern food alike.

Hard-to-pronounce Foods and How to Pronounce Them

Is there anything more embarrassing than ordering something in a restaurant and having the waiter parrot your order back to you using the correct pronunciation? Spilling red wine all over your mother-in-law's white dress might be worse, but sounding like an ignoramus is bad enough. Here's some help.

BROCCOLI RAAB: Broccoli you already know how to pronounce. Now say aaahhh! That's how the double *a* in *raab* is pronounced.

AIOLI: Simple. I. Oh. Lee. With the emphasis on *oh*. I-**oh**-lee.

ENDIVE: Is it en-dive or on-deeve? Take your pick, but if you're feeling French around the edges, say **on**-deeve.

JALAPEÑO: Don't you hate hearing hal-a-**pee**-no when we all know it should be hal-a-**pay**-nyo? Hey, it's Spanish, not English.

PAELLA: This is Spanish too. Say pah-**ay**-a, pronouncing the *ay* like the *ay* in *day*.

BRUSCHETTA: Please, not broo-shetta. This is Italian, and in Italian the *sch* is pronounced like sk. Broo-**sket**-ta. (And don't forget to roll that r.)

TARTE TATIN: Oo, la, la. The French pronounce it tart tah-**tan**, without quite finishing the n. But you most definitely will finish this delicious apple pastry.

KNOW YOUR DARK LEAFY GREENS

Kale, collards, mustard greens, chard (or Swiss chard), beet greens, turnip greens, dandelion greens, escarole, and spinach are the usual suspects. These leaves vary from blue-green kale to bright green, purple-veined beet greens, but in all cases look for rich color.

Kale and collards should have fresh, crisp, strong leaves—no limpness or withering. Avoid yellowed, brown-edged, or bruised leaves, and stems that are dry or woody. When you prep them, strip leaves away from the stems and thick center ribs; discard stems and ribs that are thicker than about one-eighth inch.

Chard, escarole, and spinach should also look perky and crisp, with no limp, brown, or slimy leaves. Trim the stem ends of chard and escarole—just chop off the bottom inch or so of the whole head. You may want to do the same with bunched spinach or you may want to nip each spinach leaf off its stem. If you buy packaged spinach, pick over it carefully; it's likely to have some rotten leaves stuck in there with the good ones.

Mustard, beet, turnip, and dandelion greens are best when young and on the small side; they should have a tender look about them. Avoid bunches with brown or yellow patches on the leaves.

Store dark leafy greens *unwashed* in plastic bags in the fridge. When you're ready to use them, wash really well (they can be quite sandy and dirty) and spin dry in a salad spinner or pat dry on paper towels.

---

10 OF THE MOST POPULAR VEGETABLES IN AMERICA

potatoes	onions	broccoli
iceberg lettuce	carrots	green cabbage
tomatoes	celery	cucumbers
	corn	

IT AIN'T EASY EATING GREENS!

Omar Morales, teenager

My entire life, I've never eaten vegetables. Well, I do eat potatoes and corn, just no dead leaves. My mother used to offer me salad, but I'd refuse. I would never eat anything that's green, except when I ate chicken soup or ordered Chinese rice. Then I couldn't avoid the little pieces already in there.

Mainly I love eating meat, like chicken, hot dogs, McDonald's, and sometimes canned meat like Spam. But whenever I see something green, automatically my mind tells me, "No, don't eat that, you don't need that, stay away from that." To me it's not a big deal. But when my editor heard about my diet, she was shocked. So she suggested I go home and cook something with vegetables in it and see what I thought.

The first thing I did was go to a library to check out some cookbooks. A lot of the books were complicated and had ingredients I didn't like. Finally I picked out a book by Dom DeLuise called *Eat This . . . It'll Make You Feel Better!* When I got back to the office I started to go through the vegetable section. I didn't like a lot of what I read. There was one recipe called "My Sister Anne's String Beans" that contained string beans and a cup of grated cheese. I don't like anything that has to do with cheese except pizza. And I didn't even know what grated cheese was, so I wasn't going to bother with that.

The one recipe that I was kind of interested in was "Mamma's Spinach and Potatoes in Broth." That first thing I saw in the ingredients was one cup of chicken broth. I didn't know what broth was, but I knew it would be good if it had chicken in it. That's when I began to get hungry. It also had potatoes. Potatoes I could trust because I've been eating them since I was little and I never really considered them part of the vegetable family. The other main ingredient was spinach, which I remembered eating when I was a baby, so I figured it was safe.

One Sunday, I decided to cook this recipe. Instead of canned chicken broth, which is liquid that tastes like chicken, I used chicken-flavored cubes that I had to dissolve in hot water. Then came the garlic. We already had garlic all cut up in a jar, so I just had to fry it with a little olive oil in a saucepan. Then I put the frozen spinach in the pan along with the chicken broth. As the spinach was breaking down into a soupy mixture, I started peeling the potatoes. I peeled five potatoes instead of four so there could be enough. Then I cut each one in four pieces and boiled them in with everything else. As it was cooking, I kept smelling it, because the aroma was so good. Then I covered it and let everything cook for fifteen minutes.

Soon it was done. Then my mom fried some chicken and we were ready to eat. "So I'm really going to eat this now," I thought to myself. Even though it smelled so good, when it actually came to eating it, I was worried. But my mom took a bite.

"It's good," she said, "not bad."

Then I took a bite. I thought it was good too.

Then my aunt came and visited for a while. She sat down and ate the meal and also liked it. I began to think eating vegetables wasn't so bad after all.

I haven't eaten too many vegetables since then. But I think maybe I'll try to in the future. After all, if I can drink something that has a bunch of small dead organisms floating in it like water, then I can eat something that's clean and fresh like broccoli and spinach.

✳✳

8 Web Sites for Finding Cooking Software

http://www.beryls.com (baking)

cyber-kitchen.com

ezgoal.com/channels/family (go to "Food and Cooking")

gourmetsleuth.com

tomdownload.com/home_education/food_beverage

eopinions.com/Home_Lifestyle_Applications-Food_Drink

bestcookingsites.com/cooking_software.htm

wsgoodcooking.com

✳✳

20 Terrific Dishes to Bring to a Warm-weather Potluck Supper

★ potato salad

★ pasta salad

★ sesame noodles

★ couscous (or bulghur, barley, rice, or wild rice) with vegetables

★ green bean salad

★ fresh corn salad

★ lentil or bean salad

★ Caesar salad

★ roasted vegetables

★ ratatouille or caponata

★ chicken wings

★ sausage and peppers

★ pork ribs

★ ham loaf or meat loaf

★ biscuits, cornbread

★ bar cookies

★ pound cake

★ fruit pie or tart

★ fruit cobbler

★ fruit salad

EUELL GIBBONS

Wild food isn't something most of us hunt for beyond the odd hand-ful of wild oregano we can pluck in a sunny summer field. But there are people whose greatest joy is stalking the woods, fields, streams, and roadsides for delicacies the rest of us wouldn't even recognize. Roots, berries, nuts, herbs, mushrooms, fiddleheads, milkweed, cattails—to an experienced forager the available variety is astonishing. That was Euell Gibbons's life work: searching out the wild foods that are invisi-ble to the untrained eye, and sharing his expertise with others.

Born in Texas in 1911, growing up in the dust bowl of New Mexico, Gibbons began foraging (so legend has it) to feed his mother and siblings when his father left to look for work. Between that time and the time he finally settled down in rural Pennsylvania in 1963, he lived in many states and practiced many trades, from carpentry to cot-ton-picking. Along his winding way he foraged and learned, asked peo-ple about the wild foods they collected, researched wild foods in libraries, and constantly experimented with preparing the wild stuff in new and delicious ways. His life was a nonfiction book waiting to be written, but Gibbons yearned to write fiction.

When he and his wife moved onto their land in Snyder County,

7 POPULAR COOKBOOKS
of the 1960s

1961: Mastering the Art of French Cooking, Volume 1, Julia Child, Louisette Bertholle, and Simone Beck

1961: The New York Times Cookbook, Craig Claiborne

1961: The Blender Cookbook, Ann Seranne and Eileen Gadden

1961: Amy Vanderbilt's Complete Cookbook

1963: The I Hate to Cook Book, Peg Bracken

1965: Michael Field's Cooking School

1965: Gladys Taber's Stillmeadow Cookbook

18 EDIBLE WILD PLANTS AND HERBS

Need we caution you? *Never* pick and eat anything you're not 100 percent sure of.

wild onion	burdock	purslane
wild garlic	pokeweed	rosehips
wild asparagus	dandelion	juniper berries
thistle	mustard	mint
milkweed	chickweed	oregano
cattail	clover	sassafras

Pennsylvania, Gibbons had failed with his novel, but *Stalking the Wild Asparagus* had emerged instead. It was delightfully eccentric, and it meshed with the zeitgeist of the 1960s—the burgeoning interest in all things organic, environmental, and natural. It was the right book at the right time, and he followed it with *Stalking the Blue-Eyed Scallop, Stalking the Healthful Herbs,* and half a dozen more. His popularity grew; he wrote a column for Rodale's *Organic Gardening* magazine and he appeared on TV and radio. And then he agreed to be a spokesperson for Post Grape Nuts cereal, and to this day if you mention Euell Gibbons to a particular generation of TV watchers, they'll say, "You mean that guy in the commercial who said Grape Nuts taste like wild hickory nuts?"

Gibbons died in 1975. His books, long out of print, are now back in reprint editions.

WHAT ON EARTH IS...
OAT BRAN?

Oat bran is the outer part of the oat grain, the hull that's removed in order to yield *groats*, the inner part of the oat grain. Groats, when steamed and flattened, become rolled oats—old-fashioned, not-instant oatmeal.

Faddish enthusiasm for oat bran happened in the late 1980s. Back then some studies seemed to point to oat bran, a soluble fiber, as a major cholesterol-kicker. Wonders of cholesterol reduction were ascribed to oat bran, and manufacturers (and marketers) stuffed it into every product they could think of. As often happens, reality was a little less exciting than fad. Oat bran wasn't magic. The experts did a U-turn and decided that a low-fat diet that included assorted foods high in soluble fiber (even oat bran) was better than an all-oat bran regimen.

FOOD SAFETY, PART I: AT HOME

Every year a lot of people get that stomach flu that's going around, and every year a lot of people think they have stomach flu when they actually have some kind of food poisoning. You *could* say, Who cares which it is? I still feel lousy, I have a fever, I'm throwing up—what difference does it make which bug caused it? In the cosmic sense it *doesn't* make a difference to your gastrointestinal system unless, of course, you've caught a *fatal* bug. But it might make a difference to your more immediate future: catching stomach flu may be out of your control, but you can take action to help avoid the food pathogens that cause food poisoning.

For openers, keep your whole kitchen clean (stovetop, countertops, interior of the fridge and freezer, sink—everything) and your fridge cold—35°F is the right temp; 0°F for the freezer. Keep cutting boards, knives, utensils, and other equipment clean too. Wash your hands with hot water and soap often when you're working with food, whether you're packing a school lunch or fixing dinner. Don't, don't, don't cross-contaminate: if you're handling raw food (especially meat, fish, chicken, eggs), be sure to wash your hands before you handle any other food, including the *cooked* meat, fish, chicken, or eggs; be equally sure to wash any utensil, plate, cutting board, and so on that's come in contact with raw food—*before* using it again. Sponges are culprits too:

---

14 DELICIOUS WILD AND CULTIVATED MUSHROOMS

cremino (or plural, cremini)	enoki	nameko (or golden needle)
portobello (or portabella)	hen-of-the-woods	wood ear
shiitake	morel	straw
oyster	porcino (or plural, porcini; also called cèpe)	black trumpet
	chanterelle	puffball

---

toss them in with the laundry, or microwave them often at full power until they're too hot to touch. Use clean dishtowels, and don't dry your hands on them if you've been handling raw food; use paper towels for quick blots—and then wash your hands ASAP.

Get perishable foods into the refrigerator as quickly as possible when you come in from food shopping; perishables shouldn't really be at room temperature for more than two hours (that goes for perishables at meals and parties as well). Leave perishables in the fridge until just before you cook, heat, or serve them; if something has to come to room temp before cooking, leave it out just until it's room temp (an hour or less) and then cook it promptly. Thaw frozen foods in the refrigerator, overnight if necessary—never, never on the kitchen counter at room temp. Put hot cooked foods straight into the fridge for storage; with today's refrigerators there's no need to wait for hot foods to cool off before you stash them.

If you have to travel with perishable food, put it in an insulated container with ice packs. Same goes for kids' lunches: if you're sending your child to school with perishable food, like tuna or chicken, add an ice pack (or a couple of frozen juice boxes) to that lunch box. And teach your child to throw away perishable leftovers when lunch is over. Pack hot soups and foods in well-sealed insulated containers to keep them very hot until it's time to eat.

Pay attention to shelf life, at home or in the market. Expiration dates, "date packaged" indications, and "best before" notices are rough

---

6 DANGEROUS WILD MUSHROOMS

According to the FDA's *Bad Bug Book*, these are a few of the direly bad mushrooms that will cause anything from horrible gastrointestinal symptoms to horrible death. Do *not* mess with these guys.

amanitas of any kind (death angel, death cap, destroying angel—scary!)	jack-o'-lantern	tigertop
	green gill	naked brimcap
	gray pinkgill	

guidelines. Expiration dates on dated foods tell you when the manufacturer expects the food to go bad, but it doesn't always go bad by that date: it might go bad *before* the date if, for example, the crate of milk cartons sat out on the sidewalk for half a day before the supermarket stock person got around to refrigerating it. We've all left even our favorite foods in the fridge for too long—week-old meat loaf, month-old Chinese take-out, two-month-old sour cream. Ditch them. Do *not* taste something to see if it's "off"; most bad bugs have no taste and no smell.

We shouldn't turn ourselves into total paranoiacs about food safety, but healthy caution is just plain smart. So follow the rule of common sense: when in doubt, throw it out. Getting food poisoning is no way to spend a weekend.

MUST OR MYTH:

Cook pork until it's well-done, to avoid trichinosis.

Times have changed. First of all, the presence of trichinosis (the *Trichinella spiralis* parasite) isn't anything like as common as it once was, and we now know that it's eliminated at 137°F, not at 185°F. On top of that, today's pork is much leaner than yesterday's, and cooking it to the previously recommended degree of doneness will produce tough, dry meat. Nonetheless, to be safe, be sure your pork roast is cooked to an internal temperature of 160°F.

The best way to do this is to insert a meat thermometer in the thickest part of the roast and let the roast cook until the thermometer reads 155°F. Remove the roast from the heat and allow it to rest for ten to twenty minutes; it will continue to cook, and the internal temperature will rise to 160°F or 165°F.

20 Foods to Ditch after a Power Loss

According to the USDA, if your refrigerator temperature rises above 40°F and stays there for more than two hours during a power loss, you have a lot of discarding to do. Here's a sampling of what to toss if that fate befalls you. (And for heaven's sake, *don't taste anything* to see if it's okay!)

fresh or leftover meat, poultry, fish, seafood

tuna, shrimp, chicken, and egg salads

lunchmeats, franks, bacon, sausage

pizza of any kind

soft cheeses (cream cheese, ricotta, cottage cheese, Brie, and the like)

low-fat cheeses

milk, cream, sour cream, buttermilk, yogurt

opened baby formula

fresh or cooked eggs and egg products

custard, pudding

casseroles, soups, stews

cooked or fresh pasta

creamy dressings

fish sauces, hoisin sauce, Worcestershire sauce

cheesecake, cream-filled pastries and pies

cut-open fresh fruit

cooked vegetables

opened vegetable juice

baked potatoes, potato salad

refrigerator biscuits, rolls, cookie dough

FOOD SAFETY, PART II: AWAY FROM HOME

Away from home can mean on the road, at your desk, in school, in a plane, on a picnic, at a game, at a restaurant. What these dining venues have in common is a certain lack of control (by you) and a lot of variables. It's unnecessary to get compulsive and overly worried about food safety away from home—we've all survived thousands of meals-on-the-go—but as we established in "Food Safety, Part I: At Home" (page 282), a little healthy caution and care go a long way toward avoiding the food pathogens that can cause food poisoning.

When you're taking food along on a car, plane, train, or boat trip, either plan on a way to keep perishables cold or don't take perishables. Never let perishable food hang out unrefrigerated for more than two hours (for example, on the picnic table or in your attaché case), and in hot weather, reduce that time to one hour maximum. Another strategy: eat perishables first, less-perishables next, and nonperishables last. In other words, munch the chicken sandwich right away, eat the peach and pear a little later, and save the box of cookies for much later. That should get you through the trip, unless it's cross-country by Conestoga wagon.

Picnics and other day trips require you to get serious about packing the food. Get your coolers into shape, meaning clean, with tight-fitting lids and plenty of ice packs. Use one cooler for food and another for beverages, since the beverage cooler will be opened often and won't stay as cold inside. Consider taking an extra cooler for extra ice packs or blocks of ice. Perishable foods should already be cold when they're packed—they should go directly from fridge to cooler. Keep coolers out of the sun and out of the hot car. All the rules that apply to indoor home cooking apply to outdoor cooking, too: wash your hands, don't cross-contaminate, and so on (see page 282 for more).

Restaurant food safety is a huge can of worms. As your mom always told you, if you saw the inside of most restaurant kitchens, you'd never eat out again. This may account for the popularity (with patrons) of open-kitchen restaurants: all is revealed. Restaurant owners love them less: all is revealed. The general rules of restaurant food safety are as follows:

★ Don't eat in a restaurant with low turnover: food hangs around for too long and some of it goes bad.

★ Don't eat raw fish or meat in restaurants. That said, if you have to eat sushi or carpaccio, eat it at a reputable place. Very reputable.

★ Watch out for specials the waitstaff pushes on you; they might be based on something extraordinary the purveyor offered the chef that very morning, but they could be based on the chef's fervent desire to unload the eighty-two pork chops and twelve pounds of crabmeat that didn't go over too well last week.

★ Restaurants usually buy fresh fish on Tuesday for Wednesday and Thursday menus and again on Thursday for Friday and Saturday menus. Reconsider ordering fish on Sunday, Monday, or Tuesday; it's probably not fresh.

★ Sunday is use-up-the-leftovers day and it's also the chef's day off. If you want to be the Sunday brunch guinea pig for specials thrown together by an assistant chef, hey, be my guest. But I won't be eating them with you.

RESTAURANT SAFETY NOTE: Right around now you're saying, What's she talking about? I've never gotten sick from restaurant food. I say, Sure you have, you just thought it was that nasty stomach flu that was going around.

WHAT IS THIS THING, ANYWAY?

It's a chinois (say "*sheen-WAH*"), an unusually shaped metal sieve. It's used for pureeing by hand, so the cone is made either of fine mesh or perforated stainless steel, and you need a spoon or a special wooden pestle to force soft food through the holes. (Some people use it for straining, too, but why buy a chinois for something an ordinary fine-mesh strainer does perfectly well?)

FOOD RATIONING
IN WORLD WAR II

The idea of food scarcity is foreign to most of us. Sure, good asparagus may be hard to find during some months of the year, but not enough coffee? Not enough sugar? Not enough hamburger? No way.

Way, during World War II.

From the spring of 1942 through the end of November 1945, government-controlled food rationing was a fact of American life, and ordinary folks had to make do with much less of some foods they'd been accustomed to having in plenty. Like coffee, sugar, and beef. Like chicken, lamb, pork, hot dogs, fats, oils, cheese, canned fruits and vegetables, canned juice, canned fish, dried beans, baked beans, ketchup, and even prepared baby food. Why? Many ships that normally transported food were being used in the massive war effort; some foods came from places cut off by the war; metal was needed for war matériel and couldn't be spared for the production of canned goods; food (a lot of it) was needed for our fighting forces and our European allies. Factor in the vicissitudes of nature and agriculture, and severe rationing was a must.

Despite the encouragement of patriotic posters and films, many citizens found rationing a tough pill to swallow. It meant an enormous change in eating habits. A coffee drinker, for instance, had to make one pound of coffee last five weeks. Protein was in short supply, and every source of it—meat, fish, poultry, eggs, cheese—was eked out and made to stretch. Recipes had to be invented or adapted to make more use of unrationed foods—eggs, fresh produce, fresh fish, bread, cereal, milk, spaghetti and macaroni, jams and jellies, mayonnaise. No food was wasted (remember the Clean Plate Club?). The ladies' magazines went into overdrive addressing the problems of the wartime kitchen for women already overwhelmed by war work and the absence of husbands and sons in the armed services.

The public had been generally unprepared for any sort of rationing, much less for a system that was complicated and got off to a disorganized start. War Ration Books were issued to everyone. The books held stamps (or coupons) with assigned point values and identifying letters. Points (plus money) got you food: so many points for this food item, so many points for that, and the numbers kept changing according to availability and—it was rumored—the whims of the rationing boards. To make matters worse, stamps had expiration dates, and it required enormous attention to detail to keep track of the dates, numbers, letters, amounts, what you could get with each kind of stamp, and how to get the most for the points. Consumers were in a constant state of confusion, frustration, and sometimes anger.

But rationing was immutable. Women simply *had* to learn to juggle the stamps (and budget the money) efficiently in order to keep their families fed. Unfortunately, all the juggling and budgeting still didn't guarantee that you got what you wanted if that chicken or can of peaches or quarter pound of sugar was unavailable in your own local store: gasoline was rationed too, and you weren't likely to waste it driving around to find a can of fruit. It was substitute or do without, and pray for the end of the war.

The Story of
GOURMET MAGAZINE

Magazines are trend followers, not trendsetters, and *Gourmet* was and is no different. That is what makes it such an interesting document (and documentation) of American culinary and cultural history: it is reflective rather than innovative. In retrospect, its evolution informs us about ourselves. A smallish number of ourselves anyway, since its target audience has always been affluent, educated, sophisticated, and adventurous—or blessed with rich fantasy lives and enough spare cash to indulge those fantasies with the purchase of an expensive magazine.

Gourmet was born in 1941, between the Great Depression and World War II, an unexpected year to launch a magazine that focused on fancy recipes, glamorous dining, wine, travel, and the Good Life. Was it hopeful or foolish? Anachronistic or prescient? The answer is, probably, all of these. The founder, Earle R. MacAusland, who ran the magazine for forty years, had a point of view: *Gourmet* was to be as much a lifestyle magazine as a food magazine. It was often Francophile around the taste buds, Brit and European in tone, and highbrow American in its peculiarly trumped-up, pumped-up writing. The good life Mr. Mac admired had its roots in Europe, though he apparently believed there was much to admire in northeastern America too. *Gourmet* was prissy, it was precious, it was overwrought, and yet it was surprisingly captivating.

It lasted. In the next couple of decades *Gourmet* expanded in scope while it continued to wallow in the past: the editors acknowledged the new internationalism of cooking by offering recipes from the far corners of the world, but they never ceased to commission nostalgic articles about lavish ways of life that had disappeared. *Gourmet* seemed to have one foot in the present, one in the past, and not even a toe in the future. But as travel became ever more accessible to Americans, the magazine made a smart move. The editors saw that their readership was shifting from the *passive* activity of reading about the pleasure of travel to the *active* pleasure of traveling. So *Gourmet* shifted from simply telling about the travels of its *writers* to actually helping its traveling *readers*—with recommendations for hotels, restaurants, sights, and experiences. That shift did a great deal to loosen the magazine's wistful (and stubborn) attachment to the bygone and push it toward a more energetic embrace of the here and now.

MacAusland died in 1980, and soon *Gourmet* was sold to Condé Nast Publications. By that time the magazine was seriously in need of (and got) a different kind of revision. Along with its usual rambling articles on lifestyle, travel, and haute cuisine the editors began to publish shorter pieces and simpler recipes—a glimmer of acknowledgment that the previous gracious, slow-moving, novelistic world of *Gourmet* had been eclipsed by the reality of faster lives, less time for cooking, more diversity in culture, and (with technology making so much information available) wider interest in everything that was happening in the contemporary world of food.

And then came the Revolution, imposed from above: a new editor-in-chief, and not from in-house. In 1999 Ruth Reichl—restaurant critic, accomplished writer, food world insider, and unmistakable modernist—was hired to bring *Gourmet* into the new millennium. The story is still changing at *Gourmet*, and even in the face of so much hip, up-to-the-minute competition from the younger, newer foodie mags, readers continue to flock to the grande dame of culinary publications.

---

12 Dated (But Still Beloved) Foods

Ritz mock apple pie ★ beef Stroganoff

franks and beans ★ tuna noodle casserole

Spanish rice ★ grasshopper pie

California onion dip ★ creamed chipped beef on toast

chocolate wafer refrigerator cake ★ Rice Krispy Squares

pineapple upside-down cake ★ bread pudding

M. F. K. FISHER

If you know who Mary Francis Kennedy Fisher is—or was; she died in 1992—you also know that one short piece about her can't begin to capture the odd and original nature of the woman. If you are as yet unacquainted with her, the bare minimum of facts may intrigue you enough to dip into some of her work, which you should do if you like food. Not that you're guaranteed to love her or her writing. She's an acquired taste, like artichokes or papaya or sea urchins. And it's possible that the less you know about her personal life, the more unencumbered your enjoyment of her writing may be. But her flavor is unique, and her quirky, even brazen assertions about the experiences of finding, cooking, and eating food paved the way for many food writers who followed.

Mary Francis Kennedy was born in Michigan in 1908, but grew up in Whittier, California, the oldest of four children. Their father, Rex, was a newspaperman, and their mother, Edith, was a mother. The Kennedys were Episcopalians in a tight Quaker town, and Mary Francis always felt like an outsider. She spent some time in each of several colleges, then

❑◈◈◈❑

And Speaking of Food . . .

M. F. K. Fisher, *Map of Another Town,* 1964

There were at least three other pastry shops as good as hers, in a town perhaps more noted for them than any other in a country dedicated to the gastric hazards of almond paste, chestnuts soaked in sweet liqueurs, and chocolate in all its richest and most redolent forms. . . . [H]er cookies and wafers and cakes were plainly made of ingredients I approved of for my children, in spite of my responsibility to their livers, and the shop always smelled right, not confused and stuffy but delicately layered: fresh eggs, fresh sweet butter, grated nutmeg, vanilla beans, old kirsch, newly ground almonds.

married Alfred Fisher in 1929 and moved with him to France, where he completed his doctorate and she began her love affair with France and continued her love affair with food. She was passionate, iconoclastic, sensual, and never cautious, and these qualities made their way into her writing.

She divorced Fisher in 1937, the same year her first book, *Serve It Forth*, was published, and the same year she married Dilwyn Parrish. Parrish, the love of her life, committed suicide in 1941 after a painful and lingering illness. In 1943 M. F. K. Fisher gave birth to a daughter, Anna (father unrevealed), and in 1945 she married Donald Friede, a literary agent, after a two-week courtship. They had a daughter, Kennedy, in 1946 and divorced in 1951. For the rest of her life M. F. K. Fisher lived in Switzerland, France, and California, raising her daughters and writing her many books. She died in Glen Ellen, California, greatly diminished by illness but writing to the end.

M. F. K. Fisher was not, by many accounts, an easy person, but she could be a seductive one. She was neither a chef nor a restaurant critic nor a food columnist; she was a writer who wrote about a basic need in an exceptionally personal way. "I am hungry," she said in a 1990 interview, quoted by Molly O'Neill in her 1992 *New York Times* obituary of Fisher, "but there is more to it than that . . . it happens that when I write of hunger, I am really writing about love and the hunger for it, and warmth and the love of it and the hunger for it." Food and eating were the metaphors she used for writing about life. Her books are what she's left us, and they are unique.

M. F. K. FISHER READING LIST: *The Art of Eating*, which comprises *Serve It Forth, Consider the Oyster, How to Cook a Wolf, The Gastronomical Me*, and *An Alphabet of Gourmets; With Bold Knife and Fork; A Cordiall Water; Not Now, but Now; Among Friends;* and many others.

---

8 NONMESSY FOODS TO EAT WHEN YOU'RE READING IN BED

grapes ★ bite-size crackers or chips

baby carrots ★ mixed nuts

malted milk balls ★ jelly beans

M&Ms ★ cheese cubes

---

15 Words That Describe How Food Tastes

salty	bland	spicy
sour	stale	gamy
sweet	sugary	bittersweet
bitter	rich	burnt
tangy	tart	mellow

15 Words That Describe How Food Smells

flowery	stinky	rancid
fruity	strong	rotten
fresh	sharp	sour
spicy	lemony	acrid
vinegary	hearty	briny

And Speaking of Food . . .

Willa Cather, My Ántonia, 1918

Anna and Yulka showed me three small barrels; one full of dill pickles, one full of chopped pickles, and one full of pickled watermelon rinds.

"You wouldn't believe, Jim, what it takes to feed them all!" their mother exclaimed. "You ought to see the bread we bake on Wednesdays and Saturdays! It's no wonder their poor papa can't get rich, he has to buy so much sugar for us to preserve with. We have our own wheat ground for flour—but then there's that much less to sell."

Nina and Jan, and a little girl named Lucie, kept shyly pointing out to me the shelves of glass jars. They said nothing, but, glancing at me, traced on the glass with their finger-tips the outline of the cherries and strawberries and crabapples within, trying by a blissful expression of countenance to give me some idea of their deliciousness.

FEINSCHMECKING: PENNSYLVANIA DUTCH SPECIALTIES

Good eating (*feinschmecking*) is almost synonymous with the Pennsylvania Dutch, a term applied to the immigrants who settled in the area around Lancaster County, Pennsylvania, in the eighteenth century, from Germany, Switzerland, France, and other parts of Europe. They were deeply religious people—Amish, Mennonites, Brethren, and Lutherans, among others—with roots in the German culture (*Dutch* is really a corruption of *Deutsch*, the German word for "German") and a tradition of farming.

Hardworking farmers needed lots of fuel to sustain them, and the meals put together by Pennsylvania Dutch farm wives were hearty and filling. Fresh, uncooked produce didn't loom large; these ladies specialized in proteins, carbs, pickling, and dessert.

Meat was on the menu most of the time—chicken, goose, turkey, rabbit, pork loin and chops, spare ribs, baked ham, homemade sausage, beef roasts, beef heart, calf's liver, bacon, and veal, all from animals raised and butchered on the farm, of course. Nothing was wasted: they made scrapple or souse from a pig's head, pickled its feet, boiled its knuckles, and stuffed its stomach.

Carbohydrates were crucial. Flour dumplings and noodles were constants, and corn was stored and used year-round in everything from

---

13 GREAT THINGS TO MAKE WITH APPLES

applesauce	apple cake	apple fritters
baked apples with caramel sauce or softly whipped cream	apple chutney	apple turnovers
	apple betty	tarte tatin
apple pie topped with wedges of Cheddar	apple dumplings	candied apples
	apple butter	apple crumble

soup to stuffing to waffles. Potatoes turned up in potato salad, croquettes, pancakes, pudding, dumplings; they were scalloped, baked, hashed, stewed, and stuffed. Even the yeast dough for bread might include potatoes. And nonpotato yeast dough was used for cinnamon buns, schnecken, raisin bread, coffee cake with streusel topping, or fastnachts—doughnuts.

Vegetables? There were cabbage slaws, sauerkraut, succotash, turnips, onions. There was no important salad tradition, with one exception: dandelion greens with bacon dressing. On the other hand, both sweet and savory pickling were major: cucumbers went into spicy relishes and briny pickle crocks; green tomatoes made piccalilli, ginger relish, and mincemeat; bell peppers, cauliflower, corn, and green beans became chow-chow. Beets, pears, peaches, cabbage, watermelon rind, even eggs got the pickle treatment. Every housewife made a stock of savory sauces like ketchup, chili, and horseradish, and fruits (apples, quinces, strawberries, and currants, to name a few) were turned into sweet fruit butters and preserves.

As for dessert, this cuisine was Pie Heaven: shoofly, crumb, raisin, schnitz (dried apple), fresh apple, apple butter, butterscotch, pumpkin, lemon, custard (and *potato* custard), molasses, berry, black walnut, rhubarb, buttermilk, and a dozen more. There were strudels, tarts, funnel cakes, fruit dumplings, cheesecakes, sponge cakes, layer cakes of all flavors, applesauce cake, pound cakes, puddings (lemon, rhubarb, date, rice, plum, carrot, and more), and cookies in abundance. If you were still hungry after all that, no worries—there was homemade fudge to nibble.

6 Fabulous Brands of Baking Chocolate

Supermarket brands of baking chocolate aren't worth using in your homemade goodies. Try one of these instead, for sensational results.

Callebaut ★ Valrhona ★ Lindt

Schokinag ★ Scharffen-Berger ★ El Rey

HEIRLOOM TOMATOES

Heirlooms are tomato varieties that have been passed along from gardener to dedicated gardener; some varieties are a few human generations old, others are more recently developed (and sticklers might argue that recent means *not heirloom*). Heirlooms are a teeny-tiny presence on the national tomato scene, but devotees, and therefore crops, are growing yearly. Why? Because heirloom tomatoes are juicy and flavorful—a far cry from the pallid, taste-free, commercially grown hybrids most of us have grown up on. Strange skins (such as purple, speckled, or striped) and strange shapes (complete with wrinkles, bumps, protuberances, and other imperfections) are characteristic of heirlooms too, which may take getting used to for a lot of consumers.

Unless you're raising them yourself, heirlooms can be hard to get your hands on. They're fragile, have a short shelf life, and don't ship well, so you're most likely to find them in your area only if a local grower is selling them (at hefty prices), either at a farm stand, at a farmers' market, or in a high-end gourmet shop or grocery chain. Restaurant chefs feature them and tend to make a big fuss about them. Like any heirloom, an heirloom tomato is a treasure.

TOMATO ADVICE: Even though ordinary tomatoes can, if needed, be held in the fridge for a day or two, heirlooms are much too fragile for that bit of bravado. Buy them ripe, keep them on the kitchen counter, and eat them pronto.

---

10 GREAT THINGS TO MAKE WITH CHOCOLATE

chocolate mousse	chocolate cookies	chocolate pudding
chocolate pie	fudge sauce	hot chocolate
chocolate cake with chocolate frosting	flourless chocolate cake	chocolate ice cream
		brownies

THE MAN IN THE WHITE TOQUE

PAUL BOCUSE

If you're interested in mini-French revolutions, you could look further and do worse than the one chef Paul Bocuse helped foment in the early 1970s. It was called *nouvelle cuisine,* and it blew French cooking (and eventually American cooking, too) right out of the water. Nouvelle cuisine left excessive butter and cream behind and depended instead on fresh seasonal food, intense natural flavors, and recipes much simpler than the classical French ones. Chefs of the nouvelle cuisine also introduced large plates bearing small amounts of food that, at the finale of the meal, sent still-hungry diners into shock when they saw the size of the tab.

Bocuse, born in 1926, came by his culinary heritage honorably, a link in a chain of chefs and restaurateurs going back a couple of cen-

11 French Stews

coq au vin

boeuf bourguignonne

daube de boeuf à la provençale

pot-au-feu

carbonnade flamande

blanquette de veau

navarin printanier

matelote normande

ratatouille

bouillabaisse

cassoulet

First Edition of Larousse Gastronomique

Larousse Gastronomique was and possibly still is the world's most amazing and extensive encyclopedia of food, though the *Oxford Companion to Food* is giving it a run for its money nowadays. Before the *Oxford Companion*, though, *Larousse* was the go-to book for everything you ever wanted to know about the classic culinary tradition of Europe (and especially France). The first edition, edited by Prosper Montagné, was published in 1938 by the French company started by Pierre Larousse back in the 1850s. Its most recent revision was in 2001.

turies. In 1959, after getting shot up in World War II and then spending years learning his culinary arts and crafts, he headed back to the family restaurant near Lyons to attempt to rescue it from disaster. L'Auberge du Pont de Collonges still stands and thrives (graced with a huge sign announcing "Paul Bocuse," lest customers drive right by it), along with several successful Bocuse-created brasseries.

There is almost no important food-world prize Paul Bocuse lacks. In 1965 his restaurant received three stars from the Michelin guide; in 1989 the Gault-Millau guide named him "Chef of the Century." On the tidal wave of his personal popularity and the popularity of nouvelle cuisine, Bocuse proceeded to expand his empire. Bocuse restaurants popped up in Tokyo, Melbourne, the Epcot Center in Florida. Bakeries were franchised; wines, teas, jams, foie gras, and other foodstuffs were merchandised. Some of it lasted, some didn't.

In 1987 he reinvented the Olympics—the culinary Olympics, called Bocuse d'Or—for promoting young chefs from all over the world, that they might one day join the pantheon of which Bocuse is such a prominent member. In 2004 the theme of the Bocuse d'Or USA National Selection, when judges decided which of seven contestants would go to the finals in Lyons, was Dover Sole and Petite Frenched Veal Rack.

BRANDY

Gin, vodka, and whisky are made year-round from sturdy grains that are harvested and stored for that purpose. Brandy is made of more ephemeral stuff—seasonal fruits. And since it's made from seasonal fruits, its excellence and abundance depend first on the ripening and harvest of the fruit and second on the quality of the distilled, aged spirits made from that fruit.

There are three basic kinds of brandy: grape brandy, pomace brandy, and fruit brandy. Grape brandy is distilled either from fermented grape juice or from crushed (not pressed) grape pulp and skins, then aged in wooden casks. Cognac and Armagnac are grape brandies, but cognac has the distinction of being double-distilled—distilled twice. Pomace brandy (such as marc or grappa) is made by pressing the grape pulp, skins, and stems left after the grapes have already been

---

12 Liqueurs and What They Taste Like

amaretto = almond

anisette = licorice

kummel = caraway

Grand Marnier = orange

Cointreau = orange

Pernod = licorice

Kahlua = coffee

crème de cacao = chocolate

crème de cassis = black currant

Frangelico = hazelnut

sambuca = anise

Benedictine = herbs and spices

---

crushed to extract their juice for winemaking. Pomace brandies are not aged much; they're not nearly as smooth and mellow as grape brandies. Fruit brandy is an umbrella term for all the brandies made by fermenting any fruit other than grapes—apples, pears, or cherries, for instance—and they're usually made from fruit wines. Don't confuse fruit brandy with fruit-flavored brandy, which is grape brandy flavored with fruit extract.

Brandy labels, you may have noticed, have mysterious alphabetical codes. Actually, the letters (and some words) comprise a rating system that's supposed to describe the quality of the brandy in terms of age. V.S.O.P. means very superior old pale, V.O. means very old, and so on, with minimum years-in-wood implied. But these are confusing terms, not always accurate, and besides, some manufacturers are starting to disregard this sort of labeling altogether. It's hard to enforce rating on a worldwide basis when there's no Brandy Police to back it up.

DISTILLATION NOTE: *Distillation* is a term we've all heard, but what exactly does it mean? It's the process of boiling a liquid and then letting the resulting vapor condense into liquid again. What happens when distillation takes place? The liquid separates into its components, becomes concentrated, or becomes purified.

MEET...

A. J. LIEBLING

A. J. Liebling (1904–1963) was a legendary journalist of his time. He's not often remembered now, but when he was writing for the *New Yorker* in the 1930s and '40s he was a large voice and a large presence, both literally and figuratively. He covered boxing (his great love), politics, politicians, and many other topics, but his dedication to food and writing about food began in Paris in 1926.

That was the year his father began to worry that Liebling might get married to the wrong girl, and so he offered his son a year abroad, in Paris, to "study." Liebling leapt at the chance and made the very best of it. He threw himself into the experience and commenced, as David Remnick put it in his *New Yorker* article written for the hundredth anniversary of Liebling's birth, "to eat, and eat as if his life, and his eventual livelihood, depended on it."

His eventual livelihood did not, as it turned out, depend on eating, since he wrote hundreds of articles and quite a few books on other subjects, but his year in Paris did produce a memoir that is part of the food-writing canon. *Between Meals: An Appetite for Paris* was published in 1962, almost at the end of Liebling's too-short life, and it details some of the food he ate, the wine he drank, and the life he lived when he wasn't at table. His slightly hyperbolic style might be considered a bit over-the-top by today's standards, but his descriptions of his days in France are *nonpareil*.

Here is Liebling on an alarming (to him) meal foisted upon him in Lyons: "Monsieur B. was sincerely a cook, but the axis of his culinary eye had shifted until he saw the main body of dinner as a perfunctory hors d'oeuvre to the sweets. His preliminary menu . . . reminded me depressingly of the Hamburg-American Line. Then squads of assistants . . . would begin to roll in trolleys of pastry and confectionary—*vacherins, suissesses, mille-feuilles, meringues, îles-flottantes de Tante Marie,* and hundreds of sugary kickshaws I was unable to identify. . . . [I]t was the first time I felt sick on *la cuisine française*."

DRINKING ETIQUETTE
FOR HOST AND GUEST

When you build a drink for your guest, make it a single, not a double; do not ambush him with more alcohol than he was expecting on the first go-round. Of course you may and will offer a second drink, but wait until the first is gone and then make the offer openly; don't surreptitiously keep topping up a half-drunk cocktail or glass of wine. This sort of act of misplaced generosity can lead to problems like lampshade-donning, obnoxious harassment of other guests, excessively loud hilarity, the accidental destruction of innocent furniture, fits of maudlin crying, throwing up in the ficus tree (if you're lucky), and worst of all, the possibility of drunk driving.

Provide some kind of food for your guests, even if they've just dropped in for a beer, and at least one nonalcoholic beverage for the nondrinkers. Absolutely do not lean on, annoy, push, or make an issue of anyone who prefers not to drink. Absolutely do not allow a drunk person to leave your home with his or her car keys; take them away by hook or crook, and either call a cab or get a friend to do chauffeur duty.

When you're offered a drink, don't waffle; say *yes, please* or *no, thank you.* If you don't want a drink, no explanation is called for. You're entitled not to drink, and it's rude of anyone (much less your host) to inquire into your reasons. If you do want a drink, a good host will list the possibilities so you can choose, and choose you must; you may not ask your host to decide for you. If you're old enough to drink, you're old enough to know what you want.

TRUE TALES OF THE DINNER TABLE:
IT'S ALWAYS SOMETHING

Lorrie Javna, writer

I was settled, finally, in a new apartment, with a beautiful new birch dining table long enough to accommodate a chunk of my immediate family. "Come for dinner on Saturday," I invited, and then sat down to plan a winter menu that everyone could eat. Not easy. In my family, everyone has a bone to pick with food.

Mom: lactose-intolerant; no wheat or any other grain except rice
Dad: diabetic; no hot spices and anyway, strongly prefers plain food
Brother: violently allergic to garlic; won't eat pasta (dieting)
Sister-in-law: vegetarian; won't eat pasta (same diet)
Niece: lactose-intolerant (runs in family); no shellfish; nothing weird

That eliminated anything made with cheese, milk, or cream; any sort of meat, chicken, or pasta; anything made with sugar; anything spicily Mediterranean, Mexican, or Chinese; anything not immediately identifiable; anything with any flavor. Keep in mind that it was winter and I couldn't fall back on tomatoes, baby lettuce, and other summer delicacies (like perfect peaches for dessert).

It took more time to figure out a menu than to cook it. On Saturday night I set it all on the sideboard and prayed that Sunday would bring no reports of night-long gastrointestinal battles.

THE MENU

Red salsa and green salsa (no garlic, no hot pepper), corn tortilla chips

Poached salmon with two sauces: lime-coriander and honey-mustard-dill

Rice with toasted pine nuts, dressed with olive oil

Pan-browned zucchini

Baked delicata squash sprinkled with nutmeg and cinnamon

Cucumber salad with (no-sugar) sweet-and-sour sesame dressing

Poached pears, fresh pineapple

18 Overused Food Phrases and Metaphors

red as a beet

red as a lobster

eat like a bird

put on the feedbag

eat humble pie

nice kettle of fish

sour grapes

salad days

egghead

rotten apple

slow as molasses

smart cookie

the whole enchilada

top banana

pea-brained

cold fish

rotten apple

What a turkey!

INDEX

Cape Cod turkey (cod), 130
Capon, Robert Farrar, 68, 261
caponata, 135
carbohydrates, 32–33, 69, 70
carrots, 51, 69, 167, 276, 293
Carvel, Tom, 266
Carver, George Washington, 80–81
catfish, 229
Cather, Willa, 294
cauliflower, 69, 167
caviar, 119, 195, 206, 236, 244
celery, 69, 118, 276
cellophane, 248
cereals, 17, 101, 115, 180, 181
Cézanne, Paul, 215
Chamberlain, Samuel, 68
Champagne, 197, 206
chanko-nabe, 10–11
Charlie the Tuna, 263
Charms, 29
chaurice, 262
Chavez, Cesar, 47
Cheerios, 101
cheese, 21, 22, 51, 110, 161, 167, 187, 212, 293
"Cheeseburger in Paradise," 37
cheesecake, 73, 112
cheesecake-on-a-stick, 23
cheese straws, 135
Cheez Whiz, 99
cherries, 55, 187, 206, 229, 244
Cherries Jubilee, 240
Cherry Garcia ice cream, 27
chestnuts, glacé, 119
Chez Panisse, Berkeley, 38
chicken, 21, 51, 209, 237
    free-range, 116
    fried, 61
    serving guests, 102, 103, 134
chicken fat, 22, 70
chicken feet, 22
chicken Kiev, 52
chicken salad, 87
chicken soup, 42
Chicken Soup Diet, 12
"Chicken Soup with Rice," 37
Chicken Tetrazzini, 41
chicken wing ice cream, 26
Child, Julia, 36, 38, 68, 263, 280
chiles, 109, 118, 212, 229

chili, 45–46, 61, 134, 207, 244
chili sauce, 141
Chinese food, 62
Chinese New Year, 190
Chinese Restaurant Syndrome, 25
chinois, 287
chip buttie, 48
Chiquita banana, 101
chocolate, 110, 118, 119, 146, 212, 249
    baking, 296
    melting, 89
    tempering, 199
    uses for, 297
chocolate bars, 14–15
chocolate bunnies, 14
chocolate chip cookie, 92–93
chocolate chip ice cream, 27
chocolate chips, 122
Chocolate Diet, 12
chocolate fudge sauce, 42
chocolate ice cream, 27, 42
chocolates, 14, 73, 135, 206, 248–49
chocolate Santas, 14
chocolate velvet cake, 67
Chocolate Watchband, 189
chop suey, 112
chores, kitchen, 157
chowderhead, 201
Christmas foods, 191
Chuckles, 15
Chunky, 15
Chunky Monkey ice cream, 27
chutney, 141, 206, 235, 271
cider, 206
cioppino, 207
cities:
    food capitals, 212
    foods named for, 112
citrus fruit, 20
Claiborne, Craig, 204–5, 210, 280
clambake, 232
clam chowder, 46, 112, 130, 200–201
clam dip, 61
clam fritters, 130
clams, 112, 167, 232
Clark Bar, 15
Clarke, Austin, 244
Clementine in the Kitchen (Chamberlain), 68
clotted cream, 124, 125
Cobb, Robert, 19

dieting, 12, 51
Diet Rite Cola, 263
Dinner at the Homesick Restaurant (Tyler), 33
dinner-date foods, 52
Dippin Dots, 23
Dirty Martini, 16
distillation, 301
dog, 22
Dogzilla, 23
Domino's Pizza, 247, 263
Doritos, 263
Dots, 15
doughnuts, 206, 247
drinking etiquette, 303
drive-in restaurants, 241–42
Dr Pepper, 120, 121
dry states, 18
duck fat, 70
Dunkin Donuts, 99
Durgin-Park, Boston, 200
durian, 22, 54

Easter dinner, 222
eating out, 51
"Eat It," 37
éclairs, 161
Edible Schoolyard Project, 39
Edison, Thomas A., 47
Edwardian menu, 239–40
eel, jellied, 22
eel ice cream, 26
Egg Beaters, 186, 187
egg cream, 130, 262
egg foo yong, 13, 112
eggplant, 147, 164
eggs, 72, 236
  allergy to, 24, 264
  deviled, 61
  freezing, 185
  fried, 147
  scrambled, 201
  soft-boiled, 42
Eggs Benedict, 41
Eggs Sardou, 41
egg yolks, 50
Eighteenth Amendment, 17, 18
Einstein, Albert, 47
Electric Prunes, 189
electrolytes, 33
elevenses, 125

Emerald Martini, 16
emergencies, foods to stash for, 289
enchiladas, 134
endive, 98, 275
English muffins, 112
enzymes, 24
epazote leaves, 109
Ephron, Delia, 25, 133
Ephron, G. H., 211
Ephron, Nora, 33
Epperson, Frank, 68
Equal, 187
ergot, 176
escargots, 22
Escoffier, Auguste, 240
Eskimo Pie, 68
Esquivel, Laura, 33
eyeballs, 11, 22

fairy floss (cotton candy), 120
farting, 47
Fast Food Nation (Schlosser), 68
fast-food restaurants, 245–46, 247
fat, body, 10–11, 70
fats, dietary, 32, 33, 69, 70
fatty meats, 50
feet, 11
fennel, 69, 98, 118
festivals, 229
figs, 118, 167, 187
films about food, 267
fingers, eating with, 159, 174–75
fish, 62, 103, 237
  allergy to, 24, 264
  how to buy, 234
  restaurant safety, 287
  what to serve with, 235
fish bladder, 22
Fisher, M. F. K., 68, 244, 292–93
fish ice cream, 26
fish oil, 70
Fitch, Noel Riley, 68
Five Quarters of the Orange (Harris), 33
Flagg, Fannie, 33
flavor enhancers, 25
flour, 115
Flying Burrito Brothers, 189
foie gras, 195
food allergies, 24–25, 264
"Food Glorious Food," 37

johnnycakes, 130
Johnson, Howard, 245–46
Johnson, Nancy, 19
Johnson & Wales University, 36
Juicy Fruit gum, 15, 54
Jung, David, 190
Junior Mints, 15

Kafka, Franz, 47
Kaga, Takeshi, 256, 257
Kander, Mrs. Simon (Lizzie), 65–66
kangaroo sashimi, 22
Kansas City steak, 112
karma, 221
Kass, Jerome, 63–64
Kellogg's cereals, 101, 181
Kennedy, Diana, 105
Kentucky Fried Chicken, 247
ketchup, 141, 217, 244
kids:
    foods they hate, 128
    foods they love, 129, 254
    recipes for, 31
kimchee, 22
Kimmel, Eric A., 133
King, Peter, 175
Kirby, J. G., 241
Kit Kats, 14, 15
Kiwi Midori ice cream, 27
knives, 100, 145–46, 158–59, 257
    sharpening, 146
kolache, 262
Kool-Aid, 266
kosher laws, 220
Kraft, 217
K rations, 101
Krispy Kreme Doughnuts, 247
Kroc, Ray, 241
Kumin, Albert, 67
kumquats, 13

La Bonne Table (Bemelmans), 196
La Côte Basque, New York, 214
lactose intolerance, 24–25, 185, 186, 187, 264
La Cucina (Prior), 33
Lamalle, Cecille, 175
lamb, 102, 236, 237
lamb's quarters, 262
Lanchester, John, 33

lard, 50, 70
Larousse, Pierre, 299
Larousse Gastronomique, 299
lasagna, 103, 134
latte, 127
Lee, Mother Ann, 132
Lee, Sara, 176
leeks, 98
Leff, Jim, 30
leftovers, 61, 62, 126–27
lemonade, 120
lemon curd, 124
lemons, 69, 110
Lender's Bagels, 61
lentils, 69
Leonardo da Vinci, 47
Le Pavillon, New York, 213–14
Let's Eat Right to Keep Fit (Davis), 95
lettuce, 79, 185, 276
Lewis, Rosa, 240
licorice strings, 15
Liebling, A. J., 302
Life Savers, 15, 29
Like Water for Chocolate (Esquivel), 33
Lileks, James, 31, 68
"Lima Beans" (Small), 250–51
Lincoln, Abraham, 207
Lind, James, 232
Lipton, Sir Thomas, 240
liqueurs, 300
liver, 25, 62
lobsters, 52, 74, 130, 229, 232, 236, 237
local foods, 31, 114
Loiseau, Bernard, 196
lollipops, 14–15
Lombardi, Gennaro, 40
London broil, 112, 141
Long Island duckling, 130
Louie, Edward, 191
low-calorie foods, 69
lox, 62, 74, 130
luau, 198
lunch boxes, 254–55
lunch counters, 122
luncheon, 252–53
lutefish, 22
lychee, 54
Lyons, Nan, 174

Rich, Virginia, 174
Richman, Phyllis, 175
rioja wine, 20
risotto, 62
Ritchie, Jean, 81
rock candy, 29
Rockefeller, John D., 41
rocket, 142
rock groups, 189
Rohwedder, Otto Frederick, 19
Romano, Michael S., 71
Roosevelt, Franklin D., 120, 207
root beer, 67, 121
root beer barrels, 29
Ruhlman, Michael, 68
rumaki, 199
Russell Stover, 248
Russian Air Force Diet, 12
Russian dressing, 112

Sabbath foods, 130
safety, food, 282–87
saffron, 195
saffron rice, 110
Saf-T-Pops, 29
sago worms, 22
St. Louis Fair (1904), 120
salad dressings, 112, 115, 185, 231
salads, 52, 62, 96–97, 134, 207, 229–30, 231
salmon, 102, 111
   smoked, 62, 74, 207
salmonella, 116
salsa, 106, 135, 141, 217, 235, 244
salt, 115, 136
   alternatives to, 136
sandwiches, 41, 176
Sanger, Amy Wilson, 133
sangría, 20
sapsago, 13
Sara Lee Cheese Cake, 101
Sardou, Victorien, 41
sashimi, 22, 161
sauces, 185
   bottled, 115
   classic, 195
   for fish, 235
sausages, 74, 173, 237
scallops, 102, 103, 237
Scheib, Walter, 83

schlag, 74
Schlosser, Eric, 68
Schonfeld, Reese, 36
scones, 120, 124, 125
scrapple, 22
sea cucumber, 22
seafaring foods, 232–33
sea slug, 22
Sendak, Maurice, 133
Sen No Rikkyu, 269
serotonin, 108
serrator, 32
sesame oil, 227
Settlement Cook Book, The (Kander), 65–66
Seven-Day All-You-Can-Eat Diet, 12
Shaker food, 132–33
Shaw, George Bernard, 47
shelf life, 283–84
shellfish, allergy to, 24, 264
Sheraton, Mimi, 244
sherbet, 123
Shibata, Grace, 267–68
shortbread, 119, 135
shortening, 70
shredded wheat, 180
shrimp, 21, 102, 103, 143, 237
   deveining, 143
   fried, 62
shrimp ice cream, 26
silkworm grubs, 22
Simmons, Amelia, 205
"Simple Cooking" newsletter, 31
Singer, Isaac Bashevis, 47
Singing Family of the Cumberlands (Ritchie), 81
Skittles, 15
slimy food, 11
Small, Peter, 250–51
Smart Dogs, 186
Smarties, 29
Smashing Pumpkins, 189
smells, food, 294
Smith, H. Allen, 46
Smith, Robert Kimmel, 133
Smithfield ham, 112
smoothies, 56
snails, 22
Snapple, 263
Snickers, 14
Sno-Caps, 15

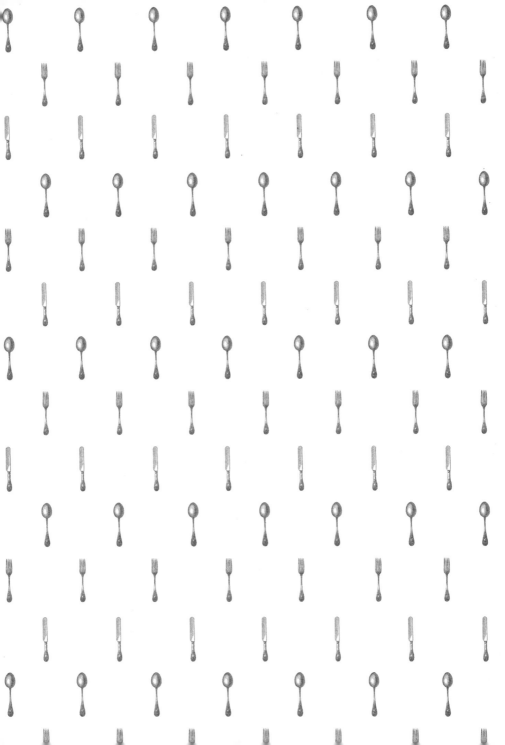